CREVASSE ROULETTE

THE FIRST TRANS-ANTARCTIC CROSSING 1957–58

Taffy Williams with our dog team. The bicycle wheel records the distance travelled.

CREVASSE ROULETTE

THE FIRST TRANS-ANTARCTIC CROSSING 1957–58

Jon Stephenson

ROSENBERG

First published in Australia in 2009
by Rosenberg Publishing Pty Ltd
PO Box 6125, Dural Delivery Centre NSW 2158
Phone: +61 2 9654 1502 Fax: 61 2 9654 1338
Email: rosenbergpub@smartchat.net.au
Web: www.rosenbergpub.com.au

National Library of Australia Cataloguing-in-Publication entry

Author: Stephenson, Jon.

Title: Crevasse roulette : the first Trans-Antarctic crossing 1957-58 / Jon Stephenson.

Edition: 1st ed.

ISBN 9781877058660

Notes: Includes index.
         Bibliography.

Subjects: Trans-Antarctic Expedition (1955-1958)
            Antarctica--Discovery and exploration

Dewey Number: 919.8904

Printed in Thailand by Kyodo Nation Printing Services

CONTENTS

Plates

The photographers are identified, otherwise by Jon Stephenson

Figures

Abbreviations

ANARE Australian National Antarctic Research Expeditions
BANZARE British Australian New Zealand Antarctic Research Expedition
BAS British Antarctic Survey
BNGE British North Greenland Expedition
FIDS Falkland Islands Dependencies Survey
GMT Greenwich Mean Time
IGY International Geophysical Year
NBS Norwegian-British-Swedish Expedition
RARE Ronne Antarctic Research Expedition
RGS Royal Geographical Society
TAE [Commonwealth] Trans-Antarctic Expedition

Foreword

Jon Stephenson's remarkable experience as a young man sparked off a lifetime passion for Antarctic knowledge, both exploratory and scientific. This, combined with scholarship, extensive research and many years of work, has resulted in the publication of this book.

Great feats of exploration are generally followed by narrative accounts composed by their leaders, and the Fuchs–Hillary crossing of Antarctica is no exception. It is rare, however, for a parallel account to be written by a member of the accomplishing team, particularly after decades of time. Fifty-odd years of study and reflection have given Jon Stephenson a maturity and balance of judgment which makes this work particularly impressive. As background to his narrative of the crossing of Antarctica, Stephenson provides much historic detail on Antarctic exploration in general.

The part that he played in the enterprise is itself noteworthy. He and Kenneth Blaiklock each drove a dog-sledge team from the South Ice to the South Pole, being the first to do it since Amundsen's party. Only one other party has travelled to the Pole with dog teams, the International Trans-Antarctica Expedition (1989–90).

Professionally, too, as a geologist, Stephenson made a major scientific contribution to the results of the expedition. An officially appointed 'Australian Observer', he provided Australian representation in what was labelled the 'Commonwealth' Trans-Antarctic Expedition.

Altogether he is to be congratulated on a highly commendable and interesting production.

Dr P.G. Law, AC, CBE
Founding Director, ANARE
Australian Antarctic Research Expeditions

Preface

Just over 50 years ago, a motley menagerie of four Cats, three Weasels, a Bombardier and 12 men, joined later by 18 dogs, set off from Shackleton Base on the Filchner Ice Shelf in the Weddell Sea. Ahead of us was a 2000-mile journey via the South Pole and on to Scott Base on Ross Island in McMurdo Sound.

Jon Stephenson and I were the drivers of the two teams of huskies and we later left South Ice ahead of the main party, to reconnoitre the route ahead. On the way we built snow cairns to assist the vehicles navigate through the heavy sastrugi. The last cairn built five days later when they would soon catch us up, we called 'Snowhenge' with three uptight pillars and two blocks across! Jon and I drove our dogs to the South Pole, the first teams to arrive there since Amundsen in 1911.

I first knew Sir (then Dr) Vivian Fuchs when he was the field commander of the FIDS bases, and base leader at Stonington Island, and I was one of the two surveyors with the team. In 1955 I was in charge of the MV *Norsel* team to set up two new bases. I heard about 'Bunny's' plans and asked to be considered for joining his Commonwealth Trans-Antarctic Expedition.

The initial response to the TAE proposal was decidedly negative. It was pointed out the expedition would involve a high risk traversing the Weddell Sea to set up the base, but also required a successful passage for the following year. Then criticism came from the risk of losing heavy vehicles traversing unknown and probably crevassed areas, which could have catastrophic results. Any Antarctic project carries risks and these have to be reduced by accepting careful procedures, in order to achieve results.

TAE was probably the most 'prestigious' of my years down south, although the first time south was the most exciting. The two years with the Belgian Base following TAE were the most enjoyable, with excellent food and wine, and nearly 60 percent of the time spent sledging in the Sor Rondane Range.

The first year of TAE at Shackleton was one of the toughest. However, in 1957, the second year, Jon Stephenson, Hal Lister and I spent the winter at South Ice at 81.7°S, and this was one of the highlights. From this six-month spell came very close friendship, which is still as strong today.

Although TAE scientific achievements had to fit in with the main crossing plans, they were accomplished in many disciplines, and also showed that heavy vehicles could traverse extremely crevassed areas with air/ground combination being very effective. It also showed that the relatively small, ice-strengthened ships could traverse the Weddell Sea in successive years. The relief of Halley Bay Base has shown this each year since 1957.

Bunny Fuchs estimated that we would take 100 days to cover 2000 miles. We did it in 99 days and travelled 2150 miles. Not a bad estimate.

Ken Blaiklock (Polar Medal with three bars; Chevalier de la Couronne; OBE)
Leader, TAE Advance Party; member, Crossing Party

Introduction and Acknowledgments

Fifty years ago I was very lucky and privileged to take part in Vivian Fuchs' Commonwealth Trans-Antarctic Expedition.

Although I returned to Heard Island in the sub-Antarctic in 1963, I spent my career in more temperate latitudes. I led expeditions to the Karakoram in West Pakistan and to Ambrym Island in the then New Hebrides. However, I concentrated over 30 years in volcanic field research in relatively remote parts of tropical north Queensland.

My obsession with Antarctica remained un-diminished, but it was not until 2000 that I revisited on a cruise. Strangely, I felt I had come 'home'.

This book describes my adventure with Fuchs' expedition. I have relied on some diary records, and have revisited the photos I took on the expedition. I used a faithful Leica 3c camera, which allowed me to record some of my impressions and experiences. The Kodak film used, Kodachrome 1, has preserved many memories, with fair colour accuracy. I have drawn the diagrams in Canvas.

The idea for this book originated on a flight from Ushuaia to Buenos Aires, returning from a Shackleton cruise in 2004. An unknown woman from California was sitting opposite me returning from a different Antarctic cruise. As we talked about mutual Antarctic interests, she learned I had been on an expedition in 1957–58. Graciously, she asked me the title of my book about the adventure. On learning there had been no such book, she insisted, 'Then you must write one'. I acknowledge her convincing encouragement to start writing, to revisit and recollect.

Many people have assisted and encouraged me, and I thank them all.

My fellow expeditioners suffered my early, angular writing efforts, and responded in various ways, from instructive comments to detailed editing. They have generously helped with personal notes about their remarkable later careers. I thank all my TAE colleagues: Ken, Roy, David, George, Hal and Rainer. Helen Lenton generously gave me information about Ralph's career. Peter Fuchs gave me essential information about his father.

Neal Sellars skilfully edited my manuscript and sensibly advised me. He has carefully preserved and helped me focus my writing purpose, while moderating my 'research' English. Rob Megarrity generously assisted me in resolving some nagging software conflicts.

David Burke met the crossing party at McMurdo Sound in 1958 and has helped me with further information, including a spur for the book title. David recovered my Australian flag at McMurdo.

I visited several polar institutions which helped me in many ways. Andie Smithies assisted me with sources from the Australian Government Antarctic Division's library in Hobart. Bob Headland at Scott Polar Research Institute showed me the startling committee minutes relating to the choice between Fuchs' plans and Duncan Carse's alternative plan. The Mitchell Library, Sydney, provided me with a scanned copy of Cook's original 'Yellow Line' map. Rita Bisley at James Cook University helped me with her knowledge and arranged borrowings for me.

Publishers have given me permission to quote some identified passages and redraw some diagrams. I acknowledge all of them for having done so. For quotations from Edmund Hillary's *View from the Summit* I thank the Random House Group Inc. I also acknowledge the satellite images from the US Geological Survey and NASA.

I have kept rewarding contact with Alec Trendall, who was the pioneer South Georgia geologist with Duncan Carse's mapping expeditions. Alec first alerted me to Carse's alternative Antarctic crossing proposal and provided me with a copy of it.

I went to the Royal Geographic Society in London, to look through the original TAE expedition's photographic files. I had taken over 800 Kodachrome photographs, which are in good condition. Justin Hobson assisted me in arranging for scanning of selected transparencies. George Lowe gave me permission to use his TAE photographs.

The printing of the colour photographs has been made possible by grants from the Trans-Antarctic Association, the Australian Antarctic Division and the Tasmanian Museum. I am especially grateful for their encouragement.

The Townsville City Council supported a TAE 50-year anniversary photo exhibition by awarding me a Queensland Government RADF grant. This helped my deliberations over photo selection.

Several veteran Antarctic explorers, Ken Blaiklock, Peter Clarkson and John Behrendt, helped me with extensive information. Charles Swithinbank has given me special information and advice, since I first met him before TAE. Peter Clarkson drew my attention to the Argentine discovery flights from Belgrano and gave me a copy of Pujato's account of their air explorations. Allesandra Mantovanelli made a translation from the Spanish. Peter Barker gave me comments on the remarkable Scotia Arc image, and I have used his published tectonic analysis.

It has been a special pleasure to renew friendship with members of the New Zealand TAE and IGY parties. John Claydon has provided much stimulation and encouragement and I have enjoyed getting to know the TAE historian, Stephen Hicks, in New Zealand.

Through John Smellie at British Antarctic Survey, I received a copy of a chapter of a thesis by Stephen Harangozo about Antarctic sea ice.

Alistair Cole crystallised a better understanding of James Cook's skill in position finding before he started using Harrison's chronometer.

Martin and Karl Kizur helped me repeatedly with their computer prowess, quickly solving the periodic problems I generated on my Macs. I have been very grateful to David Rosenberg for his positive encouragement, and to Carl Harrison-Ford for his essential editing and sensible advice.

Writing the book has been prolonged. I acknowledge the unswerving support, patience and tolerance from Jennepher, as well as her swift correction of howlers. My three daughters have maintained their interest and encouragement through these years. Most of my family have come down with me to see Antarctica, to better understand my life-long obsession with this special part of Planet Earth.

Jon Stephenson
February 2009

1 UNKNOWN ANTARCTICA

Antarctica is a huge continent, 5000 kilometres across in some regions. The outline of the Australian continent can be fitted inside it. Antarctica is buried in thick ice, and because of this is the highest continent (average elevation ~2300 metres). The average ice thickness is around 2700 metres and the highest region of its Polar Plateau rises to nearly three kilometres above sea level. A simplified map of Antarctica (Figure 1) shows its main geographic features and the routes of some early explorers.

In my last years at secondary school in Warwick, Queensland, I became obsessed by Antarctica, the ice continent. I was excited by the Scott legend and Douglas Mawson's achievements in his book, *Home of the Blizzard*. I felt compelled to learn more of these early explorers and if I wrote the word 'Antarctica' it was like a secret inspiration, a call to adventure.

I felt destined to see and experience Antarctica at first hand, to judge if its conditions were really as severe as reputed and whether I could cope with them. In the late 1940s, getting to Antarctica was impossible unless on an expedition. To do so required a qualification and relevant experience, quite a challenge in Australia. I studied geology at university and sought fieldwork in less accessible regions of Australia, from Tasmania to north Queensland.

A position arose in 1954 for a geologist on the first Australian mainland expedition by ANARE (Australian National Antarctic Research Expeditions), to establish what became known as Mawson Base. I was 24 and completing Honours in Geology at the University of Queensland. To the surprise of some of my mentors, I applied and was dismayed to not even be given an interview. I felt my last chance was gone, so I decided to go ahead with research studies and won an 1851 Exhibition Scholarship to England.

In 1954 I was studying at Imperial College, London, on the other side of the world. I embraced climbing with enthusiasm, including a summer in the Swiss Alps. Events can take unexpected turns and in 1956 I was interviewed to take part in Dr Vivian Fuchs' Commonwealth Trans-Antarctic Expedition (TAE). Circumstances can change in remarkable ways, and I was selected to take part in the party as geologist. My schoolboy dreams were soon to become a reality; I couldn't believe my change of luck.

This book describes Fuchs' achievements in leading the expedition to cross the vast and forbidding Antarctic continent in the face of severe obstacles, including opposition to his plan, a near disaster before reaching the starting point in Antarctica, and the hellish crossing into the unknown.

In hindsight, examining a map of Antarctica as we now know it (Figure 1 and Plate 1), his plan might seem straightforward. Fuchs' idea was to cross the continent by the shortest and most direct route, still over 3000 km, from the Weddell Sea to the Ross Sea. His proposal paralleled plans, made forty years before, by Bruce, Filchner and Shackleton. Fuchs' route would involve a climb from sea level to an altitude of around three kilometres, onto the vast South Polar Plateau. Modern satellite imagery shows the configuration of

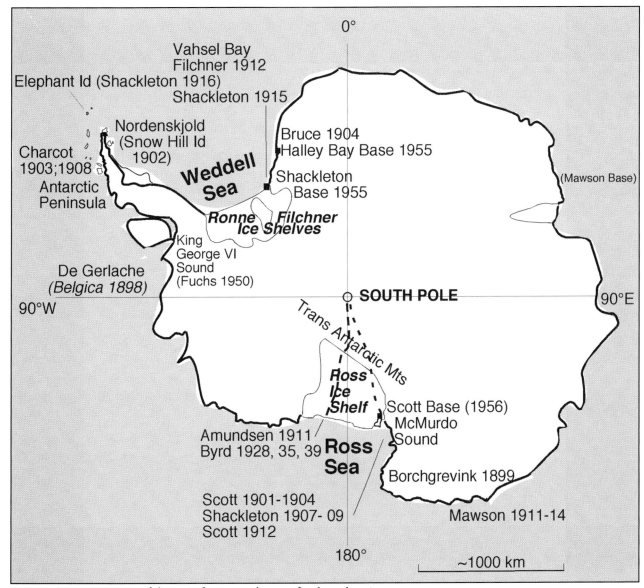

Figure 1 Antarctica: some of the main features and areas of early exploration.

the interior (Plate 2) and the TAE route. In the mid-1950s, the mountains and hazardous glaciers along this route were still undiscovered. It would be very much a journey into the unknown.

ANTARCTICA AND ITS EXPLORATION

A hostile ocean, with icy seas and high winds, surrounds the continent. Floating pack-ice with gigantic icebergs provides a severe barrier for access by ship, even in summer. Ships must negotiate a passage through it. In some regions the pack-ice can 'beset'

and crush ships, as it did to Shackleton's *Endurance*.

Only about 2 percent of the area of Antarctica shows exposed rock, but from studies of these outcrops, its geological structure has been found to be similar to the other continents, with granite, ancient continental rocks and sedimentary rock basins.

Antarctica has magnificent mountains, with peaks reaching nearly 5000 metres. There are distinct mountain chains and isolated peaks, called nunataks. Inland, the ice cap rises to the Polar Plateau, reaching 3000 metres. This plateau is vast, and to live anywhere in Antarctica is a challenge because of extreme temperatures, high winds and the prolonged winter darkness, which lasts six months at the Pole. Travel across the plateau is a major undertaking, not only because of

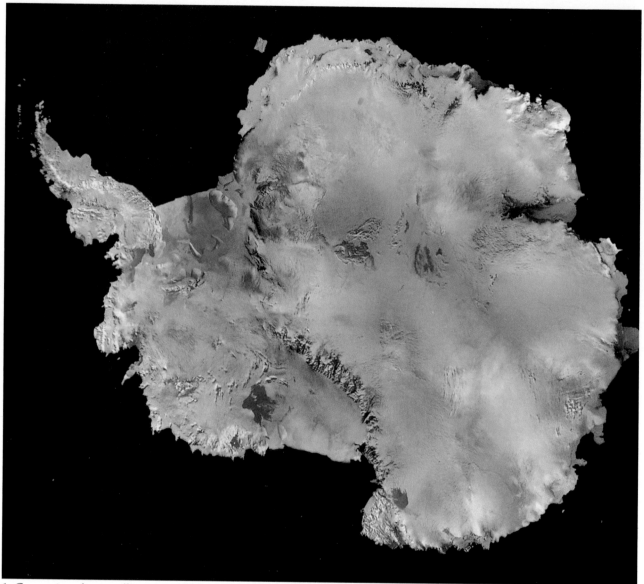

1 Composite colour satellite image of Antarctica. (Acknowledgment: NASA and US Geological Survey)

the weather. The altitude can also challenge vehicle and human performance. The surface can be soft snow and there are usually sastrugi — sharp snow features carved by the wind. In winter, temperatures can be extreme (as low as -89.6°C [-129.3°F], a surface low for Planet Earth), and in summer they typically range -10 to -49°C. The wind can be severe in summer and is much worse in winter. In some regions, there are strong katabatic winds, where the heavy, colder air on the high plateau rushes down the slope towards the coast. Winds can gust to over 100 mph (160 km/h) and blizzards make survival precarious. Antarctica has a profound influence on the weather in the other southern continents.

Snowfall accumulates, with the inland regions drier. The high plateau receives less than 5 centimetres of equivalent rainfall annually. Near the coast, summer temperatures can rise above freezing point, producing melting and streams in the mountains. Melting does not usually occur inland, and the dry snow merely compacts with accumulation, finally turning into ice. On the Polar Plateau, deep drilling has recovered the deeper ice, providing information about past climatic conditions. It also reveals the prior concentration of gases, like carbon dioxide and methane, in the atmosphere.

Antarctica's oceans are incredibly rich in marine life. Penguins, seals, killer whales and other whales live in the southern oceans and are common along the coast. Some animals venture a short distance inland and a few seals get lost and die hundreds of kilometres

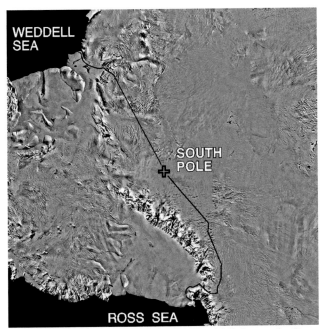

2 AVHRR satellite image, from the Weddell Sea to the Ross Sea. The topography of the continent is evident, and the TAE crossing route. (Acknowledgment: NASA and US Geological Survey)

inland. In the Theron Mountains, I was amazed to see hundreds of birds nesting in the cliffs, over 240 km from the frozen ocean, where they get their food. We saw little wildlife on the crossing journey, but petrels have been seen well inland.

Special clothing is needed and, properly clothed, it is possible to stay comfortably warm. Windproofs and layers of warm underclothes are routinely worn. Expedition equipment must include suitable transportation and shelter from the weather, and specially designed tents and huts. Fuel and other supplies need to be carefully planned, and reliable radio or satellite communication is essential.

To reach Antarctica, a robust ship is needed to negotiate the pack-ice. Aircraft must be extremely careful to respect weather conditions, and to reach and be guided to land safely on prepared landing sites.

Exploration — Early and Recent

Greek and Egyptian geographers surmised the existence of a southern continent to balance the northern continents nearly 2000 years ago.[1] The probable presence of a frozen continent was shown by the navigational genius, James Cook, on his second voyage (1772–75).[2] On this voyage he circumnavigated Antarctica and proved that even wooden ships could be used to approach the southern ice. He did not see the continent, but commented graphically on its dangers to ships:

> The risk one runs in exploring a coast in these unknown and Icy Seas, is so very great, that I can be bold to say, that no man will ever venture further than I have done and that the lands which may lie to the South will never be explored. Thick fogs, Snow storms, Intense Cold and every other thing that can render Navigation dangerous one has to encounter and these difficulties are greatly heightened by the unexpressable horrid aspect of the Country, a country doomed by Nature never once to feel the warmth of the Suns rays, but to lie for ever buried under everlasting snow and ice.[3]

Clearly, Antarctica didn't get a good report from Cook. The first voyager to actually see the main coast of Antarctica was the Russian explorer, Fabian Gottlieb von Bellingshausen, in 1820, when he also circumnavigated the continent. He saw the coast in the region of the Greenwich meridian (0°), but failed to place much emphasis on seeing the ice rising to the south, beyond the pack-ice which fringes it.

For all his warnings about the hostility of the continent, Cook did report favourably on his discovery of South Georgia in the south Atlantic, namely its abundant seal and penguin populations. Despite Cook's bleak reports, men could not resist the challenge to seek the unseen continent and extend southern commercial exploitation of seals, penguins and whales. Traditional sealing and whaling in the Arctic had been declining because of diminishing numbers, and South Georgia and the islands north of the Antarctic Peninsula were soon relentlessly exploited for their animal oil.

The exploration of the Antarctic coast progressed spasmodically via circumnavigation voyages. In 1823, James Weddell penetrated into the deep indentation, which now bears his name, south of the Atlantic Ocean. He believed that he could have sailed on to reach a supposed open ocean at the Pole. Three important international expeditions set off in 1840–41: French, American and British. The French and American expeditions discovered new coasts of the Antarctic mainland south of Australia in January 1840. A year later, the Englishman, James Clerk Ross, discovered a second major sea indentation, now known as the Ross Sea, which provides the easiest access to Antarctica. This became the standard approach route for exploring the continent, including the efforts to reach the mysterious geographic point, the South Pole, 90°S.

Although numerous expeditions had visited the Arctic regions and wintered there, the first to winter in Antarctica did so somewhat abruptly, by dint of being caught in pack-ice north of the Antarctic Peninsula. This was the Belgian expedition led by de Gerlache, in *Belgica*, 1897–99, which experienced an anxious time. The first land expedition on the continent, in 1899, was British, led by the Norwegian Carsten Borchgrevink. They wintered at Cape Adare, at the entrance to the Ross Sea. Three major national expeditions, from Britain, France and Germany, took place early in the twentieth century. The British expedition, in *Discovery*, began explorations from the Ross Sea, and Robert Falcon Scott made the first travels towards the Pole in 1903. Otto Nordenskjold led a Swedish expedition to the north-eastern Antarctic Peninsula, but his expedition ship, *Antarctic*, skippered by Carl Larsen, was crushed and sank off the northern Antarctic Peninsula. Larsen and all but one of his 20 men survived on Paulet Island. William Bruce, from Edinburgh, led an expedition into the Weddell Sea and found a route down the east coast, which later expeditions followed. French expeditions led by Jean Charcot, in *Francais* and *Pourqui Pas?*, carried out further exploration in the Antarctic Peninsula, and the German Eric von Drygalski, in *Gauss*, explored mainland Antarctica, south of Australia. Larsen established successful whaling operations on South Georgia in 1904.

Ernest Shackleton returned to Antarctica in 1908 in *Nimrod*, having taken part in Scott's first expedition. He succeeded in getting to within 180 km of the Pole. The race for the Pole accelerated, and the expeditions of Norway's Roald Amundsen, in *Fram*, and Robert Falcon Scott, in *Terra Nova*, both reached the Pole in 1911–12. Amundsen, with dogs, arrived over a month before Scott, with ponies and manhauling. Tragically, Scott and his party of five perished on the return journey. At the same time as Scott's expedition, Douglas Mawson, who had been with Shackleton on *Nimrod*, led the Australasian Antarctic Expedition (1911–14) in *Aurora*. His successful expedition operated mainly in the Commonwealth Bay region, south of Australia. Sadly, two of Mawson's companions died while Mawson survived, after a traumatic yet heroic struggle.

In 1911 a German party went to the Weddell Sea to attempt an Antarctic crossing following a plan proposed by Bruce in 1910. Wilhelm Filchner, in *Deutschland*, reached Vahsel Bay in the south-east corner. His attempt to build a base there failed, and *Deutschland* became beset and drifted north with the pack-ice during the winter of 1912. Fortunately, she emerged unscathed and returned safely to South Georgia.

Ernest Shackleton led the Imperial Transantarctic Expedition in *Endurance* in 1914–16 and reached South Georgia. Attempting to reach Vahsel Bay, *Endurance* was beset and drifted with the pack-ice until she was crushed and sank. Shackleton managed to escape with all his men to Elephant Island, near the tip of the Antarctic Peninsula, and in one of exploration's great survival epics, from there he sailed a lifeboat, the *James Caird*, to reach South Georgia with five companions. He then crossed the island with two of his men to reach a whaling station and had the three who had been left behind picked up by ship. Later, he returned to Elephant Island with Captain Luis Pardo in the Chilean tug, *Yelcho*, to rescue all the 20 men waiting there. His Ross Sea support party, in *Aurora*, laid depots for him towards the Pole but suffered many disasters, including the death of three men. Shackleton relieved them with Captain Davis, in *Aurora*.

The UK Discovery Committee was set up in 1923 to help the International Whaling Conference frame regulations to protect whale stocks being harvested in the southern oceans. *Discovery*, Scott's first expedition ship, was used on oceanographic and survey work in 1925–26 and *Discovery II* from 1929 to 1933. *Discovery II* circumnavigated the Antarctic continent in a series of voyages, reaching the edge of the pack-ice. This was only the fifth Antarctic circumnavigation and the first during winter, reaching 70°S in the Weddell Sea. A major scientific achievement on her second voyage (1933ñ35) was recording the approximate positions of the Antarctic Convergence, the junction zone where cold Antarctic waters descend under the warmer waters to their north. The Convergence is a continuous boundary surrounding Antarctica.

Richard Byrd led several American expeditions, in 1928 in *City of New York*, and in 1934, in *Jacob Ruppert* and *Bear of Oakland*, from a succession of bases called Little America, close to Amundsen's base at the Bay of Whales, south of the Ross Sea. Byrd introduced aircraft to Antarctic exploration and flew over the Pole on 29 November 1929. However, Hubert Wilkins achieved the first flights in Antarctica, on 16 and 26 November that year. In December, Wilkins made an 11-hour flight from Deception down the Antarctic Peninsula to reach 71°S. Lincoln Ellsworth (US) and Hubert Hollick-Kenyon (UK) made the first flight across Antarctica, in November 1935, from the northern Antarctic Peninsula across to Little America on the Ross Sea. This took them a month, which is indicative of the difficult flying conditions.

Australia's Antarctic explorer, Douglas Mawson, organised BANZARE (British Australian New Zealand Antarctic Research Expedition) in 1929–31. The expedition was based on *Discovery II*'s extensive cruises between 60° and 170°E, and carried out wide-ranging scientific work. Antarctic territorial claims intensified from around 1923 and involved Australia, New Zealand, France and Norway. Norwegian exploration, in *Norwegia*, and the BANZARE cruises included landings to confirm sovereignty. The Australian and Norwegian claims were reconciled, but Chilean and Argentinean claims overlapped, as they did with British territory. Disputes were resolved by the Antarctic Treaty (1961), which froze existing claims without any judgment on their validity, and decreed that no nation is required to recognise another nation's claim.

In 1934–37, a significant private British expedition, the British Graham Land Expedition led by John Rymill, in *Penola*, travelled down the west coast of the Antarctic Peninsula. It corrected an inaccurate report that there were channels across the Peninsula, originally identified by Wilkins and Ellsworth.

In 1937, Germany undertook the *Schwabenland* expedition in Dronning Maud Land, east of the Weddell Sea, using aerial photography in a region near 0°. Land claims were made via swastika darts from the aircraft, a novel way to make such claims.

After 1945, considerable exploration was undertaken in the Antarctic Peninsula by the British Antarctic Survey (BAS) from a number of established bases. American expeditions (1941–42) operated in the Ross Sea from Little America, under Byrd, and in the south-west of the Antarctic Peninsula by the US Antarctic Service Expedition, led by Richard Black. In 1947, a joint US–UK enterprise (RARE — the Ronne Antarctic Research Expedition; and FIDS — the Falkland Island Dependencies Survey) carried

out an extensive aerial and ground-based survey of the southern Antarctic Peninsula. The leaders were Finn Ronne and Ken Butler, respectively.

The US mounted its largest Antarctic operation in 1946, Operation Highjump, led by the veteran, Richard Byrd. A number of aircraft made extensive photographic survey flights around Antarctica, discovering new land. Highjump involved 23 aircraft, 13 ships and more than 4700 men.

A major Antarctic expedition, the international NBS (Norwegian-British-Swedish Expedition), took place in 1949–52. The inland area it investigated was near the Greenwich meridian in Dronning Maud Land. NBS was highly successful, undertaking pioneering research in glaciology, geology, meteorology and the measurement of ice thickness by seismic sounding.

In 1954 the Australian National Antarctic Expeditions established a new base, Mawson, near 60°E. Other bases have since been established, and extensive scientific work and exploratory journeys undertaken in this region.

THE HISTORICAL CONTEXT FOR VIVIAN FUCHS AND HIS PLANNING FOR TAE (1955–58)

Weddell Sea explorations are generally less well known than those to the Ross Sea, where the quest for the South Pole had obsessed exploration for several decades. The major Weddell expeditions are listed below.

Major Weddell Sea Expeditions Before TAE

James Cook	1775
James Weddell	1823
James Clerk Ross	1843
Otto Nordenskjold and Carl Larsen	1894; 1902–04
William Bruce	1904
Wilhelm Filchner	1911–12
Ernest Shackleton	1914–16
Discovery Committee	1929–33
FIDS and RARE (Finn Ronne)	1947
NBS Expedition	1950–52

These Weddell explorations — which are described in Appendix I — informed Fuchs in his TAE planning. The historic approaches to the South Pole had all been made from the Ross Sea, because of the inaccessibility of the Weddell Sea. It was against this historical background that Fuchs made his plans. The best approach to get ships deep into the Weddell Sea was known, though it still had a severe reputation.

Although only two ships (*Endurance*, 1912, and *San Martin*, 1955) had followed the route pioneered by Bruce in 1904, this approach seemed the most promising. Shackleton's *Endurance* had been caught and crushed, but the strength of iron ships had improved, with ice-strengthened hulls and icebreakers. The Ross Sea had no such history of sinking ships, and had been visited by many more expeditions. Although the nature of the Polar Plateau was known from the Shackleton, Amundsen and Scott expeditions, the vast interior between the southern coast of the Weddell Sea and the South Pole was still completely unknown. NBS was the only expedition which had penetrated the interior in the Weddell region. In 1955, exciting prospects for new exploration and discoveries were still open to TAE.

Fuchs grasped how important aerial support would be for the expedition. He was impressed by the way Byrd used air exploration in his pioneering work from 1928, south of the Ross Sea, and by the British Graham Land Expedition's effective use of their single aircraft in the 1930s. Finn Ronne used two aircraft on his expedition in 1947 and NBS also used aircraft during its summer visits.

Looking back after more than 50 years, TAE seems distant from the modern era, with its regular tourist voyages to Antarctica and a permanent US station at the South Pole. It is interesting that, half a century later, the memory of the journey I undertook with my fellow expeditioners is imprinted vividly on my consciousness. Time has taken its toll — most of the expeditioners have now, sadly, passed on — but not the images in my mind. They are etched sharply in my memory.

2 THE TRANS-ANTARCTIC EXPEDITION, 1955–58: A FOOTHOLD ON THE CONTINENT

Of the Antarctic expeditions which preceded TAE, the highly successful Norwegian-British-Swedish (NBS) expedition, had a major influence on the science Vivian Fuchs planned for TAE. Another expedition which influenced his planning, and provided some very experienced men for his party, was the British North Greenland Expedition (BNGE, 1953–54).[1]

The Trans-Antarctic Expedition was one of a number of expeditions which contributed to the scientific IGY (International Geophysical Year, 1957–58).[2] The IGY was the third Polar Year, proposed by Dr Lloyd Berkner (US), and involved 12 countries. Antarctica was recognised for special attention whereas previous 'years' had concentrated on the Arctic. The intention was to encourage geophysicists to conduct research on the Earth's surface and its atmosphere, via coordinated observations around the globe. The IGY was to contribute new knowledge in virtually all sectors of science, and international cooperation was noteworthy. There were about 40 research stations in Antarctica, and TAE was to carry out observations and research at three: Shackleton and Scott Bases, and a station inland from Shackleton, known later as South Ice.

TAE was a British Commonwealth enterprise, supported by Britain, New Zealand, Australia and South Africa. Its originator was Dr Vivian Fuchs. Fuchs (1908–1999) had studied at St John's College, Cambridge, where he specialised in geology. His tutor was James (later Sir James) Wordie, who had been Senior Scientist on Shackleton's Imperial Trans-Antarctic Expedition, on *Endurance*. Fuchs spent many years in exploration, first as an undergraduate on a summer expedition (led by Wordie) to Greenland in 1929 and then on four expeditions to Africa, on two of which he was leader. During World War II, he served in West Africa and Normandy, and immediately after, in rehabilitation work centred in Plön in Germany. In 1947 he was appointed Field Commander of all the Falkland Islands Dependencies Survey (FIDS) bases in Antarctica, and acquired his ice experience while leader at Stonington Base. He carried out some long dog-team journeys while at Stonington.

HOW DID IT START?

In *A Time to Speak*, Fuchs has described the circumstances which stimulated the idea of an expedition to cross Antarctica. At Stonington Island on the west side of the southern Antarctic Peninsula,[3] his party of 11 included his fellow geologist, Ray Adie.

In 1949, Fuchs and Adie undertook a long trip, studying the geology of the area, travelling down George VI Sound, south of Stonington. After a dog-sledge journey of over 50 days and 420 miles, they reached Eklund Island, which Finn Ronne and Carl Eklund had visited nine years earlier on the US Service Expedition, from its East Base on Stonington Island. Fuchs and Adie located the Americans' cairn on the island, but the start of their return journey was delayed by blizzards for several days. Confined to their tent, Fuchs records that all their books had already been read several times and Adie had been reading aloud the labels on some of their food tins. Conversation led them to thoughts of bigger and better expeditions to the interior of the continent. This was the germ of the idea that led to TAE. Two other men associated with Stonington were destined to take part on TAE, the surveyor Ken Blaiklock and pilot John Lewis. At the Stonington base, some of the men were apparently sceptical about the chance of success for the proposal, and Fuchs says bets were laid.

On his way back to England, Fuchs called on Sir Miles Clifford, the Governor of the Falkland Islands at Port Stanley, and outlined his ideas. Clifford was responsive, and arranged for the secretary of FIDS in Stanley, Ken Butler, to ask Fuchs to give Butler his plans. Fuchs was astonished by what he perceived as a 'poaching' move, and refused to provide or discuss his plans. However, Clifford wrote to the Secretary of State for the Colonies in London about the idea, which would necessitate cooperation from the New Zealand government. A sum of £45,000, during 1951 to 1954, was the cost estimate for Clifford's outline.[4]

The management of British Antarctic affairs in the 1950s became quite complex, involving three separate administrative bodies — the Falkland Islands and Dependencies administration, the Colonial Office, and the Falkland Islands Dependency Survey. While Fuchs had been away in Antarctica, the Colonial Office had approved that exploration and results from the FIDS survey were to be administered by a new office, FID Scientific Bureau (FIDSc). After returning to England in 1950, Fuchs accepted a position to set up this bureau, and started work in June 1950. He discussed his ideas for an Antarctic crossing with James Wordie, by then a significant member of the Colonial Office Polar Committee. Wordie was fully supportive and told Fuchs he would tell him 'the right moment' to submit such a proposal.

Fuchs submitted a confidential proposal in 1953, seeking government support. The media took it up after the proposal was inadvertently leaked to the press in New Zealand, and it rapidly became a talking point in the British polar community. Fuchs became aware of serious opposition from three directions — the Foreign Office, the Scott Polar Research Institute

(SPRI) and the Royal Geographical Society (RGS). Apparently, concern was based on embarrassment for Britain if the project failed, perhaps with memories of Shackleton's ITAE and *Endurance*. Someone, possibly Larry Kerwin of the RGS, said, 'leave such a journey [across Antarctica] to the Americans'. The RGS even decided a journey across Antarctica ought properly to be led by Sir Edmund Hillary, of Everest fame. Later, as Fuchs commented, at that time Hillary had never even seen sea ice. There was continuing promotion of a significant alternative project, involving the southern Antarctic Peninsula. Fuchs' proposal made very slow and difficult progress towards acceptance.

In the archives at the Scott Polar Research Institute in Cambridge there is an interesting set of notes from two meetings of the Polar Committee (30 June 1954 and 15 September 1954), held in the Commonwealth Relations Office.[5] These state that, at the meeting in June, 'the proposals of Dr Fuchs and Mr Carse were both studied'. Duncan Carse had been the youngest member of the British Graham Land Expedition (1934–37), led by John Rymill. After serving in the Royal Navy in the war, Carse had a leading role in a BBC radio series and became well known as 'Dick Barton, Special Agent'. This was to be superseded by the BBC series, 'The Archers', and Carse turned his attention to a project to map South Georgia. He was involved in this from 1951 until 1957.

Duncan Carse had submitted an alternative crossing proposal in competition with Fuchs' plan. The details of the two proposals considered by the Polar Committee are not described in the Committee's notes, beyond recording that Fuchs indicated two possible routes — one from Vahsel Bay and the other from Stonington, on the west side of the Antarctic Peninsula. The notes simply state that Fuchs' proposal was preferred for 'meteorological reasons'. These 1954 notes mention possible financial sources — UK, New Zealand, Australian, South African and Canadian. Fuchs estimated a cost of £200,000, plus air and naval support. The proposals for a Trans-Antarctic Expedition were noted to have 'a romantic appeal'. At the September meeting, it is stated that Mr B.B. Roberts was 'prepared to act on Carse's behalf, due to his absence on South Georgia'. Fuchs had provided the Commonwealth Relations Office with a memorandum of his TAE plans in August 1953.

Duncan Carse's Proposal[6]

This interesting document proposed a trans-Antarctic expedition. He distributed it to about 10 people, including Fuchs. It is detailed, and provides an interesting comparison with Fuchs' eventual TAE. The proposal is carefully written, but makes no claim that its author be the leader.

The reasons why the Polar Committee confirmed Fuchs as the TAE leader remain for a future historian to discover. However, Duncan Carse had no strong polar or leadership experience. The evaluation of his proposal had to rely on the Committee members' personal knowledge of Carse, as the Committee, being away on South Georgia, could not interview him. His plan was ambitious, and involved two parties. Its essentials are shown on the map he provided, redrawn here as Figure 2.

It is all too easy in hindsight to see its deficiencies, based on TAE's experience. His plan involved the use of Weasel vehicles, presumably modelled on the NBS experience with them referred to in Appendix I.

Ken Blaiklock has generously provided me with his assessment of Carse's plans. Blaiklock based this on his own considerable Antarctic experience:

The Carse proposals are wildly ambitious and optimistic, not only in the number of field operations but also in logistics, timing and cost. Three main problems in the program stand out.

1. Crossing party. This should be the main and probably the only effort with everything geared to achieving this. Even so, it is a risky one banking on descending through the Trans-Antarctic Mountains down an unexplored glacier. Only two routes had been previously sledged — Beardmore and Axel Heiberg. Both were ascended from the Ross Ice Shelf and I reckon it would be much more difficult finding a route descending from the plateau.

2. Reliance on Weasels. Even in the 1950's on NBSX (Norwegian British Swedish Expedition) they were somewhat unreliable at times (see Giaver's account, pages 155, 158, 181, 210).

3. The evacuation of the remaining base members to Marguerite Bay (Antarctic Peninsula) would be even more hazardous. Base E at Stonington was closed in 1950, no prospect in 1953 of being reopened until early 1961. Horseshoe Island 40 miles north would almost certainly have no sea ice to get to Stonington later in summer time. FIDS (Falkland Islands Division Survey) might be unwilling to assist as part of a private expedition, and even if they could get to Three Slice Nunatak on the Larsen Ice Shelf side (east side of the Antarctic Peninsula), the route up to the plateau and down Northeast Glacier would be hazardous in the extreme without Stonington ground support.

It is easy to comment with hindsight, but even without that, I would estimate the chances of success to be less

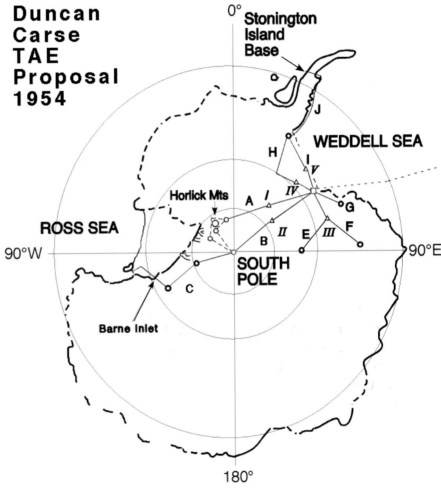

Duncan Carse TAE Proposal 1954

Crossing party routes: A, B; C
Depots: *I - V*

Figure 2 Duncan Carse's map for his proposed Trans-Antarctic Expedition.

than 50%, and some sort of emergency disaster on some part of the plans to be almost certain — Perhaps that's me being pessimistic![7]

Ken Blaiklock makes other, detailed comments on Carse's standing as a non-scientist and on his limited experience in Antarctica. In his view, there were too many projects planned, concurrently with the main crossing, and there were no contingency plans had the party needed to return to Vahsel Bay. Also, he considered that proposed rations for the crossing were inadequate for hard travelling at high altitudes.

After much deliberation, Fuchs records he calculated TAE would need a total of around £500,000, and Wordie advised him about finding this amount. Fuchs found an influential chairman for a Committee of Management in Sir John Slessor, Marshal of the Royal Air Force. Fuchs envisaged a Commonwealth expedition and he was able to address a Commonwealth Prime Ministers meeting in London in 1955 to seek their support. After this meeting, Sir Winston Churchill approved a grant of £100,000 and New Zealand, Australia and South Africa agreed to help, later contributing a total of £87,000. The Australian government contribution was £20,000 (A£25,000). Thus the Commonwealth government contributions amounted to £187,000. The relative value in today's terms of the sum of £500,000 can be estimated as over £9 million.[8] Public donations from 480 firms also provided a major contributions and £1000 from the Royal Geographical Society was the first donation received. British Petroleum was a very generous supporter, providing the expedition's vehicle and aircraft fuel, and lubricants. Nearly 4000 schools enthusiastically raised cash and other support, and a scheme arranged for them to nominate financial support for individual dogs on the expedition.

Offices for TAE were established at 64 Victoria Street, an address not far from Scott's office for his South Pole expedition, and Rear Admiral Cecil Parry was appointed secretary. A valuable appointment was Eleanor Honnywill, who joined the office staff. Fuchs needed to be replaced in his FIDSc Bureau position, and Sir Raymond Priestly succeeded him. Priestly had been south with both Shackleton and Scott. Three subcommittees were set up, with Professor H.H. Read as chairman of the scientific program. Read, as my research supervisor at Imperial College, proved to be a very important person in my later selection to

join the expedition. Sir Miles Clifford, home again on leave from the Falklands, became an enthusiastic member of the Committee of Management.

THE GRAND PLAN: THE CAST

The plans are shown diagrammatically in Figure 3. Fuchs is shown describing his adventurous plans, described in the press as 'the last great journey', in Plate 3.

An advance party of eight was to build a base on the Filchner Ice Shelf in the Weddell Sea, near Vahsel Bay,

3 Dr Vivian Fuchs discusses his plan for an Antarctic crossing, 1955. He is pointing to the site for Shackleton Bas

in 1955–56. A year later, this base would be occupied by the main crossing party, which would winter there and undertake geophysical work in conjunction with the IGY, then travel across the continent via the South Pole in the following summer (1957–58). A New Zealand party, led by Sir Edmund Hillary, would set up a base at McMurdo Sound on the Ross Sea in

1957, in the same region as Scott's first expedition. It would establish fuel and food depots for the crossing route, from McMurdo towards the Pole. An IGY scientific party would also accompany the NZ Party.

The expedition was to be mobilised with vehicles and dogs. Air support was to involve the RAF (four men) and the RNZAF (three men).

The Expedition Teams

Fuchs selected the following men for his Weddell Sea team as follows. Team members are from the UK, unless otherwise indicated.

1955–57 ADVANCE PARTY
(MV THERON)

K.V. Blaiklock, Leader, Surveyor, age 27

R.A. Lenton, Deputy Leader, Carpenter and Radio Operator, 32

Dr R.Goldsmith, Medical Officer, 28

J.J. la Grange, Meteorologist (South Africa), 28

Sergeant Major D.E.L. (Roy) Homard, REME, Engineer, 34

P.H. Jeffries, Meteorologist, 24

R.H.A. Stewart, Meteorologist, 32

Sergeant E. (Taffy) Williams, RAF, Radio Operator, 35

1956–58 TRANS-POLAR PARTY

(Most having arrived on MV Magga Dan)

Dr V.E. Fuchs, Leader, Geologist, 48*#

D.G. Stratton, Deputy Leader, Surveyor, 28*#

K.V. Blaiklock, Surveyor, 28

J.J. la Grange, Meteorologist (South Africa), 29

Sergeant Major D.E.L. (Roy) Homard, REME, Engineer, 35

R.A. Lenton, Carpenter and Radio Operator, 33

Dr H. Lister, Glaciologist, 33#

W.G. Lowe, Photographer (NZ), 31*#

D.L. Pratt, Engineer, 30*#

J.G.D. Pratt, Geophysicist, 31#

Dr A.F. Rogers, Medical Officer and Physiologist, 38#

Dr P.J. Stephenson, Geologist (Australia), 26#

ROYAL AIR FORCE CONTINGENT

Squadron Leader J.H. Lewis, Senior Pilot, 33*#

Flight Lieutenant G.M. Haslop, Second Pilot (NZ), 32*#

Flight Sergeant P. Weston, Aircraft Mechanic, 34*#

Sergeant E. (Taffy) Williams, Radio Operator, 36

*Accompanied the Advance Party on Theron (returned in February 1956).

#Arrived on Magga Dan in January 1957.

Sir Edmund Hillary and J.H. (Bob) Miller (Leader and Deputy Leader of the Ross Sea Party) and Squadron Leader J.R. Claydon (RNZAF) travelled on Theron in 1955–56.

1957–58 THE NEW ZEALAND PARTY
(HRNZS ENDEAVOUR)

Sir Edmund Hillary, Leader, 38

J.H. Miller, Deputy Leader, Surveyor, 36

Dr G.W. Marsh, Medical Officer and Senior Dog Driver, (UK), 30

M.R. Ellis, Engineer, 31

Lieutenant Commander F.R. Brooke, RN, Surveyor and Dog Driver (UK), 29

H.H. Ayres, Mountaineer and Dog Driver, 44

B.M. Gunn, Geologist, 30

G. Warren, Geologist, 23

R.A. Carlyon, Civil Engineer and Surveyor, 23

M.H. Douglas, Mountaineer and Dog Driver, 29

Dr R.W. Balham, Meteorologist and Biologist, 34

J.G. Bates, Diesel/Electric Mechanic, 31

E.S. Bucknell, Cook, 29

Chief Petty Officer P.D. Mulgrew, RNZN, Senior Radio Operator, 29

J.E. Gawn, Radio Operator, 38

Squadron Leader J.R. Claydon, RNZAF, Senior Pilot, 38

Flying Officer W.J. Cranfield, RNZAF, Pilot, 22

Sergeant L.W. Tarr, RNZAF, Aircraft Mechanic, 31

1957–58 THE IGY SCIENTIFIC PARTY

Dr T. Hatherton, Senior Scientist and Auroral Observer, 31

V.M. Gerard, Magnetic Observer, 31

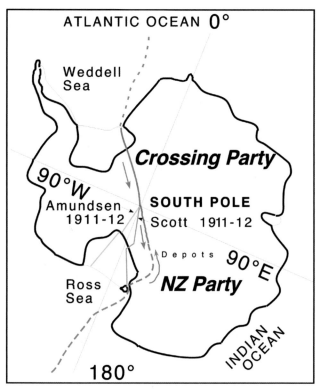

Figure 3 Overall plan for Fuchs' Trans-Antarctic Expedition.

R.H. Orr, Seismologist, 29
W.J.P. Macdonald, Solar Radiation Observer, 30
H.N.   Sandford,   Ionospheric
    Observer, 25

GETTING THERE: THE ADVANCE PARTY — 1955

MV *Theron* was an ice-strengthened Canadian sealer under
Captain Harold Marø. This 650-
ton ship was registered in Halifax,
Nova Scotia, and was chartered to
take the expedition to the Weddell
Sea. She sailed from Millwall
Docks in London on 14 November
1955. Her holds were full and her
deck space carried hundreds of
fuel barrels, two aircraft, a Sno-
Cat in a crate, a Ferguson tractor,
24 dogs from Greenland and
many other essentials, including a
prefabricated hut and workshop.
Crowds waved and shouted good
luck from wharves and jetties

along the Thames, and tugs and steamers hooted and
Captain Marø replied with *Theron's* siren.

  Theron sailed south via the Cape Verde Islands to
Montevideo. Plate 4 shows the group on board and
includes all the Advance Party charged with the
job of establishing the expedition's mainland site,
later known as Shackleton Base. *Theron* called at
Montevideo, to be joined by two of the NZ Ross
Sea Party, namely Ed Hillary and Bob Miller. The
Senior NZ Pilot, John Claydon, sailed on *Theron*
from London. The New Zealanders came to observe
Antarctic conditions in preparation for their Scott
Base plans a year later. North of Montevideo, Roy
Homard witnessed what might be seen as an ill-fated
omen for the *Theron* voyage, when a crew member
shot an albatross. Shades of 'The Ancient Mariner'!

  On 18 December 1955, a visit to Grytviken on
South Georgia was used for a short test flight by
Gordon Haslop for the Auster aircraft, equipped with
floats. Fuel was loaded at nearby Leith Harbour and
fresh water at Husvik. There were the usual icebergs
near South Georgia, and the vessel began to make her
way through the first pack-ice, moving further south
shortly before Christmas. Her choice of approach
route to reach the Antarctic coast was influenced by

4 Expedition group on *Theron*, sailing from London to Montevideo, late 1955. Back row:
David Stratton, Vivian Fuchs, Ken Blaiklock*, Ralph Lenton*, Taffy Williams*, Hannes
la Grange*, Tony Stewart*, Derek Williams (British Petroleum photographer), Rainer
Goldsmith*. Font row: Gordon Haslop, Peter Weston, John Lewis, David Pratt, John
Claydon (NZ TAE), Peter Jeffries*, Roy Homard*. The photo is from John Claydon, and
was probably taken by George Lowe. Advance Party members are marked*

the earlier Weddell explorations. If the Antarctic coast can be reached close to Kapp Norwegia, near 11°W, an open channel can usually be found along the coast, a gateway to the southern Weddell Sea. Though ice conditions in one season may be very different for the next, a ship usually has to fight its way through tight pack-ice to get to Kapp Norwegia, and can be delayed should it become trapped in the ice.

Theron was to experience over a month of frustration in the pack-ice (Plate 5). Her choice of approach route from South Georgia to eventually reach Halley Bay and the site for Shackleton Base is shown in Figure 4. An initial Auster flight was made on Boxing Day by John Lewis to find a way ahead. The vessel was severely 'nipped' by the ice, which rose on each side to deck level, and her rudder was bent. A few days later, on 20 January 1956, Captain Marø undertook a skilful manoeuvre to straighten the rudder by reversing against a solid floe, which was successful on the fourth attempt. During the weeks while they were beset, they faced a hopeless predicament, in spite of

5 *Theron*, caught in the pack-ice, Weddell Sea. Members of the team are using various tools to release some of the ice adjacent to the ship. (Photo by George Lowe)

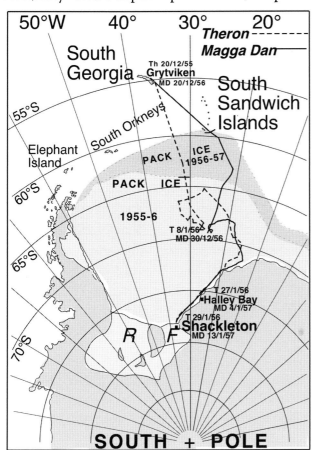

Figure 4 The routes followed by *Theron* and *Magga Dan* to get to the site of Shackleton Base. The places where the ships entered the pack-ice are shown. The pack-ice is shaded.

strenuous efforts to free the ship. However, there was time for some relaxation and Roy Homard became recognised for his affinity with wild life, when he 'called in' an Adelie penguin. He also built an igloo, but suffered snow blindness for his trouble. The ship measured its negative drift rate while beset.

Fuchs noted in his log: 'Looking back one realises that this was one of the occasions when the fate of the whole expedition must have hung in the balance'.

HMS *Protector* was in the Antarctic Peninsula area and her captain offered to sail to the edge of the ice, north of *Theron*, and help with ice reports and possible helicopter inspections. John Claydon made a critically important Auster flight on 20 January from 67°32'S, taking off from a barely long enough pool in the pack-ice. He reported that conditions should ease after another 50 miles, vital information for the Advance Party. He returned safely after a three-hour flight, sharing his landing pool with some whales. Emerging from the ice, *Theron* turned back north to make a rendezvous with *Protector*, and 10 men from *Theron* transferred for a visit, which Fuchs described as a 'great morale boost'. *Theron* then set off east, following the edge of the pack in the wake of another vessel, *Tottan*, skippered by Captain Jacobsen. *Tottan* had left South Georgia on Christmas Day, five days after *Theron*, carrying the Royal Society's IGY Expedition. She experienced heavy pack-ice on 2 January, only

25 miles from *Theron*, sought information from a TAE Auster flight, and was able to extricate herself and continue. *Tottan* reached a suitable site on the Caird Coast for siting the Royal Society IGY base a week later, at 75°36′ S, which they called Halley Bay.

Theron continued, following a similar course to *Tottan*, to reach the edge of the continent near Kapp Norvegia and enter a lead of open water, similar to that first found by William Bruce, 50 years before. (A lead is an area of open water in the pack-ice, which can give access for ships.) Currents and off-shore winds can

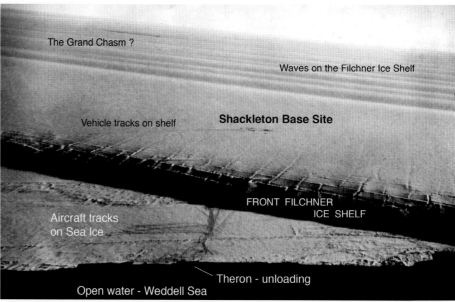

6 The site for Shackleton Base. *Theron* is unloading onto the ice, with the ice shelf behind where the base building would be erected. The crevasses under the site are clearly resolved. (High aerial photo by John Claydon)

produce an offshore lead. Shackleton used the lead in 1915 and the Argentinean vessel *San Martin*, in 1955, also used this entrance to the southern Weddell Sea to establish their Belgrano Base on the Filchner Ice Shelf.[9] By contrast, in 1911, *Deutschland* (with Filchner's German expedition) was able to follow a more direct route to reach the Antarctic coast further south (see Figure 27).

It is interesting to speculate how *Theron* came to be caught so badly in the ice. Why did she enter the ice well to the west of the entry established by Bruce in *Scotia* in 1904? Was this Fuchs' decision? Did Captain Marø have a part in choosing the route? Was Fuchs influenced by the experience of his mentor, James Wordie, who had been on *Endurance* with Shackleton in 1914? This is unlikely, as *Endurance* had gone further east.

Fuchs' journal recorded:

23rd December 'purposely entered the ice as far west as 30° W to allow diversion to the east, but there has been a general control of our movements in a south direction. Means in order to reach the 'land water' in the vicinity of Stancomb Wills Promontory we must definitely set to, say, 140° True. Ralph Lenton (TAE radio) listening radio exchange Belgrano (Argentine base) and San Martin (Argentine resupply ship). Not yet entered the ice. On 24th: ten mile pool. Forced south by such leads of open water as are to be found, in spite of a determined

effort to move east. 26th: Frustration and success with wide pool. Ice problems. That day, John Lewis did a flight and reported open pools to the south-east with wide leads; From 30 miles to the south-east he saw a water sky, 60 to 70 miles away. 27th: Good progress night, then stuck, two large thick floes. Strong NE wind ~25 knots. 28th Attempt break out. 1¾ hrs trying escape. Drifted 22 m to SW. Difficulty going E towards landwater. Several days 100 miles further from the coast, even bring us into N drift. Hoping pool aeroplane. Tottan well underway from S.G. (Georgia). We may follow more or less parallel courses ~100 m apart…31st Tottan still v good progress v little ice. Seriously thinking retracing steps to N, follow Tottan.[10]

Theron was not to escape the pack-ice for more than three weeks. I suspect she had been enticed into the pack-ice by initial good-looking leads, which at first allowed her to make good progress. When she did manage to extricate herself and follow Tottan's route further east towards Kapp Norvegia, precious time had been lost.

Only five voyages had previously penetrated this eastern part of the Weddell Sea: Bruce (1904) in *Scotia*, Filchner (1911–12) in *Deutschland*, Shackleton (1915) in *Endurance*, and *San Martin* (the Argentine vessel) in 1954 and 1955. The entry route attempted by *Theron* was close to the successful route Filchner used in *Deutschland*.

Much later, as *Theron* hurriedly reversed and entered

further east, following *Tottan*, she suffered further frustration when squally snow conditions prevented her from sighting the coast, but she progressed by using the ship's radar image of the ice cliffs down the Caird coast. *Theron* reached the site for the Royal Society Base, Halley Bay, on 27 January. Fuchs hoped to find a site for his TAE base further south and flew with John Lewis in poor visibility to find the edge of the Filchner Ice Shelf near Filchner's Vahsel Bay, 200 miles south of Halley. Fuchs had to make a quick decision whether to consider building his TAE base at Halley, or press on further south in *Theron*. From what he could see of the crevassed country inland from the coast south of Halley, he decided not set up there, except as a last resort.

Theron continued south, past where Filchner's *Deutschland* and Shackleton's *Endurance* had been caught by the ice. Captain Marø pressed on and negotiated a tense passage through a relatively narrow lead, at times down to 100 yards wide, past unusually solid ice floes, which evoked recollections of *Endurance*. On no account must *Theron* find herself caught there in similar fashion. A flight by John Claydon with Captain Marø, confirmed they were within 20 miles of Filchner's Vahsel Bay, with good conditions ahead. A second Auster flight with John Lewis and David Stratton reported there were no immediate crevasse zones inland, but they could see a distant, snow-covered mountain range. Gordon Haslop then flew Fuchs west from Vahsel Bay, to choose a suitable place where unloading might begin for the base site. *Theron* followed, and reached a place where a negotiable slope led up to the adjacent low plateau of the ice shelf, the site for Shackleton Base. Later, John Claydon took a remarkable photo (Plate 6) of the base site under low illumination, which revealed considerable crevassing. This photo, which shows near the sea edge of the Filchner Ice Shelf, also shows how effective a low sun is for seeing crevasses. The party was aware there were crevasses, which seemed to be well bridged and filled with snow, but they might have been astonished to see how many there were. The Filchner Shelf Ice is flowing north and fracturing with numerous crevasses.

Unloading began in haste, on 30 January 1956. A recent book by Anthea Arnold, *Eight Men in a Crate*, describing the Advance Party's first year at Shackleton, emphasises how *Theron* had been loaded in London

in such a way that efficient, sequential unloading was impossible. It seems to me that the *Theron* voyage was something of a learning exercise and prior logistical experience based on British Antarctic Survey vessels might not have been good preparation for TAE. The season was already advanced, the base had to be established, and *Theron* needed to get out of this situation where heavy sea ice to the north might quickly lock her in. She departed just 10 days later, but during the course of unloading, conditions got so severe that *Theron* had to leave abruptly during a bad blizzard, with five men castaway for 24 hours. David Stratton described their interesting breakfast — hot milk and sugar, with a hot sardine-tomato-sugar stew. Because of the huge task of unloading and lack of time, some materials had to be put in a temporary dump on the sea ice near the ship. Normally, everything would have been taken 50 or 60 metres higher onto the surface of the ice shelf, but because *Theron* had been trapped in the pack-ice for weeks, the situation had become critical.

Two exploratory flights were quickly made over Vahsel Bay and then south-east, where Fuchs and Lewis sighted the first inland mountain range. The next day, 7 February, Blaiklock and Haslop flew direct to these mountains, which were named the Theron Mountains. They saw a wide glacier further south and another range of higher mountains beyond that, the Shackleton Range. Unknown to TAE, these mountains had already been seen from the air by the Argentines, flying from their Belgrano Base west of Shackleton Base. The Argentine flight will be referred to later in describing other IGY explorations from the Weddell Sea (Appendix IV).

Theron was anxiously waiting for the Auster to return from this last long flight, as the pack-ice was moving in from the north. The aircraft arrived and was quickly loaded on board. The ship departed, with her open water shrunk to as little as four metres. It was apparently touch and go, and she was even trapped for two hours — more thoughts of *Endurance*. She reached Halley Bay, took their final mail, and emerged with relief into the open ocean on 10 February 1956.

Establishing Shackleton Base, 1956

The eight men watched *Theron* depart, doubtless with a degree of trepidation. There had not been a full account of the extreme winter which the Advance Party negotiated at Shackleton until the book by Anthea Arnold in 2007, based on Rainer Goldsmith's diaries. They faced the task of shifting about 500 tons of material, stacked at the foot of the ice shelf. The remainder was near the selected hut site, nearly three miles inland. They erected their tents, and Ralph Lenton prepared the Sno-Cat crate for temporary shelter while they started to build the main Shackleton hut for the approaching winter. In 2005 Charles Swithinbank told me that Fuchs was concerned by structural deterioration which developed in the NBS Maudheim hut when it became buried under deep snow.[11] Because of this concern, the Shackleton hut design was massive, and could not be completed in time for the first winter.

The Advance Party had five vehicles and the dogs. The vehicles included one Sno-Cat, two Weasels and two Ferguson tractors with special tracks. The vehicle specifications are given in Fuchs and Hillary's book, *The Crossing of Antarctica*.[12] The Weasel was made in the USA as an army vehicle for the 1939–45 war, and had served several Greenland and Antarctic expeditions. The Fergusons were farm tractors which had been modified for their Antarctic task. Arnold's book states that the vehicles were found to be poorly prepared and the sole vehicle engineer, Roy Homard, had a major task ahead of him to service them.

The Cats used on TAE have an interesting pedigree. The Tucker Sno-Cat Corporation made the Sno-Cat Model 743 in the USA, and the TAE vehicles had

been strengthened in the UK for Antarctic work. However, Roy Homard had to modify the original Sno-Cat at Shackleton. Rated 200 horsepower using petrol fuel, a Sno-Cat could travel at 6 to 8 mph when loaded, with a dry weight of 7000 pounds (3175 kg). Its traction system was unique, providing nearly 100 percent traction even when turning in soft snow. It had four pontoons, each with an open-ladder type of track around it. It could progress even in soft snow, making only a shallow indentation, whereas a man on foot would leave deep footprints. The Cat could carry a ton and haul two sledges with bakelite-polyethylene runners, each loaded with two and a half tons. Later, we used four of these impressive vehicles for the crossing journey. However, their fuel consumption ranged from only 0.8 to 2 miles per gallon (0.3 to 0.7 km per litre).

The First Year at Shackleton

Derek Williams made a fine film, *Foothold on Antarctica*, for British Petroleum.[13] This describes the *Theron* voyage and the landing at Shackleton Base in 1956. Roy Homard joked that it should have been called 'Toescrape on Antarctica', given how precarious was the Advance Party's situation.

The dump on the sea ice comprised 25 tons of coal (for the Aga stove), 350 barrels of vehicle fuel, hut and boat gear, food, clothing, sledging rations for men and dogs, as well as the dogs themselves. The site of main base was on the ice shelf, 60 metres higher and almost two miles away. The men slept in tents, but came to use the Sno-Cat crate as a home, after it had been made snow-proof and later insulated. In a prolonged north wind and warmer temperatures, it would 'rain' inside the crate, and lumpy ice grew on the floor. Establishing radio contact was proving troublesome, and vehicles suffered frequent breakdowns.

After 10 days, all the food, the hut timbers, 50 barrels of fuel and many general items had been moved from the temporary dump on the sea ice. The men started laying the hut foundations and constructing the heavy trusses. Temperatures in February continued to fall and blizzards interfered, with snow covering the work and materials and the unremitting wind made conditions severe. On 4 March 'Operation Dog-Span' moved the 24 huskies up to the base. Because they were as yet untrained to run as teams, Blaiklock left

7 The hut framework at Shackleton after the first big blizzard, which buried it. Photographer unknown.

8 Seven members of the Advance Party in the Sno-Cat crate. From left: Taffy Williams, Tony Stewart (standing), Hannes la Grange, Len Blaiklock (leader), Rainer Goldsmith, Roy Homard, Peter Jeffries. (Photo by Ralph Lenton)

Tunnelling for the buried materials was a prolonged job, but the 'catacombs' were later used as kennels for the dogs. The sun set, finally, on 20 April for four months, but work continued in the winter darkness, using kerosene pressure lamps. Ralph Lenton made his first outside radio contact on 7 May with the FIDS base at Horseshoe Island in Marguerite Bay, 1000 miles away, and news could be relayed to the London office. It was some months before they were able to raise their neighbours at Halley Bay on radio. They did have Argentine neighbours at

them chained to their steel wire and drove them up between the two vehicles — accompanied by feverish dog excitement. They were secured outside near the hut site until a tunnel was dug to house them.

The work continued during early March, and regular meteorological records were started on 1 March. By the middle of the month, the main hut framework was erected and Jeffries and Stewart began hauling the crates of wall panels into position, next to the building. On the 20th the wind rose to 30 knots and this was the first of the prolonged winter blizzards, which characterise Antarctica. It became known as the 'Great March Blizzard'. The wind eased after seven days and their tents had to be dug out and repitched. A huge snowdrift, five metres high and 70 metres long, had buried the hut panels (Plate 7).

At the coast, a large breakout had taken 300 drums of fuel, a tractor, most of the coal, the boat, many engineering stores and most of the seal carcasses stored for dog food. Blaiklock discussed the situation with his men and concluded they had ample food and sufficient fuel, if it was conserved carefully. But the chemicals for the radio-sonde balloons had gone, and this part of the scientific program had to be abandoned.

Work on the hut continued and the two gable ends were completed, the floor was laid and the roof began to take shape as the daylight shortened.

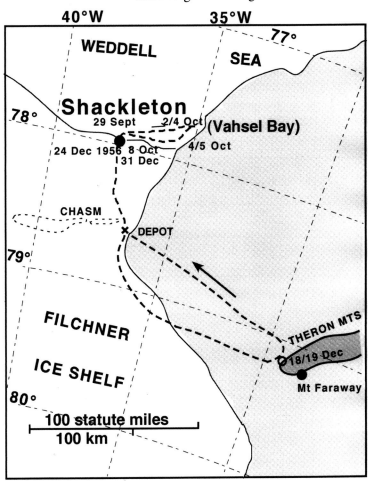

Figure 5   The route to the Theron Mountains by Blaiklock and Goldsmith with their dog team, January 1957.

General Belgrano Base, 30 miles west of Shackleton, but there was no communication with them until 1957.

Slow but steady progress continued, including digging snow out of the hut. Altogether, it was estimated that over 100 tons of snow had to be moved from the hut. Midwinter Day was celebrated in the usual Antarctic fashion, with a special Lenton menu. The crate hut table had a cloth, and special gifts were opened. The winter cold and darkness must have been severe, because everyone was still sleeping in the tents, but they did have the shelter of the Sno-Cat crate hut for meals (Plate 8). The 'Sno-House', the vehicle crate, measured 21 x 9 x 8 feet (6.4 x 2.7x 2.4 metres), and had a small kitchen bench with three primus stoves. Roy Homard made a bread oven from an empty oil drum, insulated with fibreglass. One day, Roy produced a tasty surprise with mint-flavoured peas, but refused to reveal his secret. However, this was later revealed, when blobs of toothpaste were identified.

The winter temperatures were extreme, with the minimum -63°F (-53°C). May was the coldest month, with an average -35°F (-37°C). The strongest wind, on 6 May, was recorded as 70 knots. Prolonged digging unearthed the hut panels and frame, which enabled construction to resume. On 7 August, Blaiklock and Goldsmith were the first to try sleeping in the hut, initially for only a few days, as it was still very cold. Many of the bunks had been built, but it was easier to warm the tents. Work concentrated on making the hut interior more habitable, and the big Aga coal stove and oil-burning heaters were installed. The party finally left the Sno-House in September, after eight months, and moved into the hut, with the temperature outside still -40°F (-40°C), even in bright sunshine. At the end of October, the generators and radio were running and the first voice contact was made through the BBC in London for expedition discussions, and for a BBC broadcast. That day, a Weasel and a dog team visited the Vahsel Bay sea ice and returned with a ton and a half of seal meat for the dogs.

In November, the dogs were used to place a food depot 50 miles south of the base, which was supplemented a few days later. They crossed some wide, snow-filled crevasse depressions and skirted east, avoiding the major chasm seen during one of the flights early in the year, 40 miles south of Shackleton. This located a valuable route for future use on the crossing.

Blaiklock and Goldsmith set out for the Theron Mountains, 120 miles away, on 7 December. Ten days later they camped four miles from the highest peak, Mount Faraway. Next day they had to cross meltwater streams to move camp to the foot of the rocks. Their route from Shackleton is shown on Figure 5. Blaiklock used sun observations to fix their position and they collected rock samples. Unluckily, they did not chance on the plant fossils which Fuchs found a month later. They celebrated Christmas Day at the depot, 50 miles from Shackleton, and arrived two days later, having travelled 360 miles in 20 days.

Remarkably, the Advance Party completed everything expected of them, in spite of their late arrival at Shackleton, the short summer, a hard winter and the loss of stores. In addition, a successful dog journey had already visited the Theron Mountains and reconnoitred the start of the route for the crossing.

In *Eight Men in a Crate* Arnold underlines the unusually extreme winter they experienced. Goldsmith was very critical of the leadership of TAE, especially the delays experienced by *Theron*. Specifically, he questioned why Fuchs did not have *Theron* enter the pack-ice further east and why the vehicles were not fully serviced before leaving London. He criticised the choice of a massive hut, which was difficult to build, and was also critical of some of their clothing. It is remarkable how the eight men persisted with their tasks in the face of extreme adversity and managed to build the snow-entombed hut throughout the severe winter. When the main party arrived on *Magga Dan*, everything was completed and in order. As we were not fully aware of their severe winter we probably appeared to take it all for granted. The discomfort of TAE's Advance Party's survival year had similarities to the terrible circumstances of Shackleton's Ross Sea party in 1915–16. The Ross Sea party did have huts, though badly iced-up, but were in desperate circumstances for clothing and food. The TAE Advance Party had adequate food but no hut, just the vehicle crate. Blaiklock and his team achieved the impossible for TAE, under very difficult circumstances.

THE MAIN PARTY, 1956–57

After *Theron* returned to London, everything needed for the final phase of the expedition had to be prepared. This involved provisioning of the crossing party's voyage south on the *Magga Dan*, replacement of the stores lost at Shackleton Base in March 1957, and all preparations for the crossing journey. Every detail had to be planned for the expedition's scientific work, both before and during the actual crossing. The expedition would contribute to the IGY at three stations, commencing in July 1957, for 18 months. These stations were Shackleton, an inland station later known as South Ice, and the New Zealand Party's base (later called Scott Base, on McMurdo Sound).

My Selection:
The Right Time and the Right Place

In 1956 I was completing a higher degree at Imperial College in London after I had finished a Science Honours Degree in 1954 at the University of Queensland. As stated previously, for many years, starting at school, I had developed a passion for the Antarctic and had been improving my credentials for joining an Antarctic expedition with climbing and geological work in challenging places in Australia. I was studying in Brisbane when I heard the exciting news that Everest had been climbed. I remember feeling some disappointment, having been inspired by the long history of failed attempts to climb it. This meant that Everest no longer posed an unanswered challenge; one of earth's few remaining frontiers was no more, as it were.

After arriving in London, I continued my Australian research, namely to describe and interpret the geology of a wonderful volcanic complex south of Brisbane. This was Mount Barney, a spectacular mountain and wilderness. I brought over 300 pounds of specimens with me. With my Antarctic ambitions still very much alive, I took part in rock-climbing excursions in Britain and visited Switzerland for superb and invaluable ice-climbing experiences in the Alps. I had seen my first snow in Tasmania, but saw a 'proper' snow fall one afternoon in London.

One morning in 1955, on a London bus in South Kensington, I was electrified to read a short newspaper item about Fuchs' plans for a Commonwealth Trans-Antarctic Expedition, with likely Australian participation. I subsequently found that my supervisor, Professor H.H. Read, was Chairman of the Scientific Committee of the proposed expedition. Australia had still not confirmed its financial contribution to the expedition, but was soon expected to do so.

The expedition team selection was almost complete, but a geologist had still to be chosen. Ray Adie, who was Fuchs' fellow geologist and had travelled with him in 1949 and helped stimulate his plans to cross the continent, had declined. On Read's advice — 'Do you *really* want to go, Jon?' — I made a formal application. Australia had now pledged its financial contribution and Fuchs was keen to appoint an Australian geologist. I was called to meet him and then attended a formal interview with Fuchs, Rear Admiral Parry, the Expedition Secretary, among others. The interview reviewed my geological qualifications and experience and I was then asked how well I thought I got on with people. For example, how did I settle differences and arguments? When pressed on this, I may have been a little too forthright, insisting that I believed in seeking to address differences in order to settle misunderstandings. Parry laughed, suggesting it sounded as if I settled them physically.

Later, Read told me my prospects for being selected were 'looking all right'. Fuchs had been in contact with Dr P.G. Law in Melbourne, Foundation Director of the Australian Antarctic Research Expeditions (ANARE), and asked him if he could nominate a suitable Australian. Fortunately, I had met Law about possible future work with ANARE several years before and had seen him in Melbourne on my way to England. In responding to Fuchs, Phil Law had sought the opinion of Bill Bewsher, an avid climber and wilderness bushwalker at Melbourne University. Fortunately, Bill and I had been corresponding for many years and had climbed together and he told Law, 'He's okay'.

I was thrilled to receive my official appointment letter from TAE. Now all I had to do was complete my PhD thesis in time to leave London on *Magga Dan* in November 1956. I submitted the thesis late October and had my oral examination five days before we departed. I was well aware my two examiners scarcely had time to read my work, and I felt very aware of its many deficiencies. The panel gave no hint of any decision on my examination, not even through my supervisor, and I had to wait until we reached Montevideo to get a letter to say I passed the oral examination.

In London, before departing, I was also required to meet with the Bishop of Portsmouth, the Right Reverend Launcelot Fleming, the geologist on Rymill's South Graham Land Expedition (1934–37). This 'interview', which I believe it was, apparently did not go well. Sadly, I never got to know the Bishop. In youth, one can have sketchy appreciations. I saw him as a rather formal Englishman and I felt slightly bluffed by the interview, at his club. I had met Sir Douglas Mawson, also a daunting figure on first meeting, in Adelaide on my way to England, and was very conscious of my inexperience, despite my enthusiasm. My knowledge of Antarctica was still slight and I felt I had little to say, other than expressing enthusiasm. I did not know much about Mawson, other than reading *The Home of the Blizzard*. Mawson was very gracious. He came in to meet me at the university and spent some time talking and showing me some of his rocks in the museum. I never got a chance to see him again to tell him about our expedition, as he died in 1958.

Following my selection for the expedition, I started preparations, especially for scientific equipment. I visited a manufacturer in York to arrange the loan of a Cook, Troughton and Simms polarising microscope and a universal stage for measuring the crystal direction of ice crystals. I also borrowed a photocopying stand from the Leitz Camera Company, the makers of Leica cameras, of which I had two. Such was the interest in the expedition that I was well received everywhere and helped with whatever I required. I took a crash course in surveying and the expedition flew me to Davos in Switzerland to learn from the Avalanche Research Unit how to make sections of snow for studying crystal structures with a microscope. I met Dr Sam Steinemann, who was fascinated with how snow crystals change into ice, though now working with electron microscopy in watch research at Neuchatel.

Back in London I also met some experienced Antarctic people, particularly Charles Swithinbank and a fellow PhD student at Imperial College, Allan Reece. They had been on the Norwegian-British-Swedish Expedition (NBS, 1950–52) together.

Charles was very generous and arranged for me to visit him in Cambridge. His knowledge was extensive and he had a wonderful collection of Antarctic photographs from his time with NBS. I met Hal Lister, our TAE glaciologist, and attended the release of Derek Williams' film of the *Theron* voyage. During all this, I had to concentrate on writing my thesis and completing the required maps and photographs.

It was an exciting time. I was very much aware of my good fortune in being selected as the Australian member on TAE, and was conscious that I was taking part in 'the last great Antarctic adventure'. Curiously, like others who also had such good fortune, I felt convinced I was part of the last era of Antarctic exploration. We could not have predicted that IGY would herald a sustained period of exploration and science, which accelerated into the next millennium.

The Voyage of the *Magga Dan*

Magga Dan was 1850 tons, considerably larger than *Theron*, and painted bright red. She was a newly built Danish polar vessel, chartered from Lauritzen Lines and on her maiden voyage. Joyce Fuchs, our leader's wife, had recently launched her. Her skipper was Captain Hans Christian Petersen, who had extensive Arctic experience. He was a big, bluff Dane, who was impressively skilful in handling *Magga Dan*. She was not a full icebreaker, but was a sophisticated vessel, specially strengthened for ice work. Her steel hull was an inch thick throughout and a variable pitch propeller made it unnecessary to slow or stop engines when going ahead or astern. The crow's nest contained a duplicate set of controls for a helmsman navigating the ship through ice. She had special apparatus for making fresh water from the cooling water of the diesel engines, as much as 11 tons a day. This saved the fuel and labour required on *Theron*, which collected and melted quantities of ice when she was in the ice. All the generators, engines and pumps on *Magga Dan* were duplicated, assisting repair and maintenance. A separate engine and generator in the forepeak could pump out the engine room, if this section were to be holed by ice. *Magga Dan* was very comfortable and air-conditioned.

The ship sailed on 15 November 1956, from Butler's Wharf, Tower Bridge. Two days earlier, the expedition and the ship's crew were presented to Her

Majesty the Queen, the Expedition Patron. Captain Petersen presented 11 specially chosen men from his crew, all with the surname Petersen. Fuchs' father was there, and Fuchs records the poignant experience of his German-born father, interned in Britain during World War I, though a UK resident and married to an Englishwoman.[14] Fuchs' father said: 'In my wildest dreams I could never have imagined a son of mine having tea with the Queen of England!'

Magga Dan was to carry our party down to Shackleton, and also the main Royal Society Expedition party to their base at Halley Bay.

We were soon in Madeira, sunny and warm after London. James Cook and others had called here, including Shackleton on *Endurance*, to take on wine. We were given a tour of some of the wineries, sampling three memorable varieties of madeira. The expedition was presented with a bottle of 1890 madeira, which was reserved for Midwinter Day at Shackleton. It was found to be undrinkable by David Stratton — or so he said when he emptied the bottle.

The Danish meals on *Magga Dan* were carefully presented, if slightly different. This difference involved the presentation of numerous small side dishes of food on the dining tables in the late afternoon. However, these dishes kept reappearing, becoming drier and less enticing day by day. Finally we started dealing with them, by dint of throwing them overboard. The cook did prepare a surprise afternoon tea in the form of deliciously flavoured cake. It was so tasty we quickly finished it and asked for more, which was generously provided. The cook informed us we had consumed the whole quota of cake for the week.

We continued to Montevideo, a long and increasingly warm voyage, punctuated one day by a spectacular school of many thousands of dolphins, which seemed to extend halfway to the horizon. We had blissful days and nights through the tropics and I was excited to see the Southern Cross becoming more prominent in the sky as we cruised south. I was getting to know various expeditioners, in both the TAE and the Royal Society Halley Bay parties. We had two other participants on the voyage, John Heap, a sea-ice glaciologist who later became Director of the Scott Polar Research Institute in Cambridge, and Piet DuToit, a meteorologist from South Africa. John was compiling an index for the latest volume of the *Journal of Glaciology* and I became an assistant in this task — very educational for me, planning winter research on ice and snow.

One of our team was Geoffrey Pratt, a geophysicist who used seismic methods to determine the thickness of the ice on the TAE crossing journey and took measurements of the force of gravity with a sensitive, very expensive gravimeter. Geoffrey was tall, massive and red-haired. He was a quiet man but had travelled widely working for British Petroleum, who assigned him to work in a range of outlandish places. New Guinea had his special affection, and he loved their hot curries. Normal curries were simply not hot enough, and Geoffrey was in the habit of sprinkling ours with extra curry powder. He was something of an instrument freak, proud of his very accurate watch and his camera. He explained to me the importance of measuring precise time. Geoffrey monitored the ship's chronometer against his own watch on a daily basis, to calibrate any 'instrument drift'. Over a period he seemed to become even more silent and his face longer, because the ship's chronometer seemed to be drifting significantly and increasingly. Geoffrey felt uncertain about raising this with the Captain, but eventually he isolated the problem. It actually lay with his new, special self-winding wristwatch, which had wound down through insufficient movement of his arm for the pendulum winder. From then on, he undertook an exercise round each day, climbing the ladder inside the mast.

At Montevideo we experienced contrasting profiles of Uruguayan society — affluent, cultivated people and some great restaurants with wonderful steaks, excellent wine and memorable classical musicians, and general poverty elsewhere. The naval vessels at the dock suggested a moribund navy. We waited several days for vehicle spares for David Pratt. David was one of the early appointments to TAE, and was responsible for transport and fuel. He was a qualified pilot and, when he attended his interview, hoped to gain a position as a pilot. However, the selection committee realised he would be an ideal person to organise the vehicles for the crossing journey. He was told, 'We don't want to have to walk', and was assigned to select the most suitable vehicles. David was an ebullient, enthusiastic character, who was good at persuading people in supply firms into doing far more than they intended, when first confronted with a 'Pratt scheme'.

9 *Magga Dan* at Grytviken, South Georgia, December 1956. She is moored near five Japanese whale catchers.

scenery, with rocky crags disappearing into the clouds, glaciers forming ice cliffs to the sea, and the foreshores alive with wildlife. We called first at King Edward Point, where the Falkland Islands Administration had an office. We were warmly welcomed. Nan Brown, the wife of the radio operator, was an Australian who was spending over two years there. A warm, vital personality, she wrote a book, *Antarctic Housewife*, describing her interesting time on the island, one of only two women living there. She and husband George later departed for Australia via South America and then slowly crossed the Pacific. She describes an 'illness' which began to affect her on the long journey. Its symptoms persisted in spite of being given successive unhelpful diagnoses from doctors in South America and Hawaii and it was not until she reached Australia that she was advised that she was simply pregnant. 'Not an uncommon condition for young, married women,' the doctor said.

We visited Grytviken and Leith Harbour but did not go ashore at Stromness, where Shackleton and two companions had abruptly appeared in 1915, having crossed the island after the famous open boat journey to seek rescue for the *Endurance* survivors on Elephant Island. Around a thousand men worked there during the summer in five factories along the north coast of South Georgia, most of which are accessible only by sea. The Grytviken whaling factory operations presented gruesome sights; the whole whale carcasses were being utilised by the factory. Grytivken was an interesting, thriving town with a Norwegian church and a corrugated-iron cinema. There was an extensive clothing store at Leith Harbour, another whale factory town where I bought a black leather, wool-lined cap with adjustable ear flaps, just like those worn on Shackleton's *Endurance* expedition. The air was piercingly cold and I was still learning which clothes to wear. Our photographer, George Lowe of Everest expedition fame, was in his element and delighted the hardened whaling community by strolling around wearing a Panama hat. I took the opportunity to climb a local hill, including the steep ridge behind King Edward Point, to photograph *Magga Dan* and five Japanese whale catchers in the harbour (Plate 9). Later, I saw this had been where Frank Hurley, Shackleton's remarkable *Endurance* photographer, had taken some historic photos of Grytviken, with

He searched for appropriate vehicles by visiting the US, and even talked his way into sensitive US 'dew-line' stations in Greenland, to evaluate the recently developed Sno-Cats. He arranged to get important modifications made, tested them in Norway, and then with the Advance Party at Shackleton. David Pratt and Roy Homard (already at Shackleton with the Advance Party and previously a member of the recent British North Greenland Expedition) made a very competent vehicle maintenance and repair team. The two were indispensable on TAE.

From Montevideo we sailed for South Georgia. This was a rougher, colder passage and I vividly recall suddenly seeing the nature of the island ahead, early one morning. I was unprepared for its rugged alpine his captain, Frank Worsley, and others helping to carry his heavy camera gear.

There had been a civil disturbance at King Edward Point a few days before we arrived, sparked by insobriety, and a few shots were fired at the met building. The resident magistrate, Robert Spivey, asked Fuchs to act as magistrate for the hearing. Fuchs delivered a well-received judgment, handing out £20 fines and a severe reprimand.

I was amused on first hearing Fuchs' nickname. Everyone knew him in a completely informal way as 'Bunny' and its likely origin is described in Chapter 6.

At King Edward Point we helped David Pratt build a timber 'snow harrow' to improve snow surfaces for vehicles. We visited the local cemetery and saw Shackleton's grave, with an imposing granite tombstone inscribed with numerous South American and other tributes to him. We enjoyed a dinner party and were farewelled by the 18 inhabitants. We then sailed around to the adjacent bay, many hours distant over a rough ground route, where there were three whaling settlements — Stromness, Leith and Husvik. We took on fuel at Leith Harbour from the tanker *Polar Maid*, by arrangement with the company Salvesen via our major expedition supporter, British Petroleum. Two Norwegian expedition vessels, *Polar Bjorn* and *Polar Sirkel*, arrived on their way to the new Norwegian base on the continent. We had overtaken them in the south Atlantic and had last seen them in Montevideo. *Sirkel* was impressively small. There should have been an important medical package for our doctor, Allan Rogers, on board but the only parcels were for Rainer Goldsmith, the doctor at Shackleton, a packet of soup for our chief pilot, John Lewis, and a physics textbook for our glaciologist, Hal Lister.

We left South Georgia on 20 December and that afternoon passed Clerk Rocks, 40 miles to the east, which James Cook circled in *Resolution* in 1775. Sea conditions were subdued, with only a slight swell and mild waves breaking against the cliffs, and I felt an irrepressible urge to collect some rocks as we slowly motored past. That evening, the wind suddenly rose and a wave caught the cocooned Otter aircraft, which was stored on the deck, and damaged its rudder. Peter Weston, our RAF maintenance engineer, had been doing some minor repairs on the Auster aircraft,

but to repair the 10-foot Otter rudder was a big job. Peter, who had been on the NBS Expedition six years before, was a solid, reliable person whose work on the expedition was always essential. He had a workshop in the bow of *Magga*, which rose and fell irregularly with the ship's progress. The fabric on the Otter had to be painted, and the smell of dope was nauseous. Peter completed the task, periodically retiring to be sick. He was a deceptively quiet person, with strong and unusual enthusiasms, including Egyptian archaeology.

Soon we were moving through pack-ice to find the best entry point into the Weddell Sea. This took us past the South Sandwich Islands, first discovered in misty weather by Cook in 1775. The conditions were still foggy, and we could not see anything ahead. There was a slight smell of sulphur in the air and David Stratton thought this might have been from Zavadovski Island, named by the Russian Bellingshausen, who passed this way in 1820 when its volcano was releasing fumes. David, one of our surveyors, was Fuchs' second in command and had previously spent two years with Falkland Islands Dependency Survey (FIDS) at Hope Bay on the Antarctic Peninsula. David was said to have been earmarked for Antarctic destiny by his godfather, Rear Admiral Edward Evans, Scott's second in command. Evans patted the child on the head, saying, 'One day you will go to Antarctica'. David had an amusing story about his godfather, as Ken Blaiklock recalls. Some years before, when David was first going down to the Antarctic Peninsula with FIDS, Evans said to his godson, 'Don't worry until the paraffin starts to freeze'. Ken noted that during the first TAE winter at Shackleton, this actually did happen. David was knowledgeable and widely read, and had studied geography at Cambridge. His other important role on TAE involved the expedition stores and equipment. He was expected to know exactly where they had been stored, both on the ship and later, even more critically, where they were cached in staked lines outside the Shackleton Base hut where they were quickly buried by snow. His knowledge of all the stores was usually precise.

In the South Sandwich Islands, we were not far from South Thule Island, where Geoffrey Pratt hoped to land to set up and re-zero his sensitive gravimeter. He had set it up on South Georgia, but it was decided that it was more important for us to proceed without delay. When we penetrated the pack-ice a few days before Christmas, Geoff landed on several icebergs and large ice floes to attempt work on his instrument. In calm conditions, floating ice can appear to be unaffected by any swell, but at each place Geoff found the ice showed very slow vertical movements, enough to thwart his efforts.

In sunny weather, the pack-ice produces unforgettable scenes, with extravagant colours, especially with a low sun. I found the lazy movement of the sea ice almost hypnotic. We were beginning to see the prolific Antarctic wildlife — seals, penguins and other birds. After the experience of *Theron*, beset in the pack-ice for nearly five weeks the year before, we intended to enter the denser pack-ice much further east than *Theron* had done. However, news was received that the two US vessels, *Staten Island* and *Wyandot*, were held up by heavy pack further east, north of Cape Norwegia. They were carrying the IGY expedition led by Finn Ronne, to establish a new base, *Ellsworth*, on the Filchner Ice Shelf. Captain Petersen therefore sailed *Magga* on a more direct course for Cape Norvegia, hoping to avoid the heavy pack carried east along the Antarctic coastline into the Weddell Sea. The scene was brilliant, with the wonderful contrast of the dark blue sea, the pack-ice gliding past and occasionally large, sculptured icebergs, most of which have flat tops.

Christmas Eve is festive by Danish custom, and our Christmas celebrations were observed accordingly. Clear radio contact with Shackleton allowed the new members to talk with men of the Advance Party. On Boxing Day, the Auster took a flight with John Lewis and Bill Petersen, *Magga*'s First Officer, which located the best way out of the congesting ice floes. By 28 December, an extensive sea of open water was reached and the captain was able to use the autopilot, maintaining a steady 12 knots into a stiff, southerly wind. For me, these were halcyon days, but later I felt puzzled why there were no introduction sessions for novices, as there were several of us without Antarctic experience. We did have one session on knots, and George Lowe gave us a lecture on recognising crevasses, how to stay out of them and how to be rescued from them, but I sensed his expertise was based on his experience on Himalayan glaciers.

About this time, there was an incident involving the ship's gyro compass, which was reported to have been found to be off direction by 15°. It might have been accidentally turned off for a short time. Captain Hans Christian Petersen could be jovial, or extremely sullen and severe. David Pratt described to me how he happened to climb the stairs that day up to the bridge, as we were welcome to do if no complex manoeuvres were in progress. At the top of the stairs he could see there was a serious meeting in progress, with the captain apparently admonishing his officers. David discreetly left.

Later that day, the ship reached the end of a 100-mile open lead, which closed off ahead into impenetrable pack-ice. The ship tried to continue on to the south-east and we did progress slowly, forward, reverse, forward again. A flight by Gordon Haslop and Bill Petersen indicated it would be wise to retreat, but space had to be made for the ship to turn around. Most of us had our first experience on 'land', chopping ice with axes and moving it with poles to provide some open water. I also had my first polar 'swim'. Standing on the ice, pole in hand, I stood on some thinner ice and went in up to my armpits. I quickly hauled myself out and walked back to the ship to change out of my wet clothes. I had no initial sense of cold, but suddenly the frightening, sharp cold reached my skin. Ever since, I have retained an aversion to icy water. *Magga* was turned around and, after further flight observations, began to push her way back north-east through ice floes several feet thick. Three days later, another flight allowed contact with *Tottan*, the Royal Society supply ship, only 25 miles from us but also in heavy pack-ice. The next day, both ships finally reached open water close to the coast, which consisted of continuous ice cliffs at the edge of the ice shelf. *Tottan* reached Halley Bay two hours before us.

On the Advance Party voyage in 1956, *Theron* was thoroughly beset and delayed and *Magga Dan* almost seemed determined to repeat the mistake, as the two ships' routes on Figure 4 indicate. Fuchs' journal, describing the *Magga* voyage is interesting:

23rd December. Wyandot and Staten Island held up for 12 hours north of Kap Norwegia. Petersen [Captain[would like to cut off corner following SE course, heading 160° T[true]. 24th Dec. Going SW. Capt strongly views continue 160° T. 25th Dec. I continue keep pressure on to move more East. 26th Dec. Tottan heading S somewhat

11 Cornices on the ice cliffs at Halley Bay.

10 The ice cliffs at Halley Bay. They are about 30 metres high.

E of us. 27th Dec. K.B [Blaiklock] crossed back of shelf [inland from Shackleton] easily, no sign cliff & chasm seen last year. Should now make more easting or in danger doing a Theron. 28th Dec. Open water then at 1820 cul de sac. Gordon, Bill [Haslop, pilot and first mate] flight uncompromising ice 19 m from ship. 29th Dec. Owing 15° error in gyro 85 miles W position behind. Steering W of S! Decided to turn back then NE hopefully. 30th Dec. Flight. Decided return to large NS lead yesterday.[15]

Breaching the Weddell Sea pack-ice defences is always critical for any expedition. If we study modern maps, giving the summary information of previous ship routes, access might look straightforward. Some maps show the presence of the vital, open lead along the east coast, as if it is always present. However, to reach it through the offshore pack-ice is a problem, and conditions are different every year and at different times through the season. In his preface to a reprint of Weddell's book, Fuchs makes the point that, in the modern era, it is essential that navigators should have access to aircraft observation, preferably from helicopters which can take off easily, from anywhere. We used a light floatplane, which is dependent on a take-off pool in the pack-ice. By the 1970s, satellite imagery was capable of displaying the state of pack-ice in the Weddell Sea, with up to date images to help save days of ship time. I am still intrigued by the similarity between *Magga's* course and *Theron's* (Figure 4).

The difference was that *Magga* learned from *Theron's* mistake and turned back early; whereas *Theron* lost about five weeks, *Magga* lost only five days.

What might have happened to TAE if *Theron* had not managed to free herself, with the narrow time remaining to establish Shackleton Base? Perhaps the expedition might have been forced to start from Halley Bay. *Theron* had to make a swift, second approach, with barely enough time to find a place for Shackleton Base further south and commence very late offloading, start preparations for building an expedition hut and then leave the small Advance Party of eight men, somewhat like castaways. TAE had similar difficulties getting into the Weddell Sea in both 1956 and 1957.

At Halley Bay

We arrived at the Royal Society Base, Halley Bay, on 4 January 1957, and spent an intense week unloading stores and establishing the new party. Halley was named after the famous British astronomer, Edmond Halley, well remembered for the 1759 comet named after him. He also made important magnetic direction investigations in the course of his voyages, especially his second southern Atlantic voyage in 1799, reaching 52°S, not far from South Georgia, in the *Paramore*. Halley seems to have been the first to record his experiences in crossing what is now called

12 Aerial view of the edge of the Filchner Ice Shelf, east of Shackleton. Ocean currents and the wind, holding off the sea ice, have formed the open lead. Such leads are the key to getting a ship into the Weddell Sea.

14 *Magga Dan* unloading at Shackleton.

the Antarctic Convergence, or Antarctic Polar Frontal Zone, which surrounds Antarctica, into colder waters with foggy conditions and giant icebergs.

The Halley Base had a narrow landing slope where we moored, next to *Tottan*. The coast is comprised of ice cliffs, about 30 metres high. The cliffs were spectacular (Plate 10), with sheer ice descending into the unbelievably clear water. In places, the cliffs supported magnificent cornices (Plate 11), deposited by the wind when it pours over the cliffs.

The base was about a mile inland and we worked strenuously from around 5 am each day, loading sledges for towing. David Pratt had been faced with the problem of the snow, which softens during the day and creates difficulties for vehicles, especially Weasels. The tracks dig in and can bog the vehicle. David had designed a timber grid plough, which we helped him construct on the voyage, intended for dragging behind a vehicle to turn the snow over. This would expose some of the deeper snow and accelerate

13 Aerial view of *Magga Dan*, at her 'dock', unloading at Shackleton. The vehicle trails lead up onto the shelf and the Shackleton building. (Photo by George Lowe)

'sintering' effects to harden the surface. The theory was very sound and would indeed have hardened the snow. However, the plough proved too hard to pull.

The weather became brilliantly fine and quite warm, and I soon learnt important Antarctic lessons, namely, never become separated from your windproof garments, and always carry extra clothes, even if it feels warm. By mid-morning a breeze had arisen and I was without my protective hat and anorak. I was in serious trouble and had to borrow clothes from Robin Dalgleish at Halley Bay. I learnt how important it was to wear gloves and a hat covering my ears, both of which, paradoxically, are essential to help keep your feet warm.

The clarity of the sea water was remarkable. Gazing down from beside the ice-shelf cliffs, I realised I was looking at deep, distant details of the ice cliffs descending far below the surface, seemingly almost forever, into the dark gloom of the very deep water. There were odd-shaped, luminescent jellyfish. This luminescence migrated around their bodies when I caught them in a bucket. I paid a visit with Allan Rogers to the nearby penguin rookery to admire the magnificent emperor penguins. The rookery had dead birds, many broken eggs and an overpowering smell. Allan collected a number of intact, abandoned eggs, and prepared to blow them clean on the ship by drilling a hole at each end. Sadly, they all exploded back onto him.

We saw groups of orcas, killer whales, cruising past and apparently interested in us. They were striking, swift, superbly sleek in black and white, with wonderful eyes. Our Danish cook had an idea to catch one and used an enormous baited hook attached to a large drum at the stern of *Magga*, but the orcas showed no interest, even when he managed to hit one on the nose with the bait.

The Royal Society Advance Party had reported that on clear days, with the diamond edge of transparency of pure Antarctic air, there was a hint of mountains on the far eastern horizon. The Otter took off in this direction and, after a long flight, confirmed there were indeed nunataks (isolated peaks) on a range further north. (Nunatak is an Eskimo word for a rocky mountain feature, of any size, surrounded by the ice.) Some of these peaks seemed to be as high as 3000 metres. From the plane, George Lowe observed two snow petrels near one of the peaks, presumably nesting there, nearly 150 km from the sea.

The Otter flew to Shackleton Base on 12 January, and Fuchs and others brought mail and fresh food, including oranges for Ken Blaiklock's Advance Party. *Magga* reached the region of Filchner's Vahsel Bay where a lead allowed her to follow the edge of the Filchner Ice Shelf (Plate 12). The place looked bleak and remote, with the hut and the met masts visible on the skyline, truly like the end of the earth. Our arrival coincided with a strange act by our captain. He had decided to use the ship to cut out a 'dock' in the sea ice at our unloading point, a great idea (Plate 13). However, Ken Blaiklock and his team had experienced an extremely harsh, long winter and nearly 12 months isolation. Most of them had come down to welcome the ship, but stood waiting for an hour to be invited on board, in a freezing wind. They could all have climbed safely aboard in just a few minutes. Seemingly oblivious to their existence, the

15 The Grand Chasm, inland from Shackleton. Our crossing route had to go this side of it. A future iceberg suture.

captain continued cutting out his dock. The Advance Party doctor, Rainer ('Rhino') Goldsmith, managed to get on board as the ship made one of its charging runs. The captain was extremely angry, but continued cutting out the dock. Finally, the shore party had had enough, turned and started walking back to the base. At this point, David Stratton reached for the ship's siren. It was Roy Homard's birthday, and after he and the others came aboard they enjoyed the comforts of civilisation, including a hot shower and sleeping in a warm bed.

Preparations for the Winter and Establishing South Ice Base, 1957

Unloading *Magga Dan* proceeded (Plate 14), and we were assisted by the Royal Society Advance Party, who were about to return home. The usual loading onto sledges proceeded, and in the next few days we all became adept in lifting items from the snow surface onto a sledge. Heavy fuel drums roll easily, but require a technique for getting them up the 15 centimetres or so onto a sledge by yourself. Eventually, we found we were capable of lifting a drum, rather than just one end — a real PhD qualification. I rapidly learnt to use bowline knots, which never tighten, for towing, having once taken 20 minutes to undo an impressive bind which tightened from a granny knot. We had several Sno-Cats, a Weasel and a Muskeg tractor. I was taught to drive the Bombardier Muskeg, a light Canadian tracked vehicle, after assuring David Pratt I knew how to double-declutch. However, I could not do so quickly enough to keep moving, and it took practice to get out of first gear. Eventually, I was given the job of Muskeg driver, responsible for driving the party up to the base from the ship after breakfast. Given my lack of gear-changing skill, it was appropriate that I christened the vehicle Hopalong. Hopalong needed warming up, and I liked to keep its covers on to hasten this process. Once I had to stop on the hill when the radiator started to boil — I forgot to take the covers off — wasting some precious antifreeze in the coolant. Some of my passengers decided it would be quicker to walk, but the engine cooled down so quickly I had the pleasure of pausing to pick up the hitchhikers. I was never invited to learn to drive a Sno-Cat — strictly second-year stuff. But later in Australia, filling out details for a hire car, I was able to list Antarctica in my driving experience, somewhat triumphantly.

Work continued to complete various details on the hut, technical and structural. I used a hammer for several days putting 'ruberoid' sheeting over parts of the entrance roof to keep out drift, wind-driven snow, which gets into any space if as much as a nail hole is available. The ruberoid was brittle and handling nails was somewhat difficult — you don't hold them in your mouth. Some days were down to -30°F (about -33°C) and late one still afternoon I realised I had definitely reached the frozen south when I heard the magical crackle of my exhaled breath freezing in the air. Later, I was hardly aware of this phenomenon.

I did have a chance to conclude one experiment. In a group unpacking a Sno-Cat crate, we were delighted to find a surprise package on the front seat. This comprised a wonderfully generous, enthusiastic letter of best wishes from the packers, and numerous chocolates. Being something of a chocaholic, I tried these, as did others. The chocolates were inedible, having absorbed the aromatic smells of fuel, greases and lubricants in the cocooned vehicle space. However, after about a week I noticed that the chocolates were slowly exchanging their absorbed smells with the clean air in the hut. They steadily progressed and eventually became a fine treat, which I kept as a private discovery.

The expedition planned to establish an inland station about 300 miles along the route to the Pole. The intention was to man this with three people

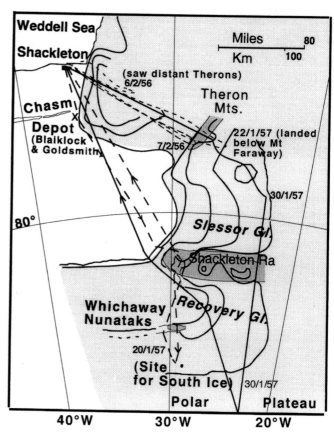

Figure 6 Exploratory flights inland from Shackleton Base.

under the leadership of Dr Hal Lister, the others being Ken Blaiklock and myself. Hal was the glaciologist and had recently been a member of the British North Greenland Expedition (1952–54). He wintered at their ice cap station known as North Ice and our inland station was called South Ice. There was an early possibility that the station might be put in by a tractor party with air support, but the nature of the inland country had first to be examined and a possible route for the traverse to the Pole had to be found later.

Exploration Flights From Shackleton

The exploratory flights inland from Shackleton are shown in Figure 6. Haslop, Fuchs, Blaiklock and Lowe made the first new flight on 20 January 1957, in the Otter. The Grand Chasm (Plate 15) was spotted the year before and the flight passed over it. A belt of huge crevasses was also evident further east, probably impossible to negotiate. Any ground route inland from Shackleton would have to avoid them. The Grand Chasm appeared to be a fracture likely to lead to a future iceberg break-off, and in the next 30 years the Grand Chasm moved north with the flow of the shelf, over a kilometre each year, until several icebergs broke away in 1986.[16]

The first January flight continued beyond the Chasm, with the Theron Mountains much further east. Further south, the flight crossed the end of a wide east–west glacier, which pushed out into the Filchner Ice Shelf with belts of severe crevasses. It became known as the Slessor Glacier after Sir John Slessor, Chairman of the TAE Expedition Committee. Beyond the glacier was the end of the Shackleton Range, from which a crevassed area extended further to the west, forming the southern margin of the Filchner Ice Shelf. Judging this to be an impassable barrier for a vehicle route from Shackleton Base to the Pole, an alternative route was sought closer to the mountains. Continuing further south beyond the Shackleton Range, the aircraft crossed another wide, west-flowing glacier. It featured bad crevasses and became familiar on the crossing journey as the Recovery Glacier. South of this 40-mile wide glacier, there was a line of nunataks marked with contours of rock strata, which were called the Whichaway Nunataks. They seemed to be the last range of mountains. About 30 miles south of the these mountains, a possible site for the inland station was noted on the edge of the Polar Plateau. No serious obstacles for a route to the Pole were apparent further south.

A flight on 22 January with pilot John Lewis visited the Theron Mountains with Fuchs, Blaiklock, Williams and Lowe. The broad snow dome behind the Theron scarp continued south to drop down to the Slessor Glacier, 25 miles wide at this point, with bad

16 Planning South Ice: Bunny Fuchs, Allan Rogers, Ken Blaiklock and Hal Lister. (Photo by George Lowe)

crevasse zones which looked impassable for vehicles. Returning, they flew along the imposing front cliffs of the Theron Mountains. They landed, and Fuchs collected specimens from the screes below the cliffs. When he stepped out of the plane after returning to Shackleton, he aroused my envy by showing me various rocks, coal and plant fossils. Fuchs suggested the plants might be *Sagenopteris*, but to me they looked the same as the Gondwana plants, *Gangamopteris* and *Glossopteris*, which I knew well from Queensland. The rocks proved to be part of Gondwana. Later, I had a chance to investigate the Theron geology myself.

The ship left to return north on 25 January. I regretted that some maturing friendships would have to be postponed and it was disappointing that three of our pioneering Advance Party had to return. Two returned to UK, while Peter Jeffries spent an extra year at Halley. The final letters were written and superfluous items were sent home on *Magga Dan*. On the way back, my baggage was rifled in dock somewhere and I lost forgettable items. Some mail was also found to have lost stamps. We had completed the franking of special philatelic mail, which fortunately went back to England safely. Fuchs had organised Falkland Islands Dependencies postage stamps with a 'TAE 1955–1958' inscription, which raised a worthwhile contribution to the expedition's finances. Later, I took a stamped envelope with me on the journey across the continent and managed to get it franked at the South Pole and at Scott Base, in spite of grumbling postmasters.

We waved farewell to *Magga Dan* and were now on our own, our tangible link to the outside world gone. Such is the naivety and optimism of youth, I felt no apprehension; it simply did not occur to me that our proposed Antarctic crossing might prove to be impossible, dangerous or disastrous. Besides, Fuchs and all his team seemed supremely experienced and competent.

A further plane flight by Haslop, Fuchs and Blaiklock at the end of January investigated possible alternative routes for the overland route south, by examining the country south from the Theron Mountains. One possibility was to cross further up the Slessor Glacier into the eastern Shackleton Range. There was some anxiety with an airlock when they changed fuel tanks and the single engine stopped, only restarting when the empty tank valve was closed. Had Haslop been unable to restart, their fate might have been sealed. Such is an ever-present danger of flying a single-engine aircraft in Antarctica. This more eastern route would have been longer and had bad crevasse zones. In the course of the return, further scrutiny was made of the original route, revealing a safer-looking route closer to the western point of the Shackleton Range. This was the route Fuchs finally chose.

I experienced mounting anxiety in relation to the cooking roster at Shackleton. There was no expedition cook and we all were rostered to serve four days, preparing meals for everyone. This was unknown territory for me, spoiled at home by my mother's cooking, and though I had lived independently as a student in a bed-sit in London and organised short-term outdoor trips with colleagues in Australia, I worried how my cooking skills could possibly cope with 16 servings. As my fate approached on the roster, I was saved in the nick of time by our departure for South Ice. Several colleagues sensed my apprehension and claimed they had been deprived of a questionable culinary experience. Even after returning from South Ice at the end of the winter, I missed the cooking roster at Shackleton, though by then I had been practising. The duty cook's productions varied from

17 The site for South Ice, near the edge of the inland ice sheet. We started to dig a pit to erect the hut. Hal Lister, George Lowe, Ken Blaiklock. The horizon was the same in all directions.

19 The almost completed hut. Hal Lister with the insulated panels.

18 The hut framework at South Ice. Lowe, Blaiklock, Lister. We had dug the pit to put down the grid foundation, and then built the framework.

20 Hal Lister installing some of his instruments on the mast at South Ice. The other feature is the Stevenson met screen.

skilled dedication and remarkable culinary skill to lining up tinned food and making sure it was opened and served hot.

On the edge of Antarctica, the prospects were thrilling. Words from Joseph Conrad expressed my feelings admirably: 'everything was so fresh, so surprising, so venturesome, so interesting'.

I soon committed the first of several foolish mistakes. The base was only two miles from the edge of the Weddell Sea and I could not resist going to have a look. I hope I mentioned it to someone, but I walked off alone with my camera to visit the edge, where the sea was intermittently freezing and breaking up. The structures in the new ice were exquisite. Realising this ice was thinner, I chose firmer ground, walking out onto firm, thicker ice. I saw that the orcas were still cruising along the coast and I found a good place to watch them. Minutes later they turned back east and startled me by swimming straight under the edge of my ice. I could see one of them studying me; there are accounts by Hubert Ponting, the photographer with the last Scott expedition, and others, about the orcas breaking up sea ice to catch penguins. Birdie Bowers, on that expedition, witnessed similar orca behaviour but the whales might have been after the ponies, caught on the ice. Some later observers, by contrast, have described benign encounters with orcas.

Planning for establishing our inland station for IGY, on the edge of the Polar Plateau, became a priority (Plate 16). It was confirmed that only three were to spend the winter at an inland station to carry out geophysical work for the IGY, namely Hal, Ken and myself. We would have no doctor, and Allan Rogers, our TAE doctor, gave us a lecture the afternoon before we left about dealing with emergencies. Perhaps my two experienced colleagues kept up with Allan's quietly impressive review of medical health, but I was soon submerged and hoped we could manage through radio communication, together with the medical reference books we took with us. Later, talking to Allan, I asked him did he ever feel concerned for us. 'Most weeks,' was his reply. The thought of appendicitis concerned me, but according to Allan, it would have been easy to handle. Even with a burst appendix, 'One could simply keep the patient sitting up, known as Fowler's position, for safe drainage'. He said the thoughts that most often disturbed his sleep were possibilities of joint infection after breaking a limb. In fact, we kept very

healthy, broke no limbs and had no serious problems.

Four of us took off with John Lewis in the Otter on 4 February — Hal Lister, Ken Blaiklock, George Lowe and myself. George would help us build the hut and then return to Shackleton. Soon after we left, Captain Finn Ronne and Captain McDonald visited Shackleton from the group building Ellsworth Base, 50 miles to the west, for the American IGY expedition.

On the flight to the site of South Ice, I saw the mountains for the first time and started forming some geological hypotheses about the types of rocks. In clear sunshine, the Shackleton Range rocks look almost uniformly black, but the Whichaway Nunataks were contoured with horizontal strata. The Theron Mountains were too distant to observe details, but Fuchs had already reported that they also had horizontal strata. There was a last small, black nunatak 25 miles further south, which we called Omega Nunatak. Beyond it, the Polar Plateau appeared to extend indefinitely. Our station was to be built on its edge. We landed and stepped out, dismayed that a slight undulation hid all the nunataks to the north. In the course of the next few weeks, all the materials needed for South Ice were freighted up in the Otter, in loads up to 2000 pounds, and we immediately began setting things up, starting with our tents and camping gear.

The South Ice Hut

Our hut site was 275 miles from Shackleton and 500 miles from the South Pole. The site was at 81°56′59″S, 28°51′40″W at a height of about 4430 feet, which was computed from 14 measurements of synoptic pressure through the next year. We were 27 miles south of the Whichaway Nunataks.

The ferry loads of hut materials, tools, furniture, scientific equipment and two years' food and fuel began to arrive, transported by Otter. The smaller Auster did not have the necessary return range. The weather was fine, and few flights had to be cancelled. The view was of the endless plateau horizon (Plate 17).

We first dug a pit the size of the hut to bury it for shelter, out of the force of anticipated heavy winter blizzards. In the pit, about shoulder deep, we laid out the metal mats and aluminium I-beam framework

21 The Whichaway Nunataks, 30 miles north of South Ice. The rocks are horizontal Permian strata with dolerite sills. A vertical dyke is visible.

22 Our tent in the Whichaway Nunataks, with Ken Blaiklock starting his survey next to out tent.

23 Whichaway Nunataks, showing the edge of the inland ice sheet, with shear bands where it flows through the Nunataks.

(Plate 18). We had not had a chance to see the hut erected in England, but there was an instruction manual. Between the four of us, we always found the next required parts from the accumulating airlifted loads and bolted these together with a floor, wall panels and the roof. The panels were about four inches thick, faced with plywood and aluminium, with a curtain of 'rock wool' inside for insulation. There were three stove and ventilation chimneys. The hut, close to completion, is shown in Plate 19 and a plan of the hut is shown in Figure 7. It was 16 feet square and proved warm, providing a comfortable home. There was even a fourth bunk.

We shovelled snow to bury the walls and roof and the wind rapidly deposited a dome of snow over the whole building. The door led out into a tunnel, and to reach the surface from the hut there was a trapdoor and a short ladder at the end of the tunnel, about 30 yards from the hut. We had side tunnels for food and fuel stores. Later I dug out a room for my snow studies. Hal created a vertical latrine pit by burning petrol outside in the tunnel, well away from the door.

On the surface we set up a weather screen with a tower, a mast and various instruments. The tower was for

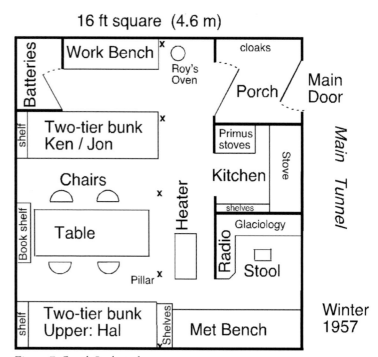

Figure 7 South Ice hut plan.

Hal's instruments and the mast carried a propeller-driven wind generator, linked to charge a bank of wet-cell batteries inside the hut. Plate 20 shows these features with Hal installing some of his instruments. South Ice was almost always windy and the generator hummed gently away, while if the wind got too strong the propeller could be furled. On the rare occasions when the wind eased almost completely, we needed to watch that the batteries did not get to drive the blade, though there was a cutout to prevent this. Once, towards the end of the winter, a gentle breeze fluctuated and fused the cutout. Our alternative for electric power was a small petrol generator, located in one of tunnels, but it was noisy, took many hours to charge the batteries and inevitably left exhaust fumes in the tunnel in spite of its outlet to the surface. Most of the time the wind generator met our requirements effortlessly, though it did require maintenance.

By 22 February, the hut was complete. Two tons of food and 10 barrels of kerosene (paraffin) had been flown in and George had returned to Shackleton.

Fuchs decided to bring each of us back to Shackleton for a few days change of scene and to collect personal items. At midnight on 23 February Blaiklock flew with Haslop to Shackleton in the Otter, leaving South Ice in a temperature of -40°F (-40°C). The flying conditions were not good, and beyond Recovery Glacier they were forced to fly between two levels of cloud. When still about 50 miles from Shackleton, Haslop could see the homing beacon ahead and decided to let down slowly through the lower cloud and follow the ground beneath. The aircraft skis suddenly touched the ground at full speed, 110 knots. Blaiklock told me Haslop did not blink, but gently ascended. The locality, an area of low snow hills, thereafter became known as the Touchdown Hills.

Eventually, the last loads had been flown in, including four drums of vehicle fuel, which formed the start of a depot for the Pole journey in the summer. On one occasion, when we had drift snow at South Ice in a moderately strong wind, Gordon Haslop arrived in the Otter and could see the station mast but not the surface beneath the drifting snow, which was about a metre thick. After making several circuits to decide the best way to land he flew towards the hut, judged when he thought he must be just above the surface and then made a slightly dropped landing. Still

uncertain if he was still moving, he eventually realised he was stationary, with the drift flowing past. Landing in drift snow became one of Gordon's specialities. If conditions were difficult, someone would talk on the radio to the pilot as he approached for landing. George Lowe undertook this vital function on one occasion, but was not told when the landing had been completed. The pilot could hear George inside as he

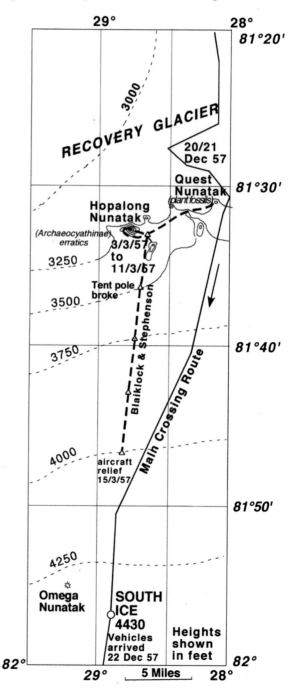

Figure 8　The Whichaway Nunataks

24 A view across to the highest Whichaway peak. The streaking is caused by drift snow, with rising wind.

walked to the hut, his voice raised because he had lost radio contact.

Castaway at Whichaway

I felt slightly restless at the beginning of March. I was ready for the winter but with the unvisited Whichaway Nunataks only 30 miles away, I realised that a short visit might be possible and worthwhile. I raised it with Bunny Fuchs when I next saw him, and he warned that the season was more advanced than it seemed and we could expect longer lasting bad weather at any time. But he must have understood how I keenly I felt, and agreed on a short visit for two men.

On 3 March, John Lewis took Hal Lister back to South Ice with David Stratton, to man the station. He took Ken and me to the Whichaways (Plate 21) for survey and geological work. This was to be a short 8 to 24 hour visit before the Otter returned for us. We landed on a broad snowfield close to the highest nunatak and, in a brisk breeze, we soon had the tent

up and prepared a hot brew (Plate 22). We had our full camping gear, with fuel and food for 10 days as sledging rations were packed in boxes, with 10 days food for two men. Even though we expected to be picked up the next day, in case of emergency we had a small sledge so that we could manhaul the 30 miles back to South Ice. Our nunatak surroundings are shown in Figure 8.

It was late afternoon, but we set off to get in a good night's work. Sunsets were now occurring, but the light was still strong enough to work in. While Ken climbed the nearby nunatak, carrying his theodolite for survey work, I couldn't wait to examine the nearby rocks. I went around the peak to examine the rocks on the west side, where there were more extensive rock exposures. As I approached the first moraines, I saw some white boulders, and I made for a large, cube-shaped rock about five feet high — limestone, perhaps? Yes. It was indeed limestone and contained numerous fossils of *Archaeocyathus*. I had studied these fossils at Queensland University. Scott's veteran

South Australian geologist, Griffith Taylor, had described such fossils. The fossils look somewhat like corals and are about 500 million years old. This was an exciting find and I was keen to locate the source. It was cold, and I had to keep moving because of it. The cold caused me to break a tooth when I foolishly bit into a frozen chocolate instead of letting it soften first. To avoid this happening again, I often toasted the edge of my sledging ration chocolate on the primus stove before eating it.

I proceeded to climb up the rock slopes to the top of the main peak (Plate 23), collecting specimens of sandstones and other horizontal sedimentary rocks and a dolerite on the summit, where it formed a sill of more recent intrusive igneous rock. It was well after midnight before I crossed the summit and returned to the tent to join Ken. Next morning was fine and, expecting the plane to return, we both worked within a reasonable distance of camp. By afternoon, with no aircraft, we felt confident it would not come that day. So I enjoyed another midnight jaunt to a more distant nunatak where I was pleased to discover some Gondwana Permian plant fossils, similar to those Fuchs had discovered in the Theron Mountains.

A change in the weather brought heavy cloud and light snow. Later, listening to our radio, we learned that bad weather at Shackleton had prevented a flight. Next day, we went out together to visit a new nunatak. The clouds had cleared, but a strong wind continued and snow drift was whirling around, reducing visibility to about 50 yards. The conditions were uncomfortable, with our cheeks and noses occasionally nipped white, frozen, so we kept an eye on each other for these signs in order to thaw them with a warm hand. It was most unlikely the plane could return until the weather improved, so we retired to our sleeping bags. I was pleased that my Antarctic adventure had really begun!

The conditions in a strong wind, carrying heavy snow drift, can create severe problems for travellers. Above us we could see cloudless sky, and from the top of a nearby nunatak I took photographs of the drift-snow scene. The landscape was an impressive sight, slowly moving with the drift which flowed through the peaks without smothering them, and there was the constant roar of the wind, drowning speech (Plate 24). The study of drift snow was a research project Hal Lister planned for the coming winter at South Ice, where it was an almost constant feature.

At our Whichaway camp we conserved our rations and fuel because, as the days passed, the weather worsened. Hannes la Grange, our weather man at Shackleton, warned us in a radio message that the weather was not expected to break for some days. Ken and I did a few more walks together and examined the moraines at the edge of the adjacent Recovery Glacier, where I collected specimens of sheared ice and saw there was no trace of any *Archaeocyathus* limestone boulders. Although we found them on every Whichaway nunatak we visited, it seemed clear the inland ice had brought the *Archaeocyathus* from the south and that there were none further up Recovery Glacier.

Time was passing, and on the eighth day we decided to implement our reserve plan and start hauling for South Ice. We left a message at the camp site and set off next morning. We faced the prospect of several days pulling our small sledge containing our tent, sleeping bags, and all our remaining fuel and food. To get through the nunataks, we first had to drag the sledge over a low saddle, through which the wind funnelled with increased force. We were wearing moccasins, soft-laced footwear, with several layers of thick socks and many duffles, blanket-like booties, inside. These were warm; boots would have been far too cold and I never wore them. We continually fell on our faces on the wind-polished surfaces and progress was frustratingly slow. I found a way of wearing crampons on my shapeless footwear, and later we shared our only pair, one each. Well muffled, we had to shout to hear one another, and every so often, plate-sized pieces of the eroding surface would come wheeling past in the wind. We got over the low saddle and I expected progress to get easier, but it wasn't.

Ken navigated, I marvelled how, with nothing to see except ghost outlines of the nunataks behind us. Whenever he checked his compass, his direction proved to be accurate. The steady wind direction was from the south-east and he made sure we walked away from the nunataks along the bearing he had taken from a slight rise near South Ice. He told me he used the looming shadow cast by the sun to estimate the bearing for our course. We plodded on for six hours, at a slight angle into the wind, and the surface became softer away from the mountains. We camped.

Tent up, struggling to control its severe flapping in the wind, anchoring it down with snow blocks and guys to pegs, then quickly inside and into our sleeping bags. We prepared a meal of biscuits and hot pemmican, with additions, which I always found a welcome meal. Then a hot drink of cocoa. In all my time on the ice, I never got tired of pemmican.

It had been a strenuous day and sleep was good, but too soon the cold, -30°F, penetrated. We slept inside a heavy pyramid tent made of ventile, with a separate, heavy groundsheet. Our stove was a kerosene primus primed with meths. We slept in our clothes inside two down sleeping bags, having taken off our moccasins. Our clothes were wool underwear (vests and longjohns), heavy woollen trousers and shirt, several wool sweaters and our indispensable light ventile windproof trousers and anoraks. We wore balaclavas and several pairs of gloves inside leather over-gloves. We wore everything we had and slept in inner and outer sleeping bags, on sheepskins and foam pads that, unfortunately, crushed flat and fragmented.

The 'night' passed, at first with deep sleep from exhaustion, warmed by our meal. But soon we woke regularly and rolled over to combat the cold, which nags at different places — hips, feet. Heads are also a problem, muffled in a woollen balaclava, and I felt annoyed about losing the precious warmth of my breath. But breathing into a sleeping bag only forms more ice.

Breakfast was hot porridge, which Ken always ate scornfully — 'silly' porridge he said, quoting the famous mountaineer Eric Shipton, even though we put heaps of butter in it — and then a mug of sweet, milky cocoa. Occasionally, Ken even added cocoa powder to the porridge — 'cocoa porridge'. Biscuits spread with butter and Marmite (resembling genuine Australian Vegemite), and thermos flasks of cocoa were prepared for lunch. The biscuits would by then be frozen and resembled cardboard. Packing up, leaving the tent and collapsing it, loading and lashing the sledge carefully were some of the unavoidable, painful tasks. Then quickly putting on our hauling harnesses, we set off again.

The second day was just as slow and arduous. Drifting snow has a way of getting into clothing, especially at the wrists behind gloves, which slowly get wet and freeze when taken off. That afternoon we stopped to erect the tent, but one of its four bamboo poles broke in the wind. I remembered the tent expert at Benjamin Edgington's, the makers in London, lamenting that China, the old source for bamboo, was cut off and that the alternative supply was inferior. Our situation was serious, and we discussed what to do. We even raised the possibility of continuing on to South Ice, but dug a triangular pit to erect the tent as a three-sided pyramid. It looked like staying up and we got inside — less space, but it worked well, though was no warmer,

The third morning was similar, and we continued on what was becoming a life-and-death journey. Although manhauling, we had been on half rations for some days. That night, in putting up the tent, I had trouble getting my frozen right glove back on and got frostbite around my wrist and blisters on my fingertips. Later, one of Ken's toes was slightly frostbitten inside his sleeping bag. The fourth day, manhauling provided similar discomforts, but in the afternoon the weather began to brighten and enabled us to see some distance ahead. The scene was one of endless, featureless snow — quite beautiful. Looking back we could see the mountains, and compass bearings confirmed the accuracy of Ken's navigation. We hauled on, wonderfully encouraged to see where we were heading. We had hopes of seeing the low hills ahead near South Ice, but could not recognise any of the landscape. We knew Omega Nunatak was further west, well off our route.

That night, the sun was setting about the usual time for temperate latitudes, around 7 pm, with a deep pinkish glow. Added to this was a full, orange moon. The cold had razor-like intensity. It was our coldest night, -50°F (-46°C). We finished our pemmican, leaving only the remnants of our food — a tin of bacon, biscuits and some scraps. The most serious problem was that our fuel was getting low. Sleep was fitful, pinched by the searching cold, with painful postures. You reach a point where discomfort and pain seem to attain a plateau, no worse than they have been for hours. The weather was still extremely cold and clear as we started breakfast next morning. We were eating our tin of bacon and had one last fill of fuel for the primus. The bacon was nauseatingly rich and greasy, and we had just started to drink our cocoa when Ken stiffened.

It was the noise of a plane approaching. Ken bounced outside to signal our safety and then quickly returned for his cocoa; it was painfully cold outside in stockinged feet at -53°F (-47°C). Soon Bunny Fuchs, John Lewis and Geoffrey Pratt landed beside us and our troubles were over. We were still only about halfway and the problem of finding South Ice, that speck on the landscape, was considerable. We would have probably tried to walk the last 15 miles without the sledge. Lister and Stratton had put out a line of flags for about 400 yards on either side of the hut. Given our circumstances, hauling our sledge, we did not dwell on the difficulty we faced in finding South Ice. Three days before, I had made a cairn in the middle of nowhere and cached my rock collection, fossils and other specimens in a sledge box. Remarkably, the first vehicle party recovered the box and specimens six months later.

I found being rescued an emotional experience, accompanied by tears. Everyone seemed strong and helpful, cheerful, and more than pleased to see us. That afternoon the bad weather returned and continued for the next six days. Fuchs and Haslop had flown out to get us on the same day we left our Whichaway camp but in the difficult, drifting conditions couldn't see us. On the morning of our rescue, they first landed where we had camped at the mountains and read our message. We flew back to Shackleton for several days respite before returning to South Ice.

In a nicely paternal way, Fuchs asked me if there was anything I would like while I was at Shackleton, and I asked to listen to some music on the record player. He agreed, and my colleagues were surprised. Fuchs did not appreciate music, and I was distinctly favoured. I chose to listen to Kathleen Ferrier singing some Mahler songs, somewhat ironically titled 'On the Death of Children'. I admired the special timbre and depth of understanding in her quite remarkable voice, with the legendary accompanist, Gerald Moore.

My first Antarctic outing had been eventful and I learned a lot, very quickly. I was pleased that this proved to be my only manhauling experience. I found it extremely strenuous, even though I was very fit. With practice, I would probably have honed the right muscles for the task, but I marvelled that Scott and Shackleton had endured this inefficient way of travel towards the Pole, as have others since. With the clarity of hindsight,

I think it was a serious mistake not to have taken two or more food boxes in the plane for our Whichaway camp. We could then have stayed there to wait for the plane to return. Occasionally, I ask myself whether we could have reached South Ice under our own steam. I doubt we could have done so, and were more than lucky to have made it back safely.

ESTABLISHING SCOTT BASE, 1955–56

The other arm of TAE, the New Zealand Party, was involved on the Ross Sea side of Antarctica. Sir Edmund Hillary was the leader and their role was to establish a base and find a good route up onto the Polar Plateau.[17] They were then to establish fuel depots for use by Fuchs' crossing party after it had reached the Pole. The locality details are shown in Figure 9.

The party comprised 18 members of TAE, together with the New Zealand IGY party of five men, making a total of 23. The expedition sailed from Wellington in late December 1956, on HMNZS *Endeavour*, under Captain Harry Kirkwood. *Endeavour* (900 tons) was a small, wooden net-layer. She was not large enough to carry all the men and supplies, but the Americans were also establishing an IGY station in McMurdo Sound and offered to help with shipping space.

Fuchs' original TAE plan envisaged a route to the Polar Plateau up the Ferrar Glacier, west of McMurdo Sound; Scott traversed a similar route on his western journey in 1903, when he discovered the Polar Plateau. Two surviving members of Scott's second expedition, Sir Charles Wright and Professor Frank Debenham, had suggested a possible New Zealand base at either Dailey Islands or Butter Point, on the west side of McMurdo Sound. Both proved to be inaccessible and otherwise unsuitable, and the base was built at Hut Point, on the east side of McMurdo Sound, close to Scott's original *Discovery* hut.

Later, the Ferrar Glacier was found to be unsuitable for vehicles, especially in its lower reaches. Bernie Gunn, one of the geologists, had visited McMurdo in the 1955–56 summer with Dr Trevor Hatherton of the IGY party and Lieutenant Commander W.J.L. Smith of the New Zealand Navy. They were members of the 'Deep Freeze I' operation and, by manhauling exploration, ruled out the Dailey Islands as unsuitable but found Butter Point and the Ferrar Glacier more promising. Gunn also made an interesting flight with the Americans and saw several other glaciers south-west of McMurdo Sound, which offered possible alternative routes to the Polar Plateau. He particularly noted the Skelton Glacier.

The New Zealand Party trained during the 1956 winter on the Tasman Glacier in New Zealand. The expedition transport in Antarctica was to comprise two aircraft, five Ferguson tractors and 30 husky dogs from the Australian Antarctic Base at Mawson. The aircraft were both single-engine — a De Havillan Beaver smaller than the Otter at Shackleton, and an Auster. The Beaver, with a freight load of half a ton, was intended for laying depots on the plateau and the Auster was for shorter flights and light loads.

On 21 December 1956, *Endeavour* left Bluff in the South Island of New Zealand. She experienced the usual dramas getting through the Ross Sea pack-ice, weathered some bad storms, and approached McMurdo Sound. Here she encountered heavy pack-ice and asked for assistance from the USS *Glacier*, a powerful icebreaker, to reach open water in McMurdo and then approach Butter Point. Hillary was offered, and accepted, a helicopter flight to reconnoitre the

way across the sea ice to the coast. This investigation was discouraging, but ground parties were landed and set off to explore the situation. Several days of effort for little return showed that it was not realistic to consider taking the 500 tons of supplies needed across 15–20 miles of sea ice to a site on Butter Point, and Hillary decided to look for a site on the east side of McMurdo. Pram Point appeared to be ideal for Scott Base, although it would require a nine-mile haul from the ship.

By 13 January, sufficient materials had been towed to the construction site on Pram Point for Randal Heke (NZ Ministry of Works) and seven men to start building ANARE-type huts from Australia. An opening ceremony was held on 20 January, after the first was erected. John Claydon records the insulation material used in the first hut was so effective that, without any heating of any kind, the hut 'acted as a perfect refrigerator' and soon everyone moved outside into the warmer sunshine.[18] The sixth and last of the main base huts was completed on 5 February. Dr George Marsh and a dog team party had been exploring the lower part of the Ferrar Glacier and reported it impassable, even for dogs. The RNZAF team had now assembled their Beaver aircraft and a flight up the Ferrar confirmed all that Marsh had reported, so therefore it was abandoned as a route. Another pathway to the plateau had to be found before winter.

Hillary had to choose, and quickly, a suitable route to the Polar Plateau, a route which Fuchs' vehicles could descend on their crossing. Figure 10 shows the southern mountains and the numerous glaciers which might have been considered. This map also shows the routes used in the first journeys to reach the Pole — the Beardmore, used by Shackleton and Scott, and the Axel Heiberg Glacier, used by Amundsen.

Remembering Gunn's sighting of the Skelton Glacier, a flight was arranged to inspect it with pilot Bill Cranfield, Hillary and others on 18 January. They flew south around Minna Bluff, a well-known landmark from the Scott and Shackleton expeditions, and then west to Skelton Inlet, the outlet of the unmapped glacier. In spite of crevassed areas, there seemed to be a possible route up the glacier towards its head, where they saw a wide, gradual slope leading up to the edge of the Polar Plateau. The next day, three dog teams with George Marsh, Richard Brooke,

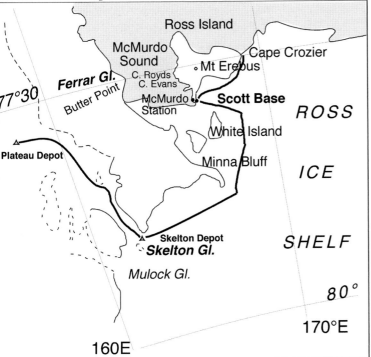

Figure 9 The McMurdo Sound region showing the routes up the Skelton Glacier and to Cape Crozier.

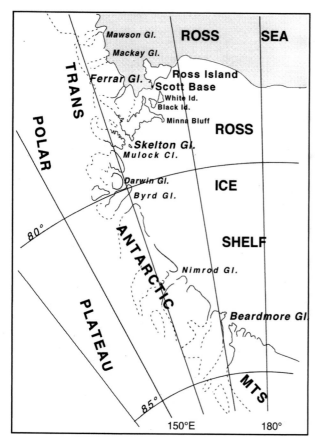

Figure 10 Possible glacier routes from the Ross Ice Shelf to the Polar Plateau. The Beardmore Glacier had been followed by Shackleton and Scott, but was impractical for vehicles because of severe crevassing.

Harry Ayres and Peter Mulgrew, left Scott Base to cross the Ross Ice Shelf to the Skelton, but they were forced to return five days later when Marsh become ill. A flight landed near the foot of the glacier on 25 January to establish the Skelton Depot. Two days later, two dog teams with four men were flown to the site for this new depot. Meanwhile, Bob Miller and Roy Carlyon set off from Scott Base with another team of dogs on the 180-mile journey across the Ross Ice Shelf. Neither had worked dogs by themselves before, but they nevertheless arrived in 11 days and began a survey of the lower part of the glacier.

The Beaver started relaying loads of food and fuel to provision the Skelton Depot. On an early flight the two geologists, Bernie Gunn and Guy Warren, were flown in with Arnold Heine, a member of the summer party, to start their geological work. They examined the major rock bluffs either side of the glacier, travelling with a manhauled sledge, and climbed Mount Harmsworth, 9090 feet. At the same time,

Brooke's Skelton reconnaissance party made steady progress up the glacier with their dog teams, having to relay loads through soft snow in the steep, middle section. They found a route which almost completely avoided badly crevassed sections and reached the long slope leading up to the plateau on 8 February.

Next day, the two aircraft flew from Scott Base to test landings on the Polar Plateau at 8200 feet (2500 metres).[19] The Beaver circled Brooke's camp and then landed in a strong wind. Having delivered mail and news, the aircraft made the critical take-off without difficulty. The Auster had been circling overhead before landing and made a somewhat sluggish but successful take-off. This was an important test for the aircraft and the Beaver returned whenever the weather permitted, flying up to 24 hours a day to stock Plateau Depot ready for the crossing party next year. It managed to do this despite temperatures in the -30°Cs and persistent winds. The field party could now descend to the region near the head of the Skelton Glacier, 10 to 15 degrees warmer, and continue mapping for several more weeks.

Meanwhile, all outside work had been completed at Scott Base, with the huts firmly tied down with wire ropes, and the covered ways connecting them completed. Nine radio masts were erected, two 80 feet high and the others 60 feet. Regular radio schedules with New Zealand were maintained via a radiotelephone service.

Endeavour sailed for New Zealand on 22 February 1957, taking the construction party and the summer party home. At the end of February all glacier parties were flown back to Scott Base. A series of fine, clear days early in March enabled long reconnaissance flights to examine the plateau for several hundred miles south of Plateau Depot. These showed that the route south would need to move further west to avoid extensive crevassing.

Hillary records that before he left New Zealand, he nurtured ideas of a more ambitious role for the NZ Party and wrote to the Ross Sea Committee: 'If organisation and time permits or an emergency occurs, the party could travel out as far as the South Pole … Fuchs seemed reasonably happy with these proposals.' Interestingly, he later commented that, 'Obviously neither the Ross Sea Committee nor Bunny Fuchs took me seriously'.[20]

The Trial Tractor Journey to Cape Crozier

Having arrived and set up Scott Base, Hillary worked on using the Ferguson tractors on a route towards the Pole, rather than use dogs and the Beaver. His engineers, Jim Bates and Murray Ellis, had modified the tractors and Hillary needed to carry out a trial with them in the 1957 summer, under conditions comparable to the planned southern journey. So he set out to repeat the famous journey made by Wilson, Bowers and Cherry-Garrard in the winter darkness on Scott's Last Expedition, from McMurdo to Cape Crozier, at the east end of Ross Island, in June–July 1911.[21] This manhauling journey took 36 days to accomplish a round trip of 140 miles. Their biologist, Wilson, wanted to obtain eggs from the emperor penguin rookery at Cape Crozier, hoping to find evidence about the evolution of these birds. The party did return with three eggs, but scientific studies on them were inconclusive.

The tractor group, which included Ellis, Bates, Mulgrew and Hillary, took three days to reach the Knoll at Cape Crozier. Mulgrew took with him a copy of Cherry-Garrard's book and they managed to find the stone hut, built 46 years before, by Wilson's party. When they excavated the snow-filled floor, they recovered interesting relics. After three days, Hillary set off to return to Scott Base. Across Windless Bight, the temperatures were around -46°F. The vehicle lights started to falter and they entered ground fog. There were ice blockages in a carburettor, but they found their way in the darkness through pressure ridges near Scott Base and got home early on 25 March. Their four-day vehicle journey stands in remarkable contrast with the heroic, 36-day effort of Wilson's party.

In April 1997, Brooke and Gunn took a dog team 20 miles south to climb the peak on White Island. On the 14th, the sun set finally for the winter. Four men, Ellis, Mulgrew, Claydon and Cranfield, manhauled across to Cape Evans in a pilgrimage visit to Scott's old hut, and the airmen tested their air emergency equipment and rations. Another party of eight crossed over with four dog teams, mainly avoiding travel on the treacherous sea ice. They found Scott's hut in poor condition, following the previous survival occupation by Shackleton's Ross Sea party in 1915–18, but the hut and its surroundings were cleaned up and rubbish

removed in January by Captain Kirkwood and crew from *Endeavour*.

During this first summer, there were many achievements by the New Zealand Party from Scott Base. Two depots were established for the crossing party, at Plateau and Skelton depots, and a satisfactory route was found from the Ross Ice Shelf onto the Polar Plateau. Scott Base was fully operational, ready for the IGY program beginning in July. The party was poised to resume operations in the spring and Hillary had proved that his modified Fergusons could be used to support his travel program.

In 1956, Peter Webb and Barrie McKelvey were completing their geology degrees at Victoria University in Wellington. They became aware of the US globemaster traffic flying down to Christchurch and then on to McMurdo and were stimulated by 'the potential excitement at the bottom of the earth'. Their enterprising story is described by Van der Kay.[22] McKelvey and Webb made eager representations to join the New Zealand section of TAE. They joined a long list of other volunteer applicants. After several rejections, they decided to ask the Americans for a lift, and were accepted. Apparently, this bypassing the system upset the hierarchy, but Professor Bob Clark made representations on their behalf and they were finally given permission to travel down on *Endeavour* as cargo handlers. They were to help unload for a week at McMurdo and then be flown home. Clark arranged a grant of £119 for film, and the Geology Department lent them a camera. They had no cold-weather clothing, but this was solved with the help of colleagues in New Zealand, lending them mountaineering down clothing and war surplus gear.

Webb and McKelvey succeeded in spending seven weeks in Antarctica, through their determination and persistence. Geological research was not a scientific discipline included in the IGY, but on the eve of their return flight to New Zealand they became aware that the Americans were mounting a geophysical party to the Trans-Antarctic Mountains and had no field geologists. Webb and McKelvey became 'honorary Americans' and transferred to the American McMurdo Base, from where they were soon transferred to a camp in the Dry Valleys area. Their project leader, Phil Smith, helped make sure they were not inadvertently flown out on a flight to

New Zealand. Barrie McKelvey has told me they took care to be out of camp on fieldwork whenever a supply plane visited, in case of a misunderstanding.

Webb and McKelvey carried out field mapping and returned the following year, publishing their findings in the first geological research papers since the work of Scott and Shackleton's geologists. The work provided the material for their masters' theses. One of the Dry Valleys is named the Victoria Dry Valley, in recognition of their original work. The region is one of the amazing areas in Antarctica which are virtually free of ice.

Webb and McKelvey continued their research on various aspects of Antarctic geology, Webb as a Professor at Ohio State University in the US and McKelvey at the University of New England in Australia. Each has made major scientific contributions to the geology of Antarctica, particularly on glacial history and old glacial deposits. The region accessible from McMurdo also proved unusually fertile for new discoveries about Antarctica's more recent Ice Age changes.

THE SITUATION FOR TAE AT THE END OF SUMMER 1957

At the end of the 1957 summer, TAE was well placed to attempt its main objective — to cross the Antarctic continent through the Pole, from Shackleton Base to Scott Base, in the 1957–58 summer. It would also fulfil its contribution to IGY from three scientific bases.

From a shaky start, which resulted in *Theron* virtually having to dump the Advance Party on the hostile Filchner Ice Shelf, TAE had firmly found its feet. Much was due to Blaiklock's Advance Party, which completed everything asked of them at Shackleton Base — completing the hut and carrying out an inland traverse to reach and survey the newly discovered Theron Mountains.

The NZ Party had brilliantly solved a major problem, namely where to site their Scott Base, by building it on McMurdo Sound, after rejecting the recommended location close to the Ferrar Glacier.

An alternative route onto the Polar Plateau, to serve later for descent by Fuchs' crossing party, had been found on the Skelton Glacier and traversed with dog teams. The first two depots, Skelton and Plateau, had been established and the Beaver aircraft was used successfully to stock them with fuel and food for the crossing party.

Ed Hillary had successfully tested the performance of his Ferguson tractors in order to use them on the following summer's journey onto the Plateau. He did so by repeating the historic 'Worst journey in the World' (to quote Cherry-Garrard) route across to Cape Crozier. Relics from Wilson's 1912 party on had been recovered from the site of their stone hut.

From Shackleton, the Otter had delivered the materials for an inland base to be built at South Ice, 500 miles from the South Pole, on the planned route for the crossing party. Three men, of whom I was one, were established there for the winter, to undertake their IGY studies.

All these preparations meant that the TAE was poised for the 1957–58 summer crossing. The NZ Party was well prepared to follow its proposed route up the Skelton Glacier. By contrast, Fuchs had no vehicle experience of the planned route to South Ice, passing the Shackleton Range and the Whichaway Nunataks. It could only be surmised there would be severe crevasse problems to negotiate across the Shelf, and the Slessor and the Recovery Glaciers. These likely problems had been identified on the Otter flights. Beyond South Ice, flights indicated the route to the Pole across the Polar Plateau would probably be easier.

For Hillary, there was the remaining challenge of negotiating the route up the Skelton Glacier with vehicles, and finding the way south to the proposed last depot, Depot 700.

TAE was now in a strong position to achieve a continental crossing. Knowing little of Antarctica, I felt no concerns. I was ignorant of the problems awaiting the Sno-Cats and the crevasses. I looked forward to my ice petrology studies during the winter at South Ice, and I was restively eager to see the new rocks in the Shackleton Range in the spring.

3 THE SECOND WINTER, 1957, AND SPRING MOUNTAIN EXPLORATIONS

Antarctic winters are a challenge, with the eternal night and severe weather. The darkness and the general invisibility of the sky also make it harder to look for changing weather. The long dark, together with the extreme cold and near-constant wind, can upset humans, confined as they are in close and crowded quarters. These effects are both psychological and physiological. The phenomenon, commonly called 'cabin fever', is well recognised in places like Canada's vast, frozen north. People are affected by the absence of sunlight, exacerbated by poor sleep patterns. Lack of sunlight affects the pineal gland in the mid-brain and its usual secretion of melatonin, which upsets biological rhythm. These effects for the wintering TAE parties were probably eased by the urgent preparations needed for the spring journeys, but there were tensions and some inevitable interpersonal conflicts. The main Shackleton and Scott Base events are well described in the books of the expedition.[1]

WINTER AT SHACKLETON BASE

The last flight to South Ice was on 25 March 1957. The Shackleton party could then concentrate on their scientific work for the IGY, formally commencing on 1 July, and prepare for the spring and summer journeys in only six months time.

There were no hangars, so the two aircraft had to be protected during winter. The mechanic, Peter Weston, removed the Otter rudder and closed every gap in the plane against snowdrift. A canvas cover protected the engine cover and a wooden shield was fitted behind the propeller. A tractor towed the plane into a wide pit, several feet deep, with the wings horizontal and the tail resting on the surface. The plane was pointed south to face the prevailing wind. These precautions would prevent the wings and ailerons fluttering in strong winds, and Peter also constructed sloping timber windbreaks, close behind the trailing edges. His preparations successfully protected the plane from the winds, which later reached 70 knots. A fence of heavy steel wire was built in front of the plane, with a two-foot gap under it on the south side to break the main wind force and minimise the snowdrift accumulation that buries everything. Drifts did form from both south and the occasional north winds, but by shovelling snow when needed, the Otter was kept clear until the spring.

The smaller Auster was easier to protect. The ailerons, elevators and rudder were locked with wooden clamps and the plane was light enough to be easily moved to face the wind. It was guyed down securely and survived the winter without much attention.

A strongly constructed vehicle workshop was erected and Ralph Lenton added a small annexe. It contained a travelling hoist to lift engines and there were benches and various electrical tools, powered by the generators in the main hut, 200 yards away. The doors were large enough to bring in a Sno-Cat. While the workshop was being built, an inflatable mobile garage, 30 x 15 x 9 feet high, provided temporary shelter. A small electric blower inflated this garage, but it was affected by temperature changes. It would slowly collapse overnight and inflate gradually in the morning sun. It served well until the rubberised cloth became brittle and tore in colder temperatures. Normal rubber becomes hopelessly brittle in extreme cold, whereas neoprene, a synthetic rubber, retains some flexibility.

Winter tunnels were prepared for the dogs. A trench 140 feet long and 4 feet wide was dug, with sawn snow blocks along the sides and a boarded, tarpaper roof. The dogs had their own alcoves to reduce the opportunities to fight. Lighting was provided 12 hours a day and the dogs had a very good winter. Their tunnels stayed above -18°C, even when the outside temperature dropped to -50°C.

Various scientific experiments were performed. Allan Rogers, our doctor, did physiological research on various subjects' energy levels, working and sleeping. He had to make some modifications to his IMP equipment (integrating motor pneumatachograph). Allan was a phlegmatic character, teased by some of his colleagues as 'Bodkin', after a notorious medical doctor, John Bodkin Adams, tried in 1957 in relation to the death of patients under his care. He would respond to this ribbing with a gentle smile. Allan was clever with his hands and, with his electronic knowledge, he soon had his equipment working properly. His guinea pigs would wear a rubber mask and a backpack and carry out routine work while the equipment monitored their breath exhalations. Geoffrey Pratt wore an IMP for a week, only removing it to eat. Allan shadowed his progress, checked on the instrument and made sure the mask stayed in position during sleep. For encouragement, Allan joined in the test with Geoffrey and found the experiment exhausting. Allan had very little medical work because of everyone's excellent health, although he did get to practise some dentistry. He was highly respected for his meticulous medical skill and his ability to repair small instruments, like watches and clocks. He also made parts for the meteorologists' instruments.

Geoffrey Pratt was the expedition geophysicist and installed the seismic equipment for the crossing in one of the Sno-Cats. He conducted experiments over several weeks with George Lowe and David Stratton, to confirm the best arrangement for burying and firing explosive charges and for laying out his geophones to record the resulting waves over various distances from the shot point. When everything worked properly, the thickness of the floating ice shelf could be measured. It came out as about 1500 feet. Geoffrey also had a very sensitive gravimeter, lent by George Woolard from the University of Hawaii. He used this to measure the force of gravity, which he did everywhere we went. He also used it to measure tidal movements at Shackleton Base where the sea floor, at around 3000 feet, was far too deep to have a conventional tide gauge fixed to the bottom. He dug a 20 foot pit, well away from the main hut, set up the gravimeter and recorded its readings photographically for 10 minutes every hour. He used a remote control, with warning lights above his bed to alert him if the instrument needed adjusting. We feared this might not work out well because Geoffrey was such a deep sleeper. However, Bunny Fuchs records that the alarm signal flashed one night at 3 am when he was on night duty, and was surprised when Geoffrey woke at once. He succeeded in getting a unique set of tide readings at the head of the Weddell Sea over a period of several weeks. However, Geoffrey's scientific report is highly technical and I have been unable to confirm the total tide range found.[2]

Waste disposal at Shackleton revealed some unexpected happenings. A 'gash pit' was made by digging a hole 18 feet deep and then igniting successive pints of petrol poured down the hole until a pit about 24 feet deep and about 2 feet in diameter was constructed. Several weeks of use, and occasionally pouring a bucket of water into the hole, deepened it further until it gave a deep, gurgling sound. A lighted ball of paper would burn like a blowtorch in the blast of air rising from the depths of the pit. The buckets of water had apparently melted down into a deep crevasse and the air emerging must have been from compression of the porous snow around a deep crevasse. We noticed a similar breeze in our borehole at South Ice. Antarctica never fails to surprise!

Under the westerly current, the leads of open water in the pack-ice in front of Shackleton Base were constantly changing. When the winds dropped, the open water would freeze over and then crack, buckle and override to form new, complex ice floes. Our South African meteorologist, Hannes la Grange, liked to prepare 'drift cards' which he put inside sealed bottles, giving the date, place of release and with instructions for finders to report their location to him. To my knowledge, no recoveries were reported, after what would have been a long passage with the pack-ice and subsequent release into the open Southern Ocean and thence to some distant shore.

There were the usual concerns about ventilation in the huts. Airflow in the radio room at Shackleton would sometimes reverse in extreme cold conditions outside. Shackleton had new coal and if the small stove heating the room burnt at too low a level during the night, the column of cold air in the upper chimney would collapse downwards, fanning the flames and filling the room with smoke fumes. Poisonous carbon monoxide would be produced, enough to be dangerous. The only way devised to reverse the flow was to cover the top of the chimney with a sack, use blowtorches to heat the metal stove pipe, and then abruptly remove the sack. The night watchman always had to monitor the room on his rounds.

Roy Homard and David Pratt decided to attempt some night fishing by making a hole in the sea ice. They made a large fish trap out of wire netting and lowered it, leaving it 250 feet down for a period. When recovered, its two wires had become twisted and coiled, perhaps by a seal. Bunny Fuchs and George Lowe one night joined Roy and David to visit the trap — a bit of novelty to help break the monotony of winter. Venturing out at night they found the way from the ice shelf down to the edge of the ocean was itself an adventure. The hole was frozen over and, when broken open, they saw countless clusters of ice crystals, an inch or more across. When the water cleared there were also krill, the tiny, pink, shrimp-like creatures which are an important part of the marine food chain. Suddenly, there was a swirl of water as a seal prepared to surface for air. Fuchs reported a continuous, vibrant purring sound — a protest or warning from the seal, perhaps. Some krill was prepared for David Stratton's birthday, as a special dish. Unfortunately, David found each krill contained a few drops of pink oil, and chose not to complete this part of his feast.

Midwinter Day celebrations were held in June, with special food prepared by the master chefs. There were presents from home, a fine party in the vehicle hut, and a spectacular 'Haslop Fireworks Display' from Gordon Haslop, spelling out 'TAE' in Morse.

The hut was slowly moving on its foundations, despite its metal-timber 'raft' foundations. It sank three inches along one side, perhaps because of the crevasses. David Stratton measured the temperature at different levels inside the hut and found a considerable gradient. It increased from around freezing on the floor to 50°F at chest height, and 70° to 80°F near the roof. Later in the year, David cut a hole in a wall panel to see how much ice had formed in the insulation and found scarcely any, a welcome result.

David made repeated theodolite observations on stars, with careful time controls from the radio signal WWV, to enable us to get a fix on the position of Shackleton Base. Ken Blaiklock had determined the base's position in the previous winter and David's measurements revealed that the base was slowly moving northwards with the flow of the ice shelf. David also determined the height of the hut above sea level to be 195 feet and the edge of the shelf 150 feet above sea level. Winter also involved checking all equipment and making arrangements for the spring journeys. This included the food ration boxes, fuel containers, and all the sledges.

In August, a glow began to appear on the northern horizon and the sun first reappeared, briefly, on 14 August. It was four days early, having been refracted up into view. While this heralded the coming of summer and was a welcome sight, the temperature was still at -50°C with a 20 mph wind. During the 'spring', the monthly average was -37°C, the minimum -55°C and the mean wind speed 20 mph, with a maximum of 63 mph.

The Emergency Auster Flight to Halley Bay.

On 17 September came the news that Dr Robin Smart, the leader at Halley Bay, was visiting the nearby emperor penguin rookery when he fell on his camera and sustained internal injuries. These seemed to get worse and his second in command, Joe McDowall, consulted Allan Rogers. Smart had refused to call for assistance previously, realising the urgent preparation underway for the journey. Allan considered that Smart needed attention and, as the

Auster was almost ready to fly, Fuchs decided to send Allan with Gordon Haslop to Halley Bay. On the 19th, the weather had improved enough for them to set off on the expected two and a half hour flight to Halley. Five hours later, the plane had still not arrived. It had flown past Halley, misled by broken ice inland from the frozen edge of the shelf ice. Gordon felt sure he was simply experiencing 'unexpected, stronger head winds', but Halley advised that his radio signal was getting weaker. He finally turned around but, with the light fading, he was forced to land close to the edge of the ice shelf. They later found they were about 50 miles north of Halley and had only one hour of fuel left. They got out of the plane and arranged a shelter camp. Later, Allan said to me, 'Steve, it was such a relief to get out of that cramped plane. I was wearing all my down clothing and could hardly even move. After more than five hours I couldn't wait to have a pee!' They had emergency RAF rations but found the kerosene can was not completely full — echoes of Scott. Using their hands and a sheath knife for nearly six hours, they dug a hole in the snow next to the well-anchored plane and sheltered there, protected by the engine cover. It was 'about the size of a two-man coffin', Gordon later reported. He periodically restarted the plane and used the radio to report they were safe, 'somewhere'.

At Shackleton, frenzied work proceeded, with day and night shifts, to prepare the buried Otter in order to rescue Rogers and Haslop. Bunny talked with Finn Ronne at the American Ellsworth Base, west of Shackleton, who immediately offered assistance, once their Otter was ready and had been test flown. Such is the spirit of cooperation in the Antarctic. The flying conditions at Shackleton were impossible, day after day, but our Otter was ready and test flown in low cloud on 29 September. The next day, Halley Bay reported improving weather and, just as John Lewis and David Stratton were about to leave, Ronne arrived with Commander McCarthy, having flown across from Ellsworth in bad conditions, bringing a special drug for Robin Smart. Ronne's party also donated two crash helmets to TAE, for likely vehicle crevasse encounters on the forthcoming journey.

Lewis and Stratton took off in the Otter into a dark, brooding, and murky sky. They soon flew into conditions causing ice to form on the wings, and were unable to climb above the cloud, with visibility of only a few hundred yards. Forced down to a lower height and unable to see through snow squalls, they found themselves iceberg hopping, which was hair-raising. They could not exceed 75 knots, even on full throttle. Lewis turned back and was relieved to find conditions had improved at Shackleton, with bright sunshine and no cloud.

Shackleton kept frequent radio contact with Halley Base, checking the weather through the night. The overcast conditions at Shackleton, a whiteout and icing up to 2000 feet, were expected to exist almost as far north as Halley Bay. But conditions did improve enough for Lewis and Stratton to set out again the next day, intending to fly at 5000 feet, above the icing conditions and below higher cloud. They reached Halley in 2 hours 20 minutes, having checked the ground over the 70 miles south of Halley for future reference. After landing to refuel, they set off north again and, within a relatively short time, the Otter was receiving the signal from the Auster's SARAH radio beacon and had found the plane and landed to refuel it. The two men were fine, though perhaps thinner. They had kept their down clothing on and their 'survival gear', namely single, lightweight sleeping bags, saw them through without frostbite, though they were uncomfortably cold. They had survival rations for three weeks and enough kerosene to make hot drinks for breakfast and at night. But they became very thirsty and, on the restricted rations, could not exercise enough to keep warm.

Reaching Halley Bay, Allan found Robin Smart had made a full recovery. Smart met the plane, wondering if he would have two patients himself. Haslop and Rogers had kept 'a bottle of a preparation calculated to hasten recovery', and shared it with Smart. Weather prevented the two planes from returning to Shackleton for four days, where final preparations were advanced for the departure of a four-vehicle party to explore the first leg of the crossing route to South Ice. At South Ice we were also about to be relieved by the Otter. Various circumstances had forced the postponement of all Fuchs' scheduled plans — the intense cold of the spring weather, similarly experienced by Amundsen, and then the aircraft emergencies. Fortunately, we were still happily situated at South Ice.

Gordon Haslop, known as 'Pedro', was a colourful,

utterly safe, focused and skilful pilot. It was said he was the only person who ironed his freshly washed clothes, including his underpants. He enjoyed his alcohol, and his colleagues on one occasion tried spiking a drink for him with black, well-stewed tea. He steadily drank it in front of them, without comment, and called their bluff. But he was a little accident-prone. His discovery of the Touchdown Hills with Ken Blaiklock has been described earlier and another incident at Shackleton happened around this time. An American plane had arrived unexpectedly from Ellsworth, which meant new faces, fellow aviators, and the opportunity for friendly exchanges. Gordon was standing with the visitors in the kitchen, in front of the big Aga anthracite stove. He was the roster cook that day and, as was his fashion, had the tins of food for lunch inside the oven, heating up. He knew exactly how long to leave them there, unopened, but then came this distraction. Suddenly, all the tins blew up, lifting the heavy door off the stove. The visitors, like the walls of the kitchen, were covered in baked beans.

WINTER AT SCOTT BASE

The scientific work at Scott Base was in full swing, centred on Trevor Hatherton's IGY group. Research topics included the aurora and the all-sky camera (Hatherton), magnetics (Gerard), earthquakes (Orr), ionosphere and the pulse transmitter (Sandford), solar radiation and tide measurements (Macdonald). The aurora was ever-present in fine weather and Hatherton is said to have sighed in relief when cloudy weather curtailed his heavy observation schedule. Hillary notes that the aurora displays were less intense than the views recorded in Wilson's classic paintings on Scott's last expedition. Occasionally they were vivid green and red, and on one occasion prompted their American neighbours, two miles away at Hut Point, to ask whether Scott Base was having a fire.

Hillary and his men had a busy winter, preparing for the planned spring travel. The sledging rations were modified and, dissatisfied with the poor performance of the field radios — 'a complete failure, designed for use in the desert' — Hillary had new sets made in New Zealand. These were flown in by the Americans in the spring and proved an outstanding success. They were battery operated, not hand winched, and transmitted only in Morse, but they could usually receive in Morse and, in good conditions, voice. Hillary's men practised and became proficient in Morse on their radios. At Shackleton we had the original hand or foot pedal-powered field sets. I found these cumbersome, but we enjoyed excellent reception when conditions were good. On one occasion, we were unable to hear South Ice from less than 50 miles away on the crossing journey, while having telephone-like clarity with the air crew at Shackleton Base, over 300 miles away. Conversations were usually short and, when wearing gloves hung around the neck, the webbing kept getting wound around the pedals.

Brooke, Miller and Carlyon were the party's surveyors and were to navigate for their field parties. Hillary, with his RNZAF navigational experience, was to guide the tractor team. In case of emergencies, he arranged for everyone to acquire some knowledge of polar navigation, and Bob Miller gave classes. I had taken classes in England and practised with a sextant on the *Magga Dan*, taking a fix on where we had just been. In Antarctica I might have been able to confirm latitude, but longitude would have taken me much longer. I knew how to find my way around in the mountains, as long as I could see them, but on the Polar Plateau I was always reliant on Ken Blaiklock's navigation.

At Scott Base there were a series of lectures, including a sequence on geology by Bernie Gunn and Guy Warren. Scott organised a similar series of lectures on his last expedition.[3] Bernie and Guy had already made extensive specimen collections and prepared microscope slides from diamond saw-cut slices, grinding them down with abrasive powder to study some of their petrological details under a polarising microscope.

Extensive modifications were made to the Weasel and the three Ferguson tractors. A crash bar was installed to protect the drivers against a fall or roll into a crevasse and canvas windbreaks were also made. The tracks were strengthened and modified for better traction in soft snow. Strong tow bars were welded onto each vehicle and 60 foot lengths of terylene towrope, with a breaking strain of eight tons, were cut and spliced, for connecting vehicles in crevasse country. It was expected that the tractor party would be very exposed on the Polar Plateau and a light, strong 'caboose', 11 x 4 feet, was erected on one of the sledges. It was fitted with a radio, cupboards, benches and a stand for two Primus stoves. It had two shelf bunks, large enough for four men to sleep, and was warmed by heat exchange from the vehicle exhaust.

The sledges, 'one of our main worries', according to Hillary, had been damaged during unloading and they were repaired and reinforced. Some had tufnol, low-friction plastic, replacing the steel runners while others had the steel runners widened to lower the pressure on the snow.

The Beaver was put away for the winter. Its wings were stored in its crate and the fuselage was towed from the sea ice to a snow-filled depression on the hillside near Scott Base. It was faced south and tied down securely with wire cables. The motor was restrained and every known opening sealed against snowdrift. Covers were not used, as these collected snow. The Beaver remained in perfect condition throughout the winter and the Auster was kept operational, parked out on the airfield behind a wire netting windbreak, with the tail facing south into the strongest wind direction. There was the occasional day with good flying weather and flying continued as long as possible. Wally Tarr would prepare the plane for flight, removing snow from the wings and fuselage with hot air blowers and freeing the motor. As the Auster was not equipped for night flying, a red light from one of the tractors was installed. It flew each month when there was clear moonlight, but after one severe storm, snowdrifts engulfed it and a month's flying was lost. The plane would do a circuit over McMurdo Sound, observing the freeze over, and report any seals or penguins.

In addition to the weekly lectures on a range of topics, a Sunday church service was held. The base had a large selection of records for the radiogram, which was rarely silent. The base enjoyed twice-weekly radiotelegraphy with New Zealand, which we became aware of as silent listeners at South Ice.

Hillary planned three summer activities. A Northern Party would travel with two dog teams along the coast, surveying and studying the geology, then climb up a glacier to the plateau and continue on to study the western side of the ranges. They would then return down the Skelton Glacier and complete

their survey. A Southern Party's role was to establish the depots for the crossing party. It would have four dog teams, start from the Skelton Depot, travel up to Plateau Depot and continue over the plateau to establish the sites for Depot 480 and the last depot, Depot 700. They were to have Beaver aircraft support to deposit the fuel drums and, when this work was done, the plan was to form two groups for survey and exploration in the unexplored sector between Skelton and the historic Beardmore Glacier. The Beardmore Glacier was on the route followed by the Shackleton and Scott Pole parties.

The third party, the Tractor Party, consisted of four men, including Hillary. They were to use the Weasel and three Ferguson tractors and leave Scott Base with enough fuel to reach D700. Hillary did not know how well his vehicles would function and had to establish a vehicle route to D700 for Fuchs to use on the crossing journey. If all went well, Hillary hoped to be able to accumulate enough fuel at D700 to allow him to push on to the Pole, but doubted if there would be time to do this if Fuchs kept to his original plan to reach the Pole by Christmas. The three NZ field parties were able to start their travels early, in September, in spite of unsettled weather and temperatures below -50°F.

WINTER AT SOUTH ICE

Hal Lister, Ken Blaiklock and I were well prepared for a six-month stay at South Ice. I can only surmise how Bunny Fuchs chose us, though we all had projects to carry out. Hal Lister was in charge and, as a glaciologist, wanted to carry out special studies on snow precipitation and on wind-blown, drift snow. Hal was very experienced, having travelled widely, and had studied Scandinavian glaciers. Glaciology was still a relatively young science. He had wintered at North Ice on the Greenland Plateau a few years before, with the British North Greenland Expedition. At 33 he was somewhat older than Ken and me, married, had served in the Royal Navy and was on the Geography staff of the University of Durham.

Ken Blaiklock was 28 years of age and also very experienced, having spent four winters with FIDS in the Antarctic Peninsula and a year as the leader of the Advance Party at Shackleton. He was a surveyor and established our station's position accurately, by star sights through the winter. He was our meteorologist and our radioman and sent the weather information daily to Shackleton.

I was 26 years old and without polar experience. My project during the winter was to study the snow beneath the surface, using microscopic techniques. My challenge was to establish how snow slowly transforms to ice, without melting. In order to get access to the deepest snow, we dug a deep snow shaft and then drilled further. We could not get deep enough to reach ice, in which the snow porosity diminishes so that the air is entrapped as unconnected bubbles. Our density measurements indicated we would have needed to go a further 15 metres to reach the ice. My work below the surface would complement Hal's surface research. This glaciological research was of great interest, being among the first such studies on the Antarctic Plateau. Hal was particularly interested in studying the mechanics of drift snow, which was occurring most of the time at South Ice, given the near-constant wind we experienced.

Hal had argued strongly for a four-man wintering party. The hut had facilities and supplies for four people and Hal judged from his experience at North Ice in Greenland that having only three men would place too many demands on us for the daily routines of cooking, maintaining power and heating, among others. This would affect Hal's own plans, which were extensive. My own work was exploratory and more elastic. Ken had the met and radio communication program, but he was very efficient and managed to undertake many other pursuits. Early in March, Hal presented the case for a fourth member to Fuchs and urged him to reconsider his decision. Bunny considered the question, but on 24 March he confirmed his earlier decision to have a party of three, doubtless aware of the tasks awaiting the main group at Shackleton. He judged that their winter program would be tight, especially including the final preparations for the crossing in the spring and summer. I believe Fuchs' decision to have only three at South Ice was vindicated, especially in view of the complications which arose with the Halley Bay medical emergency.

The last Otter flights from Shackleton took place in the last week of March. On the 22nd, I was one of Gordon Haslop's passengers and, after a delayed departure from Shackleton, he was anxious to get back early in good light. On our trip to South Ice, I looked again to see what I could of the visible geology in the Shackleton and Whichaway ranges. We landed at South Ice in drift and Gordon returned immediately. Another flight, planned for two days later, was cancelled after trouble with the preheater used to prepare the aircraft. The last flight took place on 25 March, and Gordon stayed in the plane with the engine running for a quick take-off. The Otter was due for routine maintenance, and Gordon was anxious to get back to Shackleton before sunset. He departed, leaving us alone for the winter.

We were well prepared to cope with our 'privations', a favourite term used by the RAF radio operator at Shackleton, Ellis 'Taffy' Williams. Taffy would jocularly remark how he was always keen to establish communication with 'ham' operators, so he could tell everyone in the outside world about our 'privations'. Taffy, a thoughtful person with a delicious, dry humour and a strong Welsh accent, was spending his second winter at Shackleton. Later, he shared a sledging trip with me in the Shackleton Range and I enjoyed his company. He smoked heavily and periodically announced he was giving it up. Taffy's physiology demanded he relieve himself each night at Shackleton in the small hours of the morning. This was unfortunate and uncomfortable for Taffy, especially during the first year spent in tents. He endeavoured to combat this in every conceivable way, even denying fluid intake after lunch, but to no avail. He finally accepted the situation and reverted to consuming as much fluid as he liked. Taffy was single, but was in love with Audrey, a young woman back in Wales. In his radio messages to her, which could not be kept completely private, he would sometimes recount the household tasks and responsibilities he was performing. In one message he was said to have remarked, 'I think I'll make someone a good husband'. Audrey's response was, 'Interesting skills; sounds as if you will make someone a wonderful wife'. Taffy did marry Audrey after our return home.

We lived in the small, prefabricated South Ice hut. Like the hut at Shackleton, it had an impressive temperature gradient. Later, Hal rearranged the ventilation to circulate the air inside the hut and even up the temperature, even under variable outside wind conditions. In very strong winds, drift snow came down the ventilation chimney, which had to be adjusted occasionally. I had a lower bunk and towards the end of the winter I discovered frost when I turned the plywood sheet under my mattress. I joked that I slept close to the frost line and even my pin-up, a tasteful picture of Bridget Bardot out of *Life* magazine, failed to keep the bunk warm.

Three diagrams show the plan of the hut (Figure 7), the tunnels (Figure 11) and the outside surface at South Ice (Figure 12). Our only door led into a tunnel, with various side bays. At the end of the main tunnel, about 30 yards away, was a short ladder up to a trapdoor onto to the surface. The hut had attractive wooden furniture, donated to the expedition by the Morris Company in Glasgow. There were two bunks, each with a lower and upper level, and my companions each had upper bunks. We had a tasteful dining table in polished oak, four chairs with padded seats and white-flecked backs, a bookshelf with about

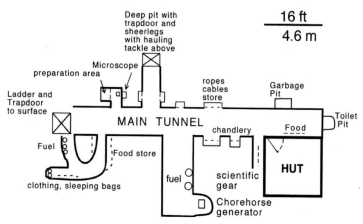

Figure 11 The tunnel system at South Ice, with our storerooms and ice section laboratory.

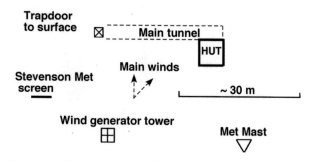

Figure 12 The surface at South Ice showing the instrument and wind generator masts, and the met screen.

60 books, and a kitchen alcove. There was a three-burner kerosene Valor stove, but it was faster to cook on Primus stoves. We also had a small oven, made for us by a Roy Homard, and a range of cooking pots, including a pressure cooker, which was used to cook some interesting concoctions. We took turns to cook. There was frozen meat from Uruguay and a supply of frozen bread, baked for us at Shackleton by Ralph Lenton, which we sliced with a saw in the tunnel. We had a year's supply of food, stored safely in a side tunnel away from the hut, and emergency equipment in case of fire, a terrifying prospect for any Antarctic building. We had several bottles of whisky, but they were seldom opened, and bottles of overproof Appleton Special rum, an expedition special from Jamaica. There was a generous supply of this rum, as there was at Shackleton, but the NZ Party at Scott Base complained they could not find theirs. We did what we could to consume ours, including what might have been their share, inadvertently shipped on *Magga Dan* to Shackleton instead of Scott Base.

There was a met and radio bench for Ken, with some of the usual instrument dials — barometers, temperature and wind gauges. Ken worked at this bench to measure aerial photos and draw reconnaissance maps of our new-found mountains. He also worked on a set of photos, provided by the US, of the mountains they discovered the previous year on a long return flight from McMurdo Sound on the Ross Sea across to our region via the Pole. These included some interesting-looking ranges, though not as spectacular as the Shackleton Range or, especially, the Theron Mountains. However, we never sighted these new mountains, as they proved to be several hundred kilometres from South Ice, and well to the west of our crossing route. At that time accurate position finding on long flights was not well developed.

Other weather observations were made outside the hut with instruments in what is known as a Stevenson screen, as well as measurements of wind direction, drift conditions, clouds and the aurora. Ken did most of these through the day, but we shared the midnight shift.

There was to have been a Morris science bench at South Ice, but this impressive piece of furniture was too heavy and bulky to take up in the Otter. Instead, it served very well at Shackleton as a cocktail bar. Ralph Lenton built a solid science bench for South Ice, which served as a carpentry and workbench for electrical tools. Hal used it frequently for making his snow research apparatus for outside measurements. He had an amazing array of instruments for his temperature and drift studies. Intensive studies of drift snow had not been made previously and Hal invented and constructed many devices. He was a master at improvisation and construction of every kind. When I visited Hal in England 40 years later, I was delighted to find he was still using such a workshop at his home in the Lake District.

Electricity for lighting, radio and power tools came from a bank of wet batteries. These were kept charged by an outside Lucas wind generator, or by a small emergency Chorehorse petrol generator in a tunnel away from the hut. The wind charger was very efficient, purring away almost silently at the top of an aluminium mast constructed by Roy Homard. Beyond a high wind speed it would furl automatically, but in strong gusts its operation was overwhelmed. In heavy conditions, we would go outside and simply furl it into the wind, like a windmill. It also had problems in light winds, but a cut-off automatically prevented the batteries from driving the propeller. This cut-off later fused in fluctuating, low wind and needed attention. The stand-by petrol generator was housed in a tunnel, some distance from our door. It was noisy and polluted the tunnels with exhaust fumes, in spite of an outside exhaust, and took hours to charge up the batteries. Later, trouble with the wind generator forced us to face possible dependence on the Chorehorse and Hal and Ken managed to reduce its noise and fume problems. Fortunately, we never became fully dependent on it.

Our radio was a 40-watt Ernest Henry transceiver. We had also been given an RAF short-wave receiver, which allowed us to tune to news broadcasts, usually from the BBC. The voice reception for our EH transceiver was excellent when conditions were good, but more often Ken had to transmit in Morse. The BBC transmitted our personal voice messages and I received family messages from Australia. My companions were amused by some Australian place names, such as Mooloolaba.

During my time as cook, I was obliged to develop some culinary skills. My success was erratic, except for a soup based on ham-aspic, the inevitable porridge and ice cream. I took advantage of our appropriately titled 'Penguin Cook Book', which explained many mysterious fundamentals including the secret of making ice cream. I was, after all, trying to study polar snow and ice, and gained an insight into the importance of crystal size, texture and air content in ice cream. The secret was to first let the mixture begin to freeze outside in the tunnel, bring it inside and whisk it vigorously to make it frothy, then refreeze it quickly in the tunnel at -30°F. If I followed this ritual, small-sized crystals and plenty of air bubbles made for smooth ice cream. My banana custard was okay, but I could never stop the dehydrated bananas turning black, whereas dried tomatoes kept their colour and were delicious. My angels on horseback and the ham-aspic soup brought words of incredulous appreciation from my companions. Encouraged by this success, I attempted a jam duff in the pressure cooker. I must have got the mix right on my first attempt and was astonished to open the cooker, remove the grease proof paper tied over the bowl inside, to find a lightly textured, tasty dessert. My stocks as a cook were rising! Unfortunately, I never got the mix quite right again. We didn't eat any pemmican, which we kept as a sledging special. I tried fruit pies in pastry cases, but these were forgettable; porridge was much easier to make, though not for dinner.

I made a bad mistake one morning, as cook, when I overfilled one of the three primus stoves. When an overfilled primus is prepared for priming in the usual way with methylated spirits, it needs leeway. If it flares, you let off some pressure, but this is likely to release a lateral fountain of kerosene. I experienced this, and to my horror the fountain reached the uncovered tub in which ice was always melting for our water. I quickly tried to scoop out the affected ice and assured myself I had averted a catastrophe, but I should have started again with a fresh block of ice. At dinner my companions instantly detected contamination in our meal. Hal and Ken quickly located the source and I felt ashamed but I chose not to admit my mistake. Fortunately, the pollution steadily diminished over the next few days as I added fresh ice. It is all too easy to contaminate food with fuel, and Scott describes having to tolerate the flavour of kerosene on a sledging trip on his first expedition. More recently, Jarvis and Tresider had to withdraw from a manhauling trek beyond the Pole through such a mishap, when fuel contaminated their food.

We recorded seeing our first aurora, Aurora Australis, on 29 March 1957. I found the auroras we saw rather disappointing. They were not much more than an arc or glow on the horizon, but perhaps the customary bad weather spoiled the display. As mentioned previously, Edward Wilson, in 1903 and 1911 on the Scott expeditions, painted the aurora in vivid colours, grey-blue to green and reddish hues. Growing up in tropical Queensland, I had high expectations about the aurora and its undulating waves, which were largely unfulfilled. Fortunately, later in the winter, when I was doing the 3 am weather observation, I did see a wonderful 'flaming aurora'. This was a pulsing structure, radiating from a point in the sky above the Magnetic Pole on the other side of the continent. It was so impressive I considered waking my companions to see it. Fortunately I did not; the display did not last more than about five minutes. Taffy Williams also saw it at Shackleton and Ken told us of a spectacular aurora display at Shackleton the previous year, a deep pink glow filling the sky and illuminating the Antarctic landscape.

Getting up to do the weather observation at 3 am was very uncomfortable and I hated my turn. After being brutally woken by an alarm, I would struggle into the bulky, cold weather gear to go outside, walk down the tunnel and climb out onto the surface. I then faced a walk over to the instrument screen with a torch to note down, or preferably memorise, the readings as well as the sky condition, wind direction, drift level, aurora and other phenomena. Then followed a rapid retreat into the hut to log everything in the met book, crawl back into bed and try to get back to sleep. However, on one occasion I was awake to see how Ken handled his visit upstairs for the weather. He stayed in his pyjamas, pulled on his lined trousers and anorak, gloves and lined slippers, then ran down the tunnel and up the stairs. He was back, minutes later, and into bed. I soon learned to wear my slippers and follow Ken's lead, but I could never match his speed.

We had newly developed terylene blankets. They were green, lightly woven and warm, and added to our comfort as we slept in our sleeping bags. The terylene could be dried easily if it became iced up. The Advance Party made good use of the versatility of the blankets at Shackleton and Ken cut up one of his to make 'duffles' to wear inside his leather gloves. The material was indestructible, and years later I used two of the blankets for their light warmth on winter nights in Townsville, in tropical north Queensland.

Our seven winter months at South Ice were not without incident. On 27 March, while changing the electric leads in our small battery area, I touched a supposed neutral wire with another lead, producing a savage spark and loud noise from the radio, fusing its aerial connection. Hal soon had it repaired, using his soldering skills. He later modified the wiring so that we could rotate the battery charging more easily.

One of the major challenges during the winter was to keep our energy sources properly charged. At different times, the two generating systems needed attention and on a couple of occasions had problems on the same day. The first wind generator problem occurred in April, and we had to bring the generator into the hut. While climbing the mast to bring it down, Ken cut his hand badly on the moving propeller, actually chipping the blade. He reluctantly accepted our advice to lie down in his bunk for a couple of hours. I helped Hal to bring the motor down, an uncomfortably cold process, climbing the mast in the wind and using bare hands to loosen the bolts. Much later, I learnt the value of shovelling snow for 15 minutes beforehand to build up reserves of warmth before working with bare hands. Ken checked the motor that afternoon and cleaned the carbon brush contacts. Hal and I replaced the motor the next morning and witnessed an extraordinary scene, one of the unanticipated joys of life in the Antarctic. To the north, we could see the full disc of the sun, miraged above the horizon. The sky was an amazing, deep steel blue and, to the east, a full moon was shining (Plate 25). The next day we had to bring the motor down again as the prop would not turn. We had to run the Chorehorse to provide power, but suffered fumes in the tunnel. I replaced the grease in the motor with special low temperature grease.

On 17 April we had a very cold hut. The Coleman stove would not burn properly and we surmised this was due either to ice in the carburettor or dust fluff in the fuel, but eventually the problem dissipated. Hal and Ken received radio messages via the Falklands whereas I did not — a depressing experience having no 'mail' when your companions get it. On the 18th we had the opportunity to test the wind generator, successfully.

The challenge to maintain machinery and instruments in the Antarctic was not the only problem we encountered. We faced the problem of altered sleep patterns. The next day, 19 April 1957, we began a curious, occasional habit for the first time. Ken usually performed the 9 am met observations followed by the scheduled daily radio link with Shackleton. He would also wake the cook for the day. That day he overslept, and it was after midday when we all awoke. This was the start of sleeping problems in the endless night of the Antarctic winter. During the winter with only three people, all affected, we found it difficult to avoid sleeping in late. There was no easy way of reversing this pattern and over several months our wake-up time got later and later, until we rose late in the 'afternoon'. There was no going back, and eventually, towards the end of the winter, the wake-up time progressed until we approached 'normal' Shackleton time again. The Shackleton party had not altered their routines. When we finally resumed normality we had 'lost' a full 24 hours and gained this as extra sleep. Ken pointed out that our bodies wanted to follow a 24 and a half hour day, and we had great problems marking our sleep rhythm cards for Allan Rogers. These cards were designed for sleep each side of midnight, not midday. When Ken used the radio to send the weather observations, he would say 'good morning' to Taffy in Shackleton and Taffy would reply 'good evening, Ken'.

Hal and Ken were well aware of this winter darkness problem and Hal related an interesting Arctic expedition experiment. Mary Lobban, a researcher on sleep rhythms, had two independent groups experience 24 hours daylight. The two groups were subjected to opposite time effects, wearing special watches which showed 24 hours apparent time. However, one group were living a 23-hour day and the other, a separate party, a 25-hour day. Their watches displayed a 'normal' sequence of time and the subjects kept to this and monitored how they felt. The 23-hour group became irritable and tired. The 25-hour group felt a little better, though

25 Moon rise at South Ice, with the figure of Hal Lister. The masts and hut ventilators can be seen. We deliberately buried the hut, to be out of the wind.

they, too, felt irritable. Antarctic sleep rhythms seem to be universally disturbed during the long winter darkness, and the problem is probably worst at the South Pole Station, where there is effectively only one 'day' each year with continuous daylight, followed by one 'night' of continuous darkness. There are real problems regulating one's sleep, and at South Ice we could read at any time we liked. At the Pole Station, there were regular movie sessions available for anyone suffering from insomnia — not available at South Ice, unfortunately.

Research by Professor Arendt of the University of Surrey into the phenomenon of sleep problems in the Polar Regions is outlined in the endnotes to this chapter.[4]

From time to time, Hal and Ken experienced mild headaches after sleeping. They had the upper bunks, and there was concern about ventilation. Hal modified the air circulation by changing one of the vents to bring cold air down into the hut rather than allowing most of our warm air to escape. The new vent brought improvements, but we needed to adjust it during very strong winds, which would bring drift snow onto the upper bunks and their occupants.

The 'nights' varied during the winter, and some full moonlit nights were calm enough for us to appreciate the remarkable scene outside. I regret that I did not take more advantage of these conditions, and absorb more of our special situation. The darkness, the deep silence when the wind stopped, and the utter sterility of our landscape, together with our isolation, were unique and special. Generally, I felt physically comfortable through the winter, and experienced a strange acceptance of the 'neutrality' of the continent and felt part of it. It was certainly not benign, but it was impersonal. I had spent a lot of time alone in exquisite, rugged Australian mountain environments, rainforest and other pristine wilderness, but the 'neutrality' of Antarctica felt deep. There were no surprises from creatures like snakes or animals, and no possibility of being visited by friends or strangers. I had no discomfort in the endless darkness, despite having an acute fear of the dark as a child. Antarctica felt completely friendly.

We celebrated Hal Lister's birthday and he had surprise parcels from his family and some small gifts from Ken and from me. We also gave him some

26 Hal Lister's birthday. He lies in his bunk and is bemused by our silly gifts.

27 Midwinter Day. A toast. Ken (Davy Crockett cap) and Hal Lister.

facetious parcels, including some useless blocks of 'wood cut-offs, elaborately parcelled endlessly inside repeated brown paper. Plate 26 shows him sitting up in his bunk unpacking these. He was very tolerant.

Midwinter Day is the longest night of the year in Antarctica, and marks the point at which you can follow the days leading towards the reappearance of the sun. We celebrated this significant day with a special traditional dinner (Plate 27). Ken produced an exotic feast — turtle soup, smoked salmon, roast chicken with stuffing, french beans, roast potatoes, fruit compote, ice cream, mince pies, Danish blue cheese and biscuits, coffee, figs, chocolate creams, marron glacés. Truly a culinary miracle! For drinks, his special menu included gin, sherry, whisky, port and rum, or juice — orange or lime. It was a very special party especially for me, the neophyte. Hal had celebrated two freezing and dark midwinters in the Arctic, and Ken five in the Antarctic.

Our days and nights usually featured drift and very cold winds. One day, I went outside to see for myself what -60°F and 60 knots felt like. I tried some manual work shovelling snow, but found I had to be very careful which way I faced, even with my anorak hood carefully positioned. I could only protect my face to a limited degree and quickly concluded there was no good reason to be outside.

The minimum temperature for the winter was -57.3°C (-71.1°F) in July, and the strongest wind was over 60 knots. The lowest temperature was recorded in still conditions, but we had a number of days with -60°F and 60 knots. We believed our privations were more extreme than at Shackleton, and the statistics supported this belief. Our monthly mean temperatures were around 10°C colder. Shackleton had a lowest temperature of -55.1°C in August 1957. We had more wind, the monthly means being 25 to 30 knots in the winter, whereas Shackleton's means were 13 to 18 knots. The maximum temperatures were -8.2°C in December 1957 at South Ice, and +2.8°C in December 1956 at Shackleton. The coldest temperature on earth, recorded at Vostok in the Russian base in Antarctica, was -89.2°C (-128.6°F) in July 1983.

Hal Lister's Winter Studies

Hal's special interest at South Ice extended the studies

on snow started at North Ice on the Greenland icecap on the British North Greenland Expedition, two years earlier. At South Ice, he was interested in all aspects of our environment, but particularly wanted to study wind-blown snow, called drift.

Hal was remarkably skilled, building and using his own apparatus, and was a genius at improvisation. He undertook pioneering research into snow behaviour above the surface and set out to measure how much snow was being transported by the wind. It is difficult to determine whether snow is falling. In a strong wind, the air is filled with snow grains eroded by the wind somewhere upwind, and driven along in a layer at the surface. With low drift, the snow can be seen to weave, snake-like, along the ground, but with stronger winds it gets thicker and obscures visibility. Drift is also very uncomfortable; not only can you not see through it, but also the fine snow grains find their way inside your clothes.

Hal cleverly designed his instruments and made special jars to mount at different heights above the ground, to collect drift. They were shaped to allow the wind to blow into them through a tube about three square centimetres in cross-section, and enter a wider chamber inside. The reduced air velocity inside allowed the drift particles to accumulate on a gauze pad. The wind then emerged through a corresponding hole, without its snow. He would then empty the contents after a measured time and melt them to find the amounts as water. Hal used up to three of these jars, at different heights, to study drift rates under different weather conditions. Drift is thickest within about a metre of the surface, and much higher there is no drift. A plane can fly with good visibility, but as it descends to land it finds visibility obscured. Hal's results are discussed in his TAE scientific report.[5] He attempted to account for the quantity of drift in relation to wind speed and height, but this needed much more time than our winter allowed.

Hal also set out to measure wind velocity at different heights, using a set of sensitive anemometers. Some had been damaged in transit, but he successfully repaired them. He also used a collector, consisting of glass microscope slides smeared with an adhesive plastic. The trapped drift grains were then studied microscopically, after the plastic had set. The trick was not to collect too many grains.

Hal was aware the anemometers could record air speed in a volume of moving air the size of the instrument cups, but he hoped to get much finer measurements. He designed an instrument using hypodermic needles, tubing and pressure gauges, to measure fine-scale velocities, such as those next to the surface. Hal used a flashgun with a camera to get pictures of drift particles and their paths through the air. Unfortunately, the camera exposure was slowed by the cold and ultimately the mechanism froze, and the camera had to be completely cleaned of lubricant.

Hal also attempted to measure the amount of drifting snow particles by measuring the 'gloom' effect they caused on a searchlight, but the cold affected his photocells and ultimately the searchlight glass shattered. He compared the apparent speed of drift at different heights from his flash photographs, and compared the camera results with the anemometers. Hal also compared visibility, routinely estimated at each meteorological observation, with drift levels. Hannes la Grange made many observations at Shackleton Base, where better measurements of distance were available.[6]

Drift has some strange ways. We experienced two main wind directions for the katabatic winds at South Ice. Katabatic winds occur as colder air gravitates down a slope. Fairly obviously, we had thicker drift associated with stronger winds and, Hal believed, after snow had fallen. With time, he reasoned, the source areas would be diminished, and on some occasions we experienced strong winds with little drift. However, under a steady, unrelenting wind, the drift would quite abruptly thin down until there was virtually none, yet a few minutes later, upwind, we could see the next lot coming. Very puzzling!

The drift particles acquired static electric charges. Inside the hut we could hear the drift as a background hiss as it travelled across the ground above the roof. Our radio aerial was a wire above the surface and the metal framework of the hut would accumulate enough static electricity from the aerial for us to feel a charge when we touched a pillar. Hal rigged a spark release and the periodic discharge, faster with stronger drift, kept us entertained. Never one to miss an opportunity to gather data, Hal measured the discharge with a voltmeter.

By the end of winter, Hal had made many drift

measurements. He and Ken had a long session, plotting the results on graph paper to identify the controls of drift density, namely height above the ground and wind velocity. The results, disappointingly, gave somewhat dispersed, inconclusive results.

Hal also undertook the more traditional glaciological studies. These involved checking a line of accumulation stakes, which extended over an area of a square kilometre, for changes due to accumulation, or deflation. Hal usually went out alone, with a compass and a kerosene pressure lamp. On one occasion he lost the line of stakes and had an anxious 30 minutes trying to locate them again to find his way home. The ever-vigilant Ken Blaiklock knew he was overdue and went out to find him.

Hal also made studies of the snow strata beneath the surface, recognising harder winter layers and coarser, more granular summer layers to identify annual patterns and accumulation in previous years. He did this in pits and measured snow densities, but for faster work he used a 'rammsonde' device. A falling weight on a metal probe drives it into the snow and progressive measurements of the penetration can be correlated with hardness, and calibrated against density. Profiles several metres deep can be measured more quickly than by digging a pit and measuring the density of successive layers. Later, Hal made rammsonde measurements every day to record the changing accumulation rates as we travelled across the continent. He found that they diminish from around 16 grams of water per square centimetre near the coast, to less than 10 grams on the Polar Plateau.

At South Ice, Hal obtained results on accumulation over the last half century. He found the general accumulation was 12 grams per square centimetre, but reached up to 17 grams in 1920 and dropped to 10 over the last decade. He also used our SIPRE (snow ice permafrost research establishment) ice drill to make drill holes up to 15 metres deep, away from the neighbourhood of the hut. He lowered a chain of resistance thermometers and carefully filled in the holes with loose, granular snow. The temperatures below about 10 metres give a good measure of the average annual temperature. At South Ice, the annual temperature was approximately -31°C.

My Snow Studies

I used a microscope to analyse snow specimens, from the surface down to the bottom of our drill hole, 45 metres (about 146 feet). I studied them in thin sections, prepared like a petrologist's thin sections of rocks. The fragile snow could be cut flat after impregnating it with an organic cement, then mounted on a glass slide, and ground down to the suitable thickness of about a millimetre on abrasive paper.

I was able to study the snow textures and shapes of the snow grains. Layered snow contains different types of snow, judged on texture. My polarising microscope also allowed me to resolve the smaller crystals of ice, which make up the grains.

I knew little about snow petrography, but had been given an introduction by Sam Steinemann of

28 Using my polarising microscope in my ice lab at about -30°C. The stage of the microscope carries a universal stage which allows tilting of an ice thin section, to set the crystallographic axes for each of about 100 crystals, and record their angles. I wore warm clothes including a down jacket and sat on an insulated seat. When I was 'acclimatised' I could work for up to an hour, before needing to go back inside the hut for a hot drink. The results were scientifically rewarding.

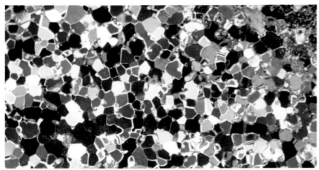

29 A thin section of the snow from near the bottom of our ice core, around 45 metres depth. Polarised light shows the individual ice crystals. The horizontal band is an old wind crust. The crystals are about one millimetre across.

Neuchatel when I visited him in Switzerland, before TAE. He recommended some aspects to study and I followed his suggestions. I studied the size of the ice crystals making up the grains and found they increased dramatically in deeper specimens. So, not only does snow density increase with depth, so too does the average crystal size. After I returned to London, I was able to find close parallels in metallurgy, involving annealing and grain growth.

With my prepared thin sections, I spent many uncomfortable hours sitting on a stool, staring at my sections through the microscope (Plates 28 and 29). I used a device called a universal stage to measure the crystallographic directions of the ice crystals. This stage needed fingertip adjustment to change its tilt angles, while watching the colours in one crystal at a time, and then reading two angles on the stage. I used a kerosene lamp with a mantle as the light source for the microscope, so that I could warm my fingers. Altogether, I must have studied about 4000 crystals. From the shallowest surface snow, the average crystal areas increase from about a thousandth of a square millimetre to about a square millimetre in my deepest specimens, which were about 300 years old.

I was excited to find that two special types of snow layers had quite different textures from normal snow. The first were thin wind crusts, which develop at the surface and become covered by later snow. They persist below the surface as very thin ice layers, and I could recognise fossil wind crusts even in my deepest specimens. The other type of distinctive snow layers was more fragile, a depth-hoar layer, with larger crystal grains. They form at shallow depths beneath the surface when evaporation occurs within the snow under certain weather conditions, presumably when the air temperature above the surface is warmer.

Both these types of snow are a problem for dog teams. Wind crusts can fracture audibly if it gets colder and contraction takes place; the noise frightens the dogs, as a thin fracture races along the surface. Hoar layers may collapse with a weak 'crump' sound, alarming the dogs because it sounds like a crevasse warning.

With my universal stage, I could measure the crystal direction of individual crystals in the snow. Most snow showed random directions, but I was astonished to find that wind crusts and depth-hoar layers both showed that many grains had their crystal axes close to vertical. This must be developed in metamorphism when the snow is subjected to strong weather changes. The crusts develop under strong wind conditions, and the hoar layers under sustained, warmer temperatures.

The ice I studied seemed impressively pure. I could drink some of my deepest 'vintage' samples when I had finished studying them. Unknown to me, Antarctic snow contains small spherical particles known as micrometeorites. Later, when we reached the Pole, I was shown some 'sludge' from the water tank at the American base. They had dug a deep 'snow mine' for their water and over the year these impurities steadily accumulated at the bottom of their tank. Micrometeorites are tiny glass spheres, 2 millimetres or less, some with very small crystals. They apparently form from splash when a meteorite hits the earth. The spheres have the same composition as the rocks where the meteorites impacted on the earth's surface. At South Ice we must have swallowed all of ours.

I used my microscope sitting in a small lab off the main tunnel and worked at around -30°C. The cold work could be painful. I needed bare fingers to manipulate the universal stage and then write down several readings for each snow grain, also recording each crystal's directions and its size. I soon learnt what to wear, always including my down clothing, jacket and long pants. I found it curious that on successive days, I could work for a progressively longer period before I could no longer tolerate the cold. After a few days away from the microscope work, I had to build up my tolerance again.

In September, South Ice experienced several days of

snowfall. The wind conditions were still, and a soft, unconsolidated layer, probably a foot thick, covered the whole surface. I had been aware that, after a time, unconsolidated surface snow could transform fairly quickly into rigid, hard material, which almost rings when struck. The soft snow would harden and become brittle, as the sand-like snow grains became cemented to one another. The recently accumulated September snow hardened in this way. In a relatively short period after that spring snowfall, stronger winds had redistributed some of the unconsolidated snow, and after the material had started to harden, proceeded to erode sastrugi in it. Sastrugi, a Russian word, are a series of ridges on the surface of the snow. These ridges can be more than a metre high, with sharp edges. The wind can further erode the sastrugi, which develops a variety of forms, and all parties encounter sastrugi when they travel across the Polar Plateau. This sastrugi make travelling difficult, for both skiers and manhauling sledges, and for dog teams and tracked vehicles. When we travelled south from South Ice two months later on the crossing journey, we encountered extensive sastrugi fields on the plateau. Some sastrugi, in the shape of 'shark snouts', can be undercut by wind erosion and develop wonderfully artistic droop features. Sastrugi are described as wind-eroded features, but I suspect that the full circumstances under which they form and evolve may not be fully understood.

Results of our Scientific Work Through the Winter

During our 196 winter days at South Ice, we kept the station running and ourselves healthy and alive. We were well occupied. Hal endeavoured to record as much as he could about every aspect of the climate and snow conditions at the edge of the Polar Plateau. The scope of his interests and undertakings was limitless, and I understood why he asked for an extra man at the station.

Ken's winter was also very busy. He did most of the routine weather observations and maintained radio contact each day. Our weather observations are compiled in the meteorological report by Hannes la Grange. On calmer nights, Ken spent many cold and uncomfortable sessions with his theodolite, taking star sights to accurately fix our geographic position

30 Ken Blaiklock taking star altitudes with his theodolite to determine the position of South Ice. We are logging the time for him.

(Plate 30). He had a good stopwatch, set from the international radio time signal, WWV. One of us would log the stopwatch time as he read out his angles. He would then calculate the longitude and latitude from *Nautical Almanac* tables, using a small Kurta calculator. He also determined a true north azimuth direction and the local magnetic variation and our records of wind direction took account of this. Ken also worked on George Lowe's aerial photographs of Shackleton Range and on the photos which the US had provided Fuchs from their 1955–56 flight via the Pole to the Weddell Sea. These mountains were well to the west of our traverse route, and yet to be accurately located. They included the Pensacola Mountains, and though Ken prepared a map of these mountains, we never saw them. Ken prepared a preliminary map of the Shackleton Range from George's photographs, which was extremely useful in our exploration work there in the spring.

I undertook new studies on snow petrology and summarised aspects of the results in papers for scientific journals (see Appendix V), but I never did complete a full report for the expedition report series, although I sent an extensive draft to Fuchs, which an ice specialist reviewed. When I returned to Australia in 1959 to Townsville, north Queensland, I was hard-pressed with teaching commitments and my research was closely related to my work at the university. I felt strangely isolated scientifically, very distant from any fellow snow researchers. My library resources were limited and I had to concentrate on other geological interests. My research speciality was igneous rocks, a curious contrast from ice. I never did rewrite the South Ice draft and Fuchs, understandably, withdrew it from the expedition publication series.

Our Social Winter

Antarctic literature records many cases of expedition blues' and tensions.[7] I'm pleased to report that at South Ice we experienced little of this. We did not know one another previously and my two, very experienced colleagues needed to be tolerant and generous towards their inexperienced companion, which they were. For my part, I was on a high after my recently acquired doctorate and was eager, with youthful zeal, to learn as much as I could in my time in Antarctica. My companions jokingly called me 'a damned colonial', to which I would respond, predictably, 'Pommy bastards'! I was probably over-assertive in our discussions, reflecting the naivety and certainty of youth. I missed listening to music and I recall the day I requested the radio operator at Shackleton to play a Beethoven symphony, which he did, as soon as the reception conditions were suitable. I had asked for the *Choral Symphony*, but the long-play record package contained several records. The music was unfamiliar and I exclaimed to Ken, probably too vehemently, 'That's not the *Choral Symphony*'. It was, in fact, the fine, First Symphony. Ken was less than impressed and chided me with, 'You are just showing off'. Ken still recalls recordings we made of Richard Strauss and *Til Eulenspiegel* but I did not get to record the Choral. My two companions were widely travelled and thoroughly experienced in cold environments, with seven winters between them, as I have noted previously. In contrast, here I was, on my first visit.

Occasionally, Hal and Ken reminisced about their previous expeditions. Hal had very interesting stories from his two winters with the British North Greenland Expedition and his earlier experiences in the Royal Navy. Ken had stories of national army service in Germany and his extensive previous work with FIDS, the Falkland Islands Dependency Survey. He was unassuming about his work in the Antarctic Peninsula and I only gradually came to realise that he had spent no fewer than four previous winters there. In addition, he was still fresh from the strenuous Advance Party winter, establishing Shackleton Base and then exploring the Theron Mountains. At times, Hal must have got tired of my youthful naivety and what he probably saw as occasional brashness, and I was aware of this. I do not recall any heated arguments, but at one period I felt discouraged by our exchanges to such an extent that I chose to withdraw, by not talking. For several weeks, I was adequately occupied on my own. Besides, I could simply listen to my interesting companions. Perhaps Ken understood my withdrawal and said nothing. As the leader, Hal must have been concerned by my silence and I once heard him ask Ken did he know why. Was I depressed by some bad news from home? Hal finally enquired into my behaviour when we were together in the tunnel outside the hut. We had a frank exchange and I can remember his saying, 'Jon, you are intelligent enough to resolve this'. I felt no offence and slowly broke my silence. Such withdrawal is apparently not unknown in Antarctica.

We could read from our somewhat limited library. Most of the books were a collection of Pan paperbacks and I found I enjoyed reading almost anything. I had a textbook on structural geology with me, but could get little stimulation from it. I set out to read more serious literature and during my stay in Antarctica enjoyed Penguin Classic volumes. With the variety of other books available, I began to develop a more critical perspective. I have never lost my Australian sense of humour, and I enjoyed passing judgment on the books I read. How interesting for my colleagues! I even established my status as a local 'professor of punk literature'. I recall several books which I found absorbing, among them were: *The Colditz Story*, *The Privileged Nightmare*, *The Diary of Anne Frank*, Eric Linklater's hilarious *Juan in America* and Russell Braddon's account of his years as a POW with the Japanese. I greatly enjoyed *Crime and Punishment*,

The Brothers Karamazov and *The Scarlet and the Black*, and later, at the start of the crossing journey, *The Confessions of Jean Jacques Rousseau*. I even managed to read Mickey Spillane's *Kiss Me Deadly*, our birthday present to Hal, genuine pulp literature. We had some poetry and I well remember Oscar Wilde's 'The Ballad of Reading Gaol', especially his description of 'the tent of blue / which prisoners call the sky'. Very apt, in Antarctica.

We listened to the news on short-wave radio whenever we could. The BBC had interesting material and we followed closely the disputes between Russia and the West. Negotiations in relation to nuclear testing seemed consistently hopeless.

Once or twice we intercepted communications from Scott Base to New Zealand. They obviously had a wonderfully efficient home conversation link, and this served to underline our isolation. However, we could eavesdrop on conversations between the New Zealanders, who we did not know, and their wives/girlfriends at home. We were never able to find the return wavelength to hear the women's voices, though we got to hear their first names. We could only imagine the other half. I found to my surprise how much I missed hearing female voices. Months later, we met the absent women in Wellington. After revisiting Scott Base in 1994, Ken said he wondered if the easy NZ communication might have had dubious advantages, intensifying the feelings of isolation rather than easing them.

By August, I felt it was time to have a 'bath' and change my clothes, not having done so for over four months. This was a sponge bath and I tried to make sure I kept the floor dry to avoid new ice. In one way the bath proved a mistake, because I felt I shed some skin insulation and felt colder. The positive outcome was that the new clothes were much warmer.

Our bodies had acclimatised in various ways through the winter and this was dramatically demonstrated to me one night when I woke to find the heating stove had gone out, releasing kerosene vapour in the hut. As cook, I had failed to refuel it. I got up, quickly filled the stove with kerosene and then relit it, using a wick on a long wire, placing this inside until the flame took hold. Half asleep, I withdrew the glowing wire and grasped the end with my bare my hand. There was a sizzling sound and a burning smell. I felt no pain,

but released it. No harm was done, but the depth of the painless wire burn indicated how my skin had thickened during the winter.

The sun reappeared on 1 September, an occasion which I felt had spiritual overtones and we went outside to celebrate this event. My main impression, with the sunshine on my face, was that I could feel no warmth; I might as well have been feeling the heat from a candle across a room. But summer was finally coming, with warmer days and improving weather, more than welcome after a dark and seemingly endless winter.

One day in the spring, Ken and I skied across to our nearest nunatak, the Omega Nunatak. Ken knew where it should be, but I felt some apprehension in case the weather changed and I wore extra clothes in case we had to ski back into the wind. We found the nunatak, but I voiced my disappointment when I recognised the rock. I grumbled to Ken, 'Bloody dolerite!' We spent 20 minutes looking around but could not find anything else. I collected a large specimen, with directions marked on it for later palaeomagnetism studies, and we skied home into a mild wind, which fortunately eased. By the time we reached the hut I was too warm. Once inside, I peeled off my anorak and Hal laughed on seeing the thickness of the snow condensation in my sweater against my back.

We began packing up for our relocation to Shackleton Base. This was via the Otter on 7 October. Gordon Haslop arrived in the Otter with Allan Rogers and Fred Morris, on loan from the Halley Bay base. After a jubilant meeting with handshakes and backslapping, Ken and I were flown out first, to prepare for planned fieldwork with dogs in the Shackleton Range. Hal was to follow on the next flight. Meanwhile he explained to the newcomers how the station worked. Gordon flew us further east than usual, over the Shackleton Mountains, past Mount Flat Top. Ken was able to check his reconnaissance map and I again attempted to identify the visible rocks. My previous guesses that there were extensive sedimentary rocks had to be revised, because I could see veins and reefs of quartz in what were probably metamorphic rocks.

Close to Shackleton Base, we flew over the four vehicles which had just embarked on the first leg of the crossing to explore a route up to South Ice (Plate

31 The four vehicles which had just left Shackleton to find the route to South Ice, 7 October 1957.

31). Fuchs and three others had left Shackleton that afternoon in three Weasels and one Sno-Cat, slowly moving south, pulling heavy sledges of fuel. They made an impressive sight, alone in the vast snow plain of the ice shelf. They were to find the journey to South Ice difficult and dangerous. It was to take them five weeks, and only two vehicles would arrive. They would then fly back to Shackleton to complete the final preparations and repeat this difficult leg to South Ice with all the other vehicles. This would be the start of the main Antarctic crossing via the Pole.

We landed at Shackleton and enjoyed spending time with of our Shackleton colleagues again. Apart from Gordon Haslop, Allan Rogers and Fred Morris, they were the first new faces for six and a half months. We were greeted warmly all round, but faced with all those people, I felt strangely antisocial and later enjoyed sitting alone, thumbing through their book collection. George Lowe was excited to see me, and we talked non-stop for an hour. It didn't take me long to cover the South Ice events, but there seemed much to hear about the winter at Shackleton, which I felt George had found a tense period.

SPRING 1957: MOUNTAIN EXPLORATIONS FROM SHACKLETON

Exploration on the Shackleton Range

After Fuchs and the first vehicle team left Shackleton on their exploratory journey to South Ice, preparations continued for the main journey. But before that departure, the plans involved some exploration and fieldwork in the Shackleton Range. Fuchs' vehicle trip to South Ice is described in Chapter 4.

Fuchs needed a careful ground reconnaissance of the Ice Wall, beyond the edge of the ice shelf beside the Shackleton Range, one of several critical and difficult sections on the route to South Ice. He had planned a tentative route for the crossing, but first he had to check this route and find a way through several obstacles, including the Ice Wall. Then came the challenge of the wide and severely crevassed Recovery Glacier.

Two dog teams were to be flown out from Shackleton in the Otter, to establish a base camp near Mount Provender on the western end of the Shackleton Range, close to what was later called Nostoc Lake, a frozen meltwater lake. Later, we found living algae, *Nostoc sp*, visible inside its ice. This lake was west of the Ice Wall, and a dog team working from the Nostoc base should be able to find a route up the Ice Wall.

The dogs had been in training through the winter. After I returned to Shackleton from South Ice, I was given guidance in dog handling, as we were to use them in our fieldwork. This involved a run with two of our dog experts, Ken Blaiklock and David Stratton. George Lowe also took part and we had both dog teams. They took us on a hectic run, south from Shackleton Base. The dogs were unbelievably excited and strong after a spell in the dog tunnels. There was one pup in my team, a magnificent-looking young dog with long brown and white hair. He was born either on *Theron*, or after arriving at Shackleton, and was a fine Antarctic husky. He was named Marø, in honour of *Theron's* skipper. Marø behaved like an adolescent and was strong enough to accelerate the sledge on his own. He was tethered near the back of the team, to learn, but he soon made the sledge overrun the forward dogs. He was simply having fun, but the other dogs were not amused. After we returned, the other dogs turned on him and gave him his first dogfight. He was overwhelmed and his perfect, clean coat was quickly stained with his blood. Growing up can be hard, especially for a new sled dog. We rescued him, but his perfect ears were now ragged. He lost some of his youthful exuberance and learned not to work too hard in the team. I found driving these well-trained dogs did not require much experience, but it's a different story with an untrained team.

I took to driving dogs readily. They were always eager to be off, and the sledge had to be restrained with a peg driven deep into the snow. The command to prepare the dogs and get them poised for a concerted strain, ready to jump off, was a clear call, 'Now dogs', and then 'Huit' (hoo-it) would launch them in unison. The encouragement call was also, 'Huit, huit' and the call to stop was a long, drawn out, sigh-like, 'Arrhhhh now.' Their ears would go up, and they would look back and stop. On the run, the call 'Irrrrah, irrrrah' was for the two lead dogs to veer left and turning right was 'Auk, auk'. It seemed straightforward enough, but you had to act as if you were really the boss and knew what you were doing. You needed to let them know if you were angry and we even had a whip, which I

can't recall using, except when a dogfight started. Unfortunately, in a dogfight, they were often unable to differentiate between another dog's leg and your hand, so we kept our gloves on.

Feeding them was easy, but you had to be sure they were all tethered properly or be overwhelmed in the rush. You needed to be quick in distributing each dog's food, and sometimes a dog would try to steal its neighbour's meal. They enjoyed seal meat, but on journeys we fed them dog pemmican. This looked a bit like the pemmican we ate, and was wrapped in greaseproof paper. In my first attempt at feeding the dogs I tried to take the paper off, bringing an incredulous shout from my companion; the dogs simply wolfed down everything, paper and all, and I never made this mistake again. They slept on the snow, and as it got colder inland they had a delightful way of preparing their 'bed' by walking it down, circling tightly until it was ready. If there was a wind blowing, they curled up in a ball and allowed the drifting snow to cover them. Next morning, after snow or in windy conditions, there was no sign of any dogs, just some inconspicuous mounds. When called, they would slowly break out, covered in soft snow, seemingly happy. Working with the dogs was a wonderful experience, and I felt privileged and sometimes sorry for my colleagues, who spent their lives dependent on cold, hard, unfeeling vehicles. The dogs didn't need much maintenance and were friendly, cheerful companions, as long as they had enough to eat and were given a reasonable distance to cover. Walton has expertly described the fine traditions of dog training in the Falkland Islands Dependency and our dog handling routines followed their well-developed methods.[8]

The initial dog flight to the Shackleton Range (Plate 32) had to be aborted because of weather, but the first team, the Black and Tans, was flown out successfully on 11 October, with David Stratton and George Lowe. There were some concerns about how the 10 dogs would react in the plane, tethered around the 12-foot Nansen sledge. However, once they were airborne they seemed to enjoy their flights. Maybe the noise and vibration helped them relax, and the cabin heater was turned on full. They spent most of the flight staring out the window, an amusing sight (Plate 33).

32 The Shackleton Range: delectable, unexplored mountains.

33 Husky dogs in the Otter with Ken Blaiklock on the flight to the Shackleton Range. They stopped fighting and liked to stare out the window.

The second team was to follow next day, but bad weather delayed this for two days. Meanwhile, I injured my right hand handling one of the dogs in their tunnel. The exuberant animal sprang just as I was releasing its tethering clip, which put an impressive gash in my finger. I returned to the hut and found Ralph Lenton, who attended to my injury. I looked like I was about to pass out, so he gave me a glass of whisky. Allan Rogers was at South Ice and John Lewis flew me across with Ralph to the US IGY Ellsworth Base, about 50 miles to the west, for treatment. This proved to be an interesting experience, as their film show was just starting. John Behrendt, a member of the US ream, described John and Ralph's startled reactions when the base commander, Finn Ronne, arrived in the cinema with his 'adjutant', who called everyone to attention.[9] After some bewilderment, John and Ralph complied. Our party did not go in for that sort of thing, and besides, we did not have a cinema!

Meanwhile, the Ellsworth doctor, Clint Smith, was attending to me. He assured me it was not the bone I thought I had seen in my wound, only the tendon sheath. He stated how pleased he was to meet me and

34 Mount Provender, close to our air camp near Nostoc Lake in the Shackleton Range. The yellow rocks near the summit are marble.

to have a real medical case to deal with after a quiet winter. He carefully cleaned and stitched the wound and explained how to remove the stitches in a week's time.

At Ellsworth, I met the American geophysical team and was excited to hear news of their work. Ed Thiel, a seismologist, was co-leader of the IGY traverse group, which consisted of his fellow seismologist, John Behrendt, two glaciologists, Hugo Neuberg (Thiel's co-leader) and Paul Walker, and a geologist, Augie Aughenbaugh. We talked of many things and I told them about the Whichaway geology and the Gondwanaland fossils. The geophysical team later carried out a productive traverse from Ellsworth across the ice shelf into the Dufek Massif, about 470 miles south of Ellsworth Base, which is outlined in Appendix IV. I also briefly met Finn Ronne, whose previous contributions to Weddell exploration are described in Chapter 1 and Appendix I. He was courteous, but his real interest was in news of Fuchs' progress.

Ken and I flew in with the second dog team to the Shackleton Range Air Camp at Mount Provender on 13 October. David and Ken went off with their dogs to examine the Ice Wall to look for a route for Fuchs'

traverse vehicles, while George and I did some geology near the camp with our team. Over the next few days, David and Ken found a route up the Ice Wall through some badly crevassed country, and flagged it for the vehicles.

I looked at the local rocks and had to revise my interpretation of them, which I had first based on the view from the Shackleton Range flight, when I convinced myself the rocks would be metamorphic. Near the Air Camp, the first rocks contained pink feldspar and seemed to be layered; I initially identified them to be banded gneiss, a metamorphic rock. The next day I saw they were arkosic sandstone, a sedimentary rock, with an important unconformity on the higher metamorphic rocks on Mount Provender.

George and I did our first dog run, crossing the glacier so that I could examine what were obviously sedimentary mountains to the south. We were novice dog handlers, but the dogs were probably bluffed by George's strongly assertive confidence. We swept across some obvious crevasses, which the dogs seemed fully aware of, and looked back to see if we knew where we were going. The sedimentary rocks were completely different from those I had seen previously, but I could not find any fossils in Shackleton Range rocks, then or later. We returned to the Air Camp and, because my wound had now been healing for a week, I got George to remove the 25 or so stitches. He claimed to know exactly what to do, and confidently cut off both knots on each stitch. He then had trouble removing the remaining thread with tweezers, resulting in pain for the patient. Little healing had occurred and the wound promptly reopened. Bandaged, it was a struggle for me to write, and I could only use my geological hammer awkwardly with my left hand. On my return to Shackleton Base and the warmth of the hut, the finger healed in a few days and I now have to look hard to find the scar. From our camp on Nostoc Lake, I climbed the ridges to the north to reach the yellow marbles near the top of Mount Provender (Plate 34). Returning after a long day, I had to descend a glacier below the ridge. I was very tired and decided to climb down the face rather than go around over the broken rocks. It was not very high, perhaps 150 feet (46 metres), but I was wearing moccasins. A fall down the 40° face would have been serious. The glacier got steeper and there was some blue ice to be negotiated. Fortunately, the ice was scalloped and my moccasin gripped enough for me to descend safely, greatly relieved.

Taffy Williams, the RAF radioman, was flown in as a replacement so George Lowe could continue his photographic work. Taffy and I tried our first dog run and the dogs rapidly showed who was really in charge. It wasn't us! They did a U-turn of their own volition but we managed to sort them out eventually. Shortly afterwards, David and Ken returned to the camp from their Ice Wall trip. As usual, Ken yelled 'tea' 20 minutes before reaching our camp near Nostoc Lake, which we had ready when they arrived.

The next day we all left to lay

a depot 18 miles further south, near the head of the Blaiklock Glacier. The map showing our journeys is in Figure 13. We parted at this point and Taffy and I turned back, while David and Ken continued on to map further south and east. I planned to return to continue the geological mapping I started in the western section of the Shackleton Range and David Stratton, as leader of the party, agreed for us to go off by ourselves. I realised I could achieve more by concentrating in a smaller area rather than travelling with the surveyors, who wanted to map as far as possible through the mountains.

My choice proved a productive as well as a delightful experience, despite an uncompromising start. When I tried to investigate the rocks at the point of a long ridge we had followed down the glacier, there was an inaccessible wind scoop, a deep bowl in the ice created by the wind, and I could not reach the rocks. However,

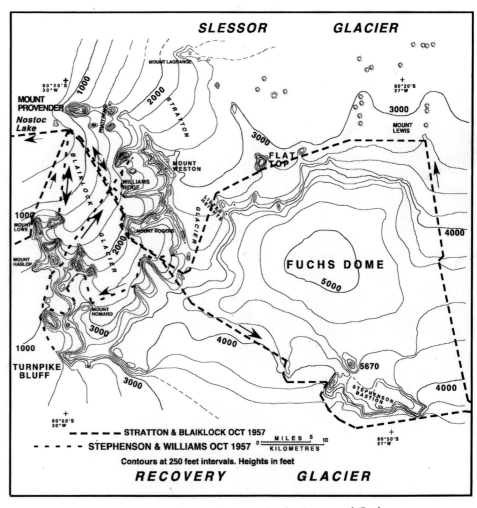

Figure 13 Shackleton Range map showing the routes by the Survey and Geology parties, using dog teams.

35 A steep ice ridge in the Shackleton Range, west of Nostoc Lake.

36 A necklace moraine in a glacier, with the Blaiklock Glacier beyond.

37 A frozen melt lake in the Shackleton Range. It is surrounded by patterned ground (polygons and stripes). The patterns disappear under the ice cliff behind.

38 A tableland surface in the Shackleton Range. Many of the mountains have plateau summits.

39 The angle where a younger erosion surface has been cut into the older tableland surface above.

40 Taffy Williams with our dog team. The bicycle wheel records the distance travelled.

41 Turnpike Bluff. From out tent, my route goes up the ridge.

the mountains proved to be very interesting geologically and visually stunning (Plate 35). Some of the glaciers had unusual *necklace* moraines, which I presumed were formed by basal thrust faults in the glacier (Plate 36). From elevated viewpoints there were interesting details in the landscape, including some frozen meltwater lakes and patterned ground (Plate 37). It was good chance to concentrate my geological work at the western end of the range, and establish a broad geological framework. David and Ken collected rocks for me on their journey, much further east around Mount Flat Top, and I was able to correlate three different rock groups. I had mapped about 30 localities and climbed several of the peaks. I recognised the presence of a very old land surface (Plate 38), which had been covered during a higher glacial level and then affected by successive decreasing ice levels which cut down into the earlier levels (Plate 39). David and Ken's specimens enabled me to extend the presence of the three rock groups much further east. Between 1967 and 1989, the Shackleton Range become a region of major geological interest, so I was fortunate to do the early work in this interesting area.[10]

Taffy and I worked around the western mountains (Plate 40), reaching the last peak to the south, Turnpike Bluff (Plate 41), south of which is the huge Recovery Glacier. The Whichaway Nunataks are south of this glacier. We eventually returned to mountains south of

Nostoc Lake, several days before our rendezvous with the Otter. But even Taffy's skill could not establish radio contact with Shackleton, but one day I was sure I heard an aircraft. The next day I saw the Auster disappear to land at the Air Camp near Nostoc Lake. I judged the weather as safe and I left Taffy in our tent behind Mount Gass, next to our tethered dog team, and set off on skis over the six miles to see if there was anyone there. My skiing skills were improving, but I had problems turning on a downhill run, especially on hard snow.

When I reached the Air Camp, I surprised Gordon Haslop and George Lowe in their tent, next to the Auster. Gordon was not entirely welcoming, asking me how would I have got back if the weather changed. And where was my sleeping bag? However, I slept in the aircraft engine cover and next day Gordon flew me back to Taffy. We still had no radio communication with the other dog party and started off for the depot on the glacier, our agreed rendezvous. At the same time, David Stratton and Ken Blaiklock reached the Air Camp with their dog team. David took off with Gordon to tell us to turn back, in preparation for an air transfer in the Otter to South Ice. The weather had been closing in, and from the Auster with Gordon, David saw us drive over a steep snow bank in the semi-whiteout, and in a very undignified way capsize

42 Theron Cliffs. John Lewis stands next to the Auster aircraft. The strata include sedimentary rocks with plant fossils and coal. The cliffs above are a dolerite sill.

our sledge. He got Gordon to land nearby and, rather sanctimoniously, stepped out of the plane to help us right our overturned sledge. He then told us about returning to the air camp to prepare for evacuation to South Ice.

However, it was soon Gordon's turn to be embarrassed. In the conditions, he had trouble taking off. In whiteout it becomes impossible to interpret slopes and Gordon tried to take off using Taffy as a reference, but his takeoff strip sloped uphill. Seeing a moraine approaching, he turned to miss some large rocks, but broke the Auster's back ski and a replacement had to be flown in from Shackleton Base. So we had the pleasure of taking Gordon and David with us back to the Air Camp. Revenge, as they say, is sweet. It was all good-natured banter.

Nostoc Lake was close to the Air Camp. It contained relatively thick ice and in places you could look down several metres through clear ice formed from meltwater to see 'floating' rock

clusters and numerous bubbles. There was also some plant material, resembling cabbage, in the ice and I collected some for identification. Such was my ignorance that I failed to put it in a preservative such as formalin. We had no biologist with us, but I am sure Allan Rogers would have advised me. By the time I showed the specimens to a botanist in London, the algal plant remains had deteriorated and could only be identified generically. I was also intrigued by the soil polygons in some of the soils on the hill slopes, which are common in cold regions. These are linked to polygonal patterns in exposed soil. I was also surprised to find gypsum in places, which is normally found in temperate, semi-arid regions. Had this area experienced a warmer period recently?

All the questions raised by the unknown mountains, their geology, previous ice levels and details of some soil polygons and gypsum, were immensely interesting

43 The Theron Mountain scarp forms the face of the mountains on the north-west side. The escarpment runs for about 45 km and is up to 300 m high.

geologically and I was sorry to leave. I could tell that some of the soil polygons were appearing from under the small mountain glaciers, and appeared to be fossil polygons.[11]

We flew out with our dogs and sledges to South Ice. Hal was back, and never being enamoured of Spam, one of the tinned meat products, I was dismayed to find he was feeding it to the first dog team, who appreciated it. It also happens that I liked Spam. We then flew back to Shackleton to help in final preparations for the main journey, awaiting Fuchs' return. He and the first vehicle party were still negotiating difficult crevasses on their route-finding journey from Shackleton Base. They were reduced to two vehicles and I remember being unable to understand why this first journey from Shackleton to South Ice took them five weeks. I don't think my colleagues understood either, but we were soon to find out.

A Short Visit to the Theron Mountains

I was flown back to Shackleton to prepare for the journey with the rest of our vehicles to South Ice, following the newly found route. There was still time for me to make a short visit by air to the Theron Mountains, which Fuchs had visited briefly in February, and found coal and plant fossils. John Lewis was scheduled to fly me out in the Auster on 18 November. But he had trouble with the radio and we had great difficulty taking off in the complete calm and warm sunshine. We tried several times before John was finally able to coax the plane into the air. He then began to circle the base and gave me some flying lessons while he valiantly tried to fix the radio. He landed again, removed the radio, and took it inside the main hut for repair. I waited in the Auster, feeling new depths of frustration, but quite soon John had us in the air again for a short flight, to land in front of the spectacular Theron cliffs (Plates 42 and 43).

Ken Blaiklock and Rainer Goldsmith visited a locality close to this point early in 1957. From his quick survey and the use of aerial photos, Ken produced the map shown in Figure 14.

Ever thorough, John stayed with the plane in case he had to restart the engine or turn the plane around, should the weather change. I collected more fossils and other specimens, and some coke produced from coal by the heat of an adjacent intrusion. The cliffs were awesome, with hundreds of nesting birds (Plate 44). Brook and Beck have described this remarkable nesting site.[12] The birds fly over 150 miles (240 km) to reach the pack-ice north of Shackleton, catch fish and then return to feed their chicks. Brook and Beck identified Antarctic petrels, snow petrels and south polar skuas, all breeding in these mountains. Antarctic petrel colonies are uncommon, and this site may be the most southerly of only nine that are known.

I wanted to collect from rocks from as high as possible on the highest feature, Mount Faraway. It was easy climbing the left skyline buttress and crossing the first glacier to the outcrops beyond. I could see there was a discontinuity, always of interest to a geologist, further on in the horizontal strata.[13] When I reached this the scene was spectacular, with the view along the Theron escarpment to the south-west. However, after many hours, John was becoming anxious about the changing weather and signalled me to return urgently. Sadly, I had to leave Mount Faraway for the next visitors.

This was effectively the end of my 'geological holiday'. While others had been finding the route through the crevasses to South Ice, or completing final preparations for the main journey, I had been thoroughly enjoying studying the previously unseen rocks in spectacular mountains.

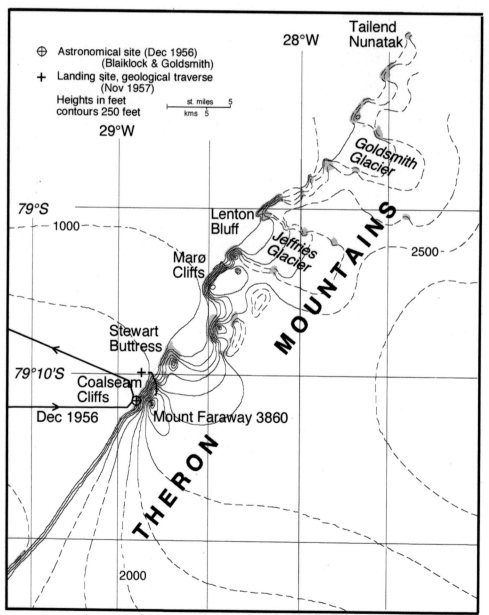

Figure 14 The Theron Mountains showing the Blaiklock–Goldsmith route in 1956 and the geological visit in the Auster in 1957 which landed at +.

44 Dolerite cliffs east of Mount Faraway next to the Glacier. There were numerous birds nesting here, and one can be seen near the base of the cliff.

4 CROSSING THE CONTINENT: CREVASSE ROULETTE

When the 1957 winter passed, the time for the expedition's main purpose was upon us. The prospects for a first Antarctic crossing were challenging, but imbued with the optimism of youth, it never occurred to me we would not succeed. This optimism was not based on knowledge or experience; I was totally ignorant about vehicle travel across snow, and especially how to negotiate crevasses. Flying to South Ice before the winter, we had seen many crevasse belts along the proposed vehicle route, but I don't think any of us could anticipate what travel across the seemingly endless Polar Plateau would involve for our vehicles. No one had used vehicles to reach the Pole previously — Amundsen used dogs, Scott used ponies and manhauling, and the IGY American Pole Station (Amundsen-Scott) had been established and supplied by air.

Fuchs succeeded in getting to South Ice in October–November, with two vehicles out of the four he set out with from Shackleton Base. After Fuchs and his four-man party had been flown back to Shackleton Base, the expedition now had to drive the remaining vehicles to South Ice, along his route. We now had to set off on the unexplored sector to the Pole. Beyond the Pole, our route was through the NZ depots to Scott Base, through previously unexplored territory.

In this chapter I will first describe the original ground journey to South Ice, based on Fuchs and Hillary's *The Crossing of Antarctica*.[1] The main party crossing will then be described in three sections: the repeat of the first South Ice journey;

South Ice to the Pole; and finally, from the Pole to Scott Base.

In July, Fuchs developed tentative schedules for the crossing, which had to be significantly modified. Fuchs was remarkably persistent in doing so, and I consider his modifications to the expedition schedules were brilliant, without compromising any of his original plans,

The original plans were severely interrupted by the Halley Bay medical emergency in late September and early October, involving Robin Smart. The other serious delay resulted from the first ground exploration of the 'crevasse roulette' section of the route, from Shackleton to South Ice. Rather than three weeks as planned, it took us five. When the main party came to repeat this leg, though we now knew the route, it still took us more than four weeks.

Because of these delays, Fuchs was denied the opportunity to undertake any personal geological fieldwork. He was restricted to his discoveries in the Therons, an afternoon climb in the western Shackletons, and some fossil collecting in the Whichaways. Nevertheless, the plans for further geological work in the Therons and extensive fieldwork in the Shackletons were both fulfilled. Remarkably, on the crossing journey Geoff Pratt's seismic and gravity workstations were sustained, together with Hal Lister's glaciology. Beyond South Ice we saw no more mountains, but other important research continued, including the careful survey of the route and regular weather observations.

THE FIRST GROUND JOURNEY: SHACKLETON TO SOUTH ICE

The South Ice reconnaissance started with four vehicles — three Weasels and Geoffrey Pratt's Sno-Cat, Haywire, fitted with the electronic equipment for his geophysical work. Bunny Fuchs set off with David and Geoffrey Pratt, and Roy Homard. Ken Blaiklock and Rainer Goldsmith had investigated the first part of the route south from Shackleton 10 months before with their dogs, and had placed a small depot 50 miles inland. The party's role was to explore this first leg of the crossing route for vehicle travel.

A major obstacle existed 30 miles south of Shackleton, in the form of the Grand Chasm. Blaiklock and Goldsmith had found a route around its eastern end, but reported there were wide, 'well-filled' crevasses. Finn Ronne and his aircraft party had visited Shackleton in August, just as our Otter was preparing to fly up to Halley Bay following the Robin Smart accident. With characteristic American generosity, their pilot donated two crash helmets for our vehicle drivers, as TAE had none. These two helmets have survived but were scarcely used, even though we took them with us. We found them to be too cumbersome when worn inside a vehicle.

The party set off on the afternoon of 7 October 1957, and soon had vehicle problems. Roy had to turn back in his Weasel and return to Shackleton in order to replace a sheared axle. Only Roy and Hal Lister had crevasse experience, having travelled with Weasels in Greenland. Fuchs notes that no one else knew how thick a crevasse bridge needs to be to carry a Weasel, Sno-Cat or heavily laden sledge. He comments that at first the party was a little foolhardy but, through mistakes, quickly developed 'infinite patience and sensitive assessment'.

Crevasses are fractures in the snow and ice which form because of ice flow. Some are obvious, as gaping clefts, but the wind can build bridges across a crevasse by depositing drift snow, and conceal the crevasse below. A snow bridge will often sag and is easily recognised in good light, but other bridges don't sag and in diffused light, under cloudy conditions, are very difficult to see. A bridge can be thick enough to appear strong, but may have weak edges. They can be treacherous, even for a person on skis. If you are on foot, it is always wise to wear skis to spread your weight, or travel roped to a colleague or a vehicle for protection.

The vehicle party soon met their first crevasses after leaving Shackleton. They experienced snow bridge collapses and had to solve their initial vehicle recovery problems. Following his Greenland experience, Roy had fixed metal brackets onto the sides of each Weasel and the Sno-Cats, for towing them forward. Fuchs arranged air reconnaissance to investigate more troublesome country ahead, and John Lewis arrived in the Auster with Roy. John flew Fuchs to inspect a bad patch of crevasses ahead.

Further west was the Grand Chasm (Plate 15), a mile-wide zone of broken ice. The vehicle route avoided it, passing well to the east. The Chasm was about 40 miles inland, roughly parallel to the coastal edge of the Filchner Ice Shelf, and over the following decades it got progressively wider. The edge of the shelf broke off along it in 1986, creating three major icebergs, which carried away all three IGY base sites — Shackleton, Belgrano and Ellsworth. The Chasm is evident in satellite images of Antarctica, recorded before the breakaway occurred (Plates 1 and 2).

Fuchs decided to withdraw to Blaiklock's 50-mile depot, strike four miles west through the narrowest part of the ice shelf between the known crevassed area and the Chasm, and then continue south. Fuchs describes how they could hear incessant glacier noise at their camp, due to ice movement beneath, which he likened to the sound of metal construction work. Hammering noises increased rapidly as the temperature increased, peaking around midday. Satellite and synthetic aperture radar (SAR) imagery is now available, and Figure 15 shows an example of the state of the ice shelf today. This image of the edge was taken after the Chasm icebergs had broken away. SAR penetrates below the surface and displays crevasses.

The vehicles proceeded, roped together like climbers with thick terylene safety lines, breaking strain 15 tons, and double steel-wire ropes. Driving with these ropes required close concentration to avoid jerking or running over them. The three vehicles continued and judged when to turn south, confident they were clear

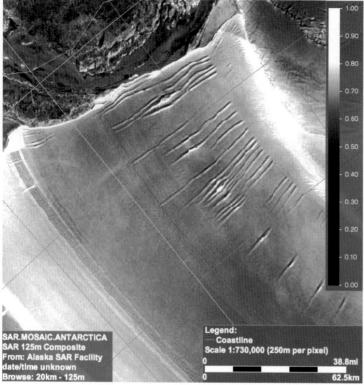

SAR.MOSAIC.ANTARCTICA
SAR 125m Composite
From: Alaska SAR Facility
date/time unknown
Browse: 20km - 125m

Legend:
    Coastline
Scale 1:730,000 (250m per pixel)

Figure 15 An SAR (synthetic aperture radar) image by satellite, around 2000. It shows the Filchner Ice Shelf with big crevasses and flow lines. Shackleton Base would have been well off this coastal position, but in 1986 Shackleton broke away on a massive iceberg. (Acknowledgment: NASA and the Alaskan Satellite Facility)

of the difficult area. It was not until the main journey in late November that Fuchs realised how lucky they had been to avoid more trouble.

Fuchs' Weasel had mechanical problems, but they continued another 70 miles in poor visibility until one evening they could see the Shackleton Range ahead in the distance. The Weasels experienced trouble in soft snow over hard sastrugi, whereas the Sno-Cat travelled majestically, with its independently articulated tracks. One Weasel broke two suspension U bolts, which became a relatively frequent occurrence. Making repairs was uncomfortable in -28°F (-33°C), even in fine, clear weather.

The dog teams had been flown in to the Shackleton Range and David Stratton and Ken Blaiklock undertook a reconnaissance of the Ice Wall from Nostoc Lake, well ahead of Fuchs. They flagged a route up the Wall for the vehicles. The vehicles travelled another 35 miles before encountering the next groups of crevasses. After one near miss, they backtracked

for five miles and then went west. The vehicles were again roped, and continued at only 5 mph. Fuchs' Weasel lurched backwards above a 'dark abyss that widened downwards in all directions', resting on its rear flotation tank and 'held by the sledge tow bar'. The vehicle recovery was complicated and took several hours. The team had established a routine of probing with long poles to locate the crevasses, and even had to do this to find a safe place to erect the tents. The way ahead called for further air reconnaissance, but radio contact from this location was proving difficult. In the meantime, there was no alternative but to probe the route with crevasse poles. Probing the snow at every step to confirm a safe route and marking the way with flags was an extremely slow process. The alternative, Fuchs noted, would have been to risk losing vehicles and men. Crevasse incidents continued for several days, in spite of the beautiful, sunny weather.

Radio contact with Shackleton was finally achieved and Lewis flew in the 200 miles from Shackleton to fly Fuchs over the ground. This flight confirmed they were in a severely crevassed area and needed to take a different route. Further east, the narrowest width of this crevasse belt was 10 or 11 miles, where the northern margin of the Slessor Glacier pushed out into the ice shelf. Fuchs wrote: 'If we can break through that belt we have a chance of good going beyond. It will certainly be a tough job and a dangerous one, but if we are to have a trans-Antarctic journey it has to be attempted, and somehow we must be successful.'[2]

This was at a critical point on the crossing journey. Fuchs devised a plan for an Air Camp in the Shackleton Range, near Nostoc Lake, in order to use the Auster for studying the route ahead. The next day, the vehicles retraced their route for six miles. They had taken three days to advance only a few hundred yards into this crevasse minefield.

After the Air Camp was established, Haslop flew Fuchs in the Auster and found that the dog-team route, flagged by David and Ken up the Ice Wall, looked forbidding, with open trench-like crevasses curving towards one another from the Wall. The intervening stretch was crossed by countless crevasses. The next 10 miles were difficult, and required careful probing to find a safe way through, very slowly and with many crevasse incidents. It took over a week to negotiate this section and finally turn the south-west corner of the Shackleton Mountains. The Recovery Glacier lay ahead; it was 40 miles wide and from the air, impressive crevasse belts were evident. Fuchs' Weasel finally stopped and was abandoned, together with a sledge. Now only two vehicles remained, a Weasel and the Sno-Cat, and they transferred the sledge loads to these. Finding a good route across the Recovery Glacier involved similar air scouting, followed by ground probing and flagging to locate a safe route. With the exploration of the first leg of the route still incomplete, Fuchs must have felt his plans to cross Antarctica were more than fragile, and under severe threat.

The party finally reached South Ice on 14 November, where Hal Lister and Hannes la Grange welcomed them. This first leg from Shackleton had taken 37 days and they had travelled 400 miles. Fuchs would have felt disheartened by the prolonged, tense effort in finding a way to South Ice, with the awful prospect of having to do it all again with the main party and our other vehicles. Fuchs' vehicle team flew back to Shackleton. The rest of us, making final preparations for departure were not aware of the severe difficulties ahead of us. We were soon to find out.

THE SECOND MAIN PARTY JOURNEY: SHACKLETON TO SOUTH ICE

The route to South Ice is shown in Figure 16. Six vehicles finally set off on 24 November, around 7 pm — three Sno-Cats, two Weasels and the Muskeg tractor. A vehicle party from the Argentine station, Belgrano, 20 miles west of Shackleton, arrived just before we left. The RAF air contingent — Lewis, Haslop, Williams, Weston and Geoffrey Pratt — waved us off, as did the four Argentines in their orange windproofs. Geoffrey was to take Hal's place at South Ice. The RAF group were to fly our two TAE planes to Halley Bay and return the two Royal Society volunteers, Ivory Beney and Fred Morris, who had been helping with our preparations. They would leave the Auster there for returning to England, when *Magga Dan* arrived to resupply Halley Bay. They would fly back to Shackleton in the Otter.

Fuchs' early plan had estimated 14 November as a tentative date for the crossing departure, and we

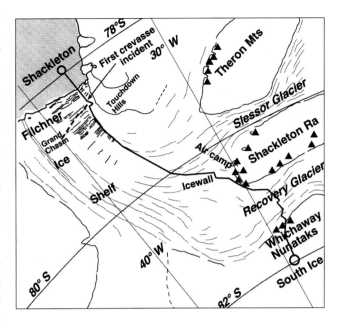

Figure 16 The vehicle route from Shackleton to South Ice. The topographic features are sketched from an SAR image. The position of the Grand Chasm is shown with Shackleton in 1957. Both drifted north until the Chasm widened to release icebergs for Shackleton to drift away in 1986.

were now over five weeks late. The question was: could we make up time travelling to South Ice? The crossing party comprised Fuchs, David Stratton, Roy Homard, David Pratt, Ralph Lenton, Allan Rogers, Ken Blaiklock, George Lowe and myself. The vehicles all had nicknames; The Sno-Cats were Rock 'n Roll (Fuchs), Able (David Pratt), County of Kent (Roy Homard) and Haywire (Geoffrey Pratt). The Weasels were Rumble (Rogers), Wrack and Ruin (Lowe), and I drove the Muskeg Bombardier tractor, Hopalong. Hal Lister would join us shortly from South Ice, and Geoffrey Pratt would wait for us there with Hannes la Grange.

We had travelled 17 miles south by 10.30 pm. I tented with Allan Rogers and was 'outside man' that night, helping with the refuelling while Allan prepared our meal inside. The vehicles had given no trouble, the Sno-Cats cruising comfortably in top gear though pulling about four tons each on their sledges. Allan's Weasel gave some oil trouble, which proved next morning to be an unconnected pipe. My Muskeg went well in what for it was deep snow, pulling only a ton on two sledges. A dog sledge carrying food followed at the end of this bizarre procession of vehicles. The terrain we crossed had long, broad undulations, about a mile across and 50 to 100 feet high, which I could see when the vehicles ahead dropped out of sight. Ralph had a good radio schedule with Shackleton Base at 8 pm.

Next morning, Ken and I started a rammsonde profile. A rammsonde is a rod with markings, and by dropping a weight on the rod, can be used to record the penetration with each blow. In this way, a snow hardness profile can be drawn up. We had only reached a metre when it was time to leave. We met the first crevasses just before midday. They were narrow enough to drive straight across, but were well hidden, and the bridges collapsed as we crossed. Hardly reassuring! There were more crevasses after lunch,

45 The first big crevasse on the Filchner Ice Shelf, which almost got Fuchs and Stratton's Sno-Cat. Four men earnestly discuss how to recover it: Roy Homard, David Pratt pointing, David Stratton and Bunny Fuchs. (Photo by George Lowe)

including a wider chasm, 10 to 15 feet wide, which forced us to cross it at a safer point. Ken took over driving the Muskeg while I travelled behind David Pratt's Sno-Cat to keep an eye on a dog sledge, with top-heavy fuel drums, should it tip over.

At 4 pm a frightening incident occurred. Visibility was bad and Fuchs and Stratton were leading in their Sno-Cat, Rock 'n Roll, when they experienced a severe lurch, and found their stalled vehicle was astride an enormous chasm (Plate 45). The crevasse had clean, vertical sides, with the blue depths continuing out of sight into blackness. It was almost wide enough to engulf the vehicle, and the snow bridge had collapsed when the front pontoons were two-thirds across. Had they been only 10 degrees off course they would have dropped right in, with the sledges following. Fuchs and Stratton had difficulty getting out of their vehicle, but emerged on Stratton's side and climbed out onto the rear pontoon, above the deep void below.

I felt shock. My first reaction was that the situation for the vehicle was hopeless. It was lost. I took some black-and-white photos, leaving the 'scoop' photos to George Lowe, as our official photographer.

An immediate challenge was to recover the precious vehicle. The front pontoons were already skewed at odd angles. The Sno-Cat was emptied, and its two sledges unshackled and towed away. Prolonged discussions took place on how to attempt a recovery. First, a safe place was found, 200 yards away, for the two Weasels to cross the crevasse safely and tie onto the front of the stricken Sno-Cat in tandem, with steel wire ropes. The Weasels were left in gear, ignition off, to act as anchors. Meanwhile, the other two Sno-Cats hooked up to pull the stricken Rock 'n Roll out backwards. The Muskeg was tied to the front starboard pontoon, which had jammed at an angle against the edge of the crevasse, to rectify its angle as movement began. The diagram (Figure 17) shows the recovery situation. The two Weasels proved over-efficient as anchors, and were allowed to ride gently backwards on the clutch as the Snow-Cat was towed backwards.

The two other Sno-Cats succeeded in dragging the stricken Cat backwards, until its weight came to rest on the near side of the crevasse. The Muskeg had been holding the front pontoon in position, but then the other pontoon dropped out of position. Pulling the Cat backwards would have damaged it,

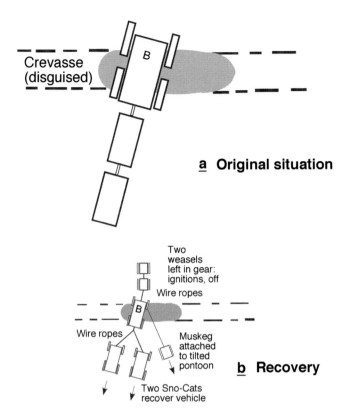

Crevasse
(disguised)

<u>a</u> **Original situation**

Two
weasels
left in gear:
ignitions, off

Wire ropes

Wire ropes

Muskeg
attached
to tilted
pontoon

<u>b</u> **Recovery**

Two Sno-Cats
recover vehicle

Figure 17 The first vehicle recovery on the main crossing journey. The stricken Sno-Cat was successfully pulled out backwards, a procedure taking five hours.

by pivoting it further against the crevasse edge. It called for a complicated manoeuvre. David Stratton was coordinator and did some digging with a shovel on the lip of the crevasse, providing room for the pontoon to swing into position, tied to the Muskeg. Unfortunately, a wrong move jammed the pontoon even more seriously, but eventually the Sno-Cat was extricated. The recovery had taken five hours — very efficiently, considering the situation.

This sense of relief and feeling of achievement were tempered by questions about damage to the Sno-Cat. Were the hydraulics affected? Was there axle damage? Steering? Happily, and amazingly, tests showed no apparent damage. Nothing short of a miracle! After retrieving their sledges, the Sno-Cats crossed the crevasse at a safe point and joined the other vehicles to make camp. Another section of snow bridge over the big crevasse had collapsed from vibration. We had travelled only 13 miles but what a day!

It is easier to analyse an incident afterwards, which we did. The crevasse bridge had collapsed before the vehicle occupants were aware there was a crevasse

ahead. A depression was evident, but the light at the time was very poor. In sunshine, it would have been more prominent.

The weather cleared and around 5 pm. The Otter flew over us on its way to South Ice with Geoffrey, to collect Hal, and saw our predicament. It returned at 11.30 and landed to deposit Hal.

The next morning, we left at 9.30. Allan had to arrange space in his Weasel for Hal by lashing some gear on a sledge. Visibility was perfect and we pushed steadily on. Wide crevasses were probed carefully and avoided. Fuchs' Sno-Cat developed a coolant leak, taking several hours to fix in a sharp wind with drift, while the rest of us tried to keep warm. Continuing, we passed over more obvious crevasses, having probed them first. Just before 6 pm, we all crossed a nasty-looking crevasse, which Roy and Ralph bringing up the rear reached just in time to witness its bridge collapse only a few feet in front of them, revealing a great cavern rivalling that of yesterday. After many attempts they found a way around and joined our camp half a mile further on. That day we covered only nine miles.

Next day, 27 November, we set off, probing for hidden crevasses, working in pairs with aluminium rods and ice chisels, testing every yard. Though laborious and time consuming, this was the only method we had for finding crevasses and everyone undertook this vital routine (Plate 46). When we found a safe route through, we marked it with flags. I worked with George, and after several hours we happened to be in front, finding few crevasses except

46 Our only crevasse detection method: team members probing with long rods to see if there is space beneath. Fuchs, Stratton, Lowe, Lister.

the obvious ones. We skied on, and after recognising the October journey's five-week-old tracks crossing the route, we returned to the vehicles for lunch. The reconnaissance allowed every vehicle to drive over the probed ground, in this case for only two miles. We resumed probing and drove another mile. The ground was still dangerous and we travelled slowly, at two or three miles per hour, with the vehicles roped together with terylene hawsers. We camped after only another three miles.

Another day followed, probing through crevasse country, still chastened by the earlier incident, and covered only a couple of miles. Ken's depot, laid a year before with Rainer on their dog journey to the Therons, was still two miles ahead. I probed with Ken and he expressed exasperation not to be racing along with the dogs. It took us all next day to reach the depot.

Our slow and deliberate progress continued, and beyond the depot we travelled five miles west before swinging south again, delayed by Sno-Cat troubles. This pattern of travel continued, with an easier section in a long leg approaching the Ice Wall. The last day of November was surprisingly warm and almost still, and we sat eating our lunch with our shirtsleeves rolled up. We pushed on. It got colder, and Ralph had to relieve me in the unheated Muskeg. The Muskeg really was a cold vehicle, and Ken had to relieve Ralph before long. By contrast, Hal's Weasel was overheating. He stopped for Roy to look it over and soon after was on his way, overtaking us. We signalled to him because he had lost a sledge, but fortunately only a short distance back. We had a long day, at times following David Stratton skiing ahead, but travelled 25 miles. We camped towards midnight in a balmy +5°F (-15°C).

The following day was another clear, warm day, and only trouble with one of Fuchs' pontoons limited us to 41 miles. The following days saw us rolling steadily forward, with occasional vehicle problems. The Shackleton Range came in view on 3 December and I found it difficult to recognise the peaks from the north. The route followed compass headings set by Fuchs in Rock 'n Roll and every five miles we passed a flag left by the October party. We made 65 miles that day, quite an achievement.

Next day, we began breaking small crevasses, but our leading Sno-Cat was untroubled by them and pressed on at a steady 5 mph. The following vehicles inspected the crevasses before attempting to cross them. Around noon, we overtook Rock 'n Roll, which had broken into a crevasse, wide but not as spectacular as the earlier monster. The rear of the Sno-Cat had dropped in, snapping the coupling to the sledges behind, then dropped further. After we had probed a safe crossing further along, David tried pulling Rock 'n Roll out with Able but failed, and the stricken vehicle dropped in a foot more. Roy linked Able to County of Kent, and the two vehicles recovered Fuchs' vehicle. The accident happened within 50 yards of a chequered flag, and on the first journey, crevasses had not been encountered for another couple of miles. The weeks of warmer weather had steadily weakened some of the crevasse bridges.

As well as snapping the sledge coupling, the accident had also sheared part of the main aluminium alloy rear chassis. Our engineers immediately located the only spare we had and set about the replacement, a long task. Fuchs was anxious to keep to the original route, but the light was so poor that we continued probing in case we lost the old tracks. Most of us had the afternoon off, and I dug a glaciology pit several metres deep next to the wall of the crevasse to examine it more closely. The crevasse was about 10 feet wide and around 60 feet deep. It narrowed in both directions away from the point of the collapse. Our day had brought us eight miles and we saw birds, which was surprising, because we were now over 200 miles from the ocean.

It was 5 December when we set off again, prodding. Fuchs thoughtfully kept changing the prod pairs around, and I had interesting conversations with different colleagues. That day I worked with Fuchs and he talked about a number of things, including the expedition's progress. He was already very much aware of a possibly late arrival at Scott Base, and he realised our ship, Endeavour, might have already departed without us to avoid getting beset for the winter. He contemplated flying out, rather than staying another winter, and stressed the undesirability of flying out with the US Air Force. He maintained that any flight would have to involve the RNZAF. On many occasions he voiced the importance of not seeking help from the Americans, perhaps as a result

47 Another of our numerous crevasse incidents. Able is caught by a crevasse bridge collapse. Our aluminium bridges are being put in place for the Sno-Cat to be hauled out successfully. It almost fell off the bridges.

of early opposition and the suggestion from the Royal Geographical Society that a crossing should be left to the Americans.

We did not move camp that day, but followed the probed route a short distance next day and resumed probing until late, in very warm sunshine, without a breath of wind. It was so warm I enjoyed working without a shirt. The following day was similar, and we moved a little further and camped around midnight. After a tiring day we made a later start the next day, setting off after lunch, with the vehicles again roped together. Within a short distance, David Pratt's Able fell into a 12-foot crevasse, which had been crossed by all the other vehicles. Fortunately, the crevasse was partly filled with snow. We shovelled more snow into the crevasse to build up the collapsed snow bridge under the vehicle and used two aluminium crevasse bridges, being carried on the Muskeg, for the first

time. These were placed under the vehicle and secured by wire ropes to 'dead men' in the soft snow (Plate 47). A dead man consists of a wooden block buried in soft snow, which is stamped down over it, and is capable of taking an enormous strain. The towing by the other Cats led to a happy ending. Able was towed forwards, with two Weasels behind to prevent the back dropping in abruptly. The Cat lurched alarmingly on the aluminium bridges and might have tilted over had we not shouted 'full speed ahead', which probably saved the day. There was no damage, but this recovery had taken another five hours. We camped late, at 11 pm. Ralph had an excellent radio schedule with the Pole, where it was -10°F (-23°C).

David Pratt drove a tank in Normandy during the D Day landings in 1945 and experienced the tensions associated with this offensive, with the ever-present fear of mines. He joked that driving through our TAE 'crevasse roulette' course had similarities, except that instead of being blown up he had to be prepared for the reverse, suddenly dropping down.

On 8 December, the Otter arrived from Shackleton and flew back and forth overhead as we prodded ahead through the crevasses. Then, to everyone's astonishment, John Lewis landed near the vehicles, though he had been instructed to continue eight miles further to land and unload. He was several hundred yards back and we continued prodding, while Fuchs walked past us and muttered, 'I hope he takes off as luckily as he landed'. Presumably, severe words were spoken, and the now-empty Otter made a remarkably short take-off. Fuchs returned with mail the Americans had brought across to Shackleton the night before, ferried from Punta Arenas.

The letters were distributed but some, disappointingly, missed out on mail. Fortunately, David Pratt later found more mail for us all, packed with some vehicle spares, which had also come down with the Americans. These evened up the distribution. The RAF men had missed these letters and did not get them until they flew up to South Ice. Mail was always very important to us in the isolation of Antarctica. After lunch, having lashed on the new spares, we moved off along the probed route until 7 pm. Fuchs advised us to get an early night as he planned a long day, to start travelling at night, partly for the better surfaces but also to relieve the sunburn some of us had been suffering. This again showed Fuchs' sensitivity to his team's needs.

We started off probing, expecting to at last reach the foot of the Ice Wall. Fuchs intended to keep moving until 2 am, camp, and change to Greenwich Mean Time (GMT), a three-hour advance. We then had the prospect of an 18-hour sleep in order to shift to GMT, 12 hours behind Hillary's NZ time. After a second stretch of probing, Ralph made soup for everyone's thermos. We moved off around 9 pm local time and continued on slowly from the end of our probed route. David Stratton and Hal were able to ski ahead as the crevasses had become fewer, and we camped around midnight. Roy cut his left thumb while breaking up pemmican. Allan dressed this. Then, with Roy and Ralph he joined us for tea and a yarn, but I was unable to stay awake.

We indeed slept until 5.30 pm GMT, and had breakfast at 8 pm. We then set off with four colleagues to reconnoitre the crevasses on the Ice Wall. There were some wide crevasses, which looked safe enough, but we made a detour. It was cold, and the nearby mountains looked just as impressive as they had on our dog traverse, eight weeks before. In the 'afternoon', we climbed the Ice Wall in the vehicles. The soft snow troubled the Muskeg, and the two Weasels, roped together up ahead, had to assist. The Wall looked something like the sea front at Shackleton Base, but with a rise of about 700 feet and less steep. At the top, we went on another half mile to reach the Weasel which had been abandoned in October. Several hours were spent stripping it for spare parts, including its rubber tracks. Fuchs skied ahead to find a better way around the large hole produced on the previous journey, and as we were moving on to rejoin Fuchs, the leading Weasel, driven by Allan, dropped one side into a four-foot crevasse. Hal had been sitting on top as scout and was thrown off, unhurt. The Weasel recovery was not difficult; David Stratton pulled the vehicle upright, then George pulled it out backwards with his Weasel. We camped at 9.30 am.

December 12–13 was another fine day, and we started off with a few hours probing. The large hole from the first journey was spectacular, 20 feet across and about 40 deep, and had formed just 15 feet from the Weasel, being towed at the time by the Sno-Cat. The bridge collapse happened just as the Weasel was about to cross the crevasse, and the soft snow on the crevasse bridge had bogged it. The vehicles, by then the last two left on the advance journey, could both have fallen in. The snow debris was about 20 feet down and it might have been impossible to retrieve them. After more probing, we moved off, roped together as usual. The Muskeg was in difficulties, and it felt like it was swimming. We continued, unroped, from the end of David and Ken's flagged dog-team route. The weather deteriorated as we reached four large crevasses, previously crossed successfully, and after more probing we crossed them, again roped together. We were now approaching the south-west corner of the Shackleton Range but had poor visibility, and we camped around 8 am, three or four miles further on.

Around 9 am, I drove off in the unladen Muskeg with Fuchs, David Stratton and Hal to go to the nearest mountain, just north of the corner of the Shackleton

Range. The Muskeg skipped along without its load and we drove two miles, almost to the rocks. We walked up the mountain and paused on top, where Fuchs and Hal seemed disappointed by the erosion surface, covered in moraine and hummocky with bouldery soil polygons. Fuchs suggested a hypothesis, based on the distribution of weathered quartzite boulders, namely that the ice had retreated rapidly because these rocks seemed confined to the highest slopes. The lighter coloured quartzite boulders gave a curious, patchy colouring to the hillside. We returned in improving sunshine, to hear that Ralph had also been out to a nearby mountain, skiing.

Next day, 13–14th, we departed before 10 pm GMT, in fine weather but with a chilling wind. We crossed some extraordinary ice-dome sastrugi, two to three feet high. The glazed surfaces testified that high winds occur here. The Muskeg loved these conditions, and seemed less troubled by sharp sastrugi than the other vehicles. We were now moving onto the infamous Recovery Glacier and we camped on the edge of the initial crevasse belt after covering 31 miles. The first journey led us to expect this to be the worst and widest of the Recovery crevasse areas.

We set off again, around 8.30 pm, prodding our way ahead. The party seemed a bit disgruntled, perhaps tired and because of the return to laborious prodding. The usual prodding and short advances were repeated, past some enormous crevasses. Allan and George spent five hours on a short but very severe section. The crevasses were shown up by large drift hummocks up to 10 feet high, scattered across the landscape — a strange scene. We camped about 11 am, with the prospect of a 'lie-in' until 10 pm. Very welcome! The following day was a maintenance morning for the vehicles, then prodding continued for a mile. The weather began to change from north to east with cloud, but we advanced 17 miles. On the 17–18th we had poor weather and bad visibility, with some snow. We travelled about three miles west to gain entry into the next narrow crevasse belt, but the lack of visibility forced a halt. I went back with David Stratton to the previous campsite to retrieve his compass, and the Muskeg did an easy 9 mph without its load. The poor visibility continued and we eventually camped, and David skied ahead for a mile to try to identify the previous route. The following day proved to be a lie-

in, because of more snow and poor visibility, and I had a chance to continue reading Rousseau's *Confessions*. In the afternoon, Allan and I enjoyed a social call to Bunny and David's tent for a long chat, accompanied by cocoa and shrimps on biscuits.

Out next day, 18–19th December, brought more bad weather and looked like another forced lie-in, but we eventually got moving by 11 pm GMT. Some skied ahead and we did some probing, but found no crevasses and drove on, roped together, to reach what we called the 'echelon belt'. This was a series of elongated pinnacles arranged in a stepped, alternating pattern, which we could not see well because of the poor visibility. They form an area of hummocks over 10 feet high, and would have been spectacular in sunlight. The hummocks conceal some very large crevasses, formed by faster flowing ice. We drove through, roped, and then continued a further three miles at a funereal speed. Another three miles west, unroped, we approached the last crevasse belt before South Ice. The Whichaway Nunataks lay close ahead and we camped at 6.30 am, in improving weather.

That afternoon we moved about a mile to the first crevasses, and Hal and I began probing. The sun came out but then went in again, and poor visibility returned. There were some frightening-looking crevasses, and this belt had perhaps the worst ones we encountered anywhere. On the first journey, this short section took a full day to negotiate. Ken Blaiklock had a close call when he broke through a crevasse on skis. He saved himself by his elbows but lost his skis. We moved up to the limit of probing, and I continued after lunch with Roy. The crevasses were nasty and Ken had another near disaster when the bridge he was probing collapsed, leaving him kneeling on his skis, straddling a very deep hole. We retrieved him gingerly, and returned to camp at the vehicles. I arrived there early and was walking without my skis, beside one of the sledges, about halfway along the line of six vehicles. I felt the ground suddenly give way under me and just managed to catch myself on one elbow and my chin, on the lip of a large snow bridge which had given way. After struggling back onto firm ground, I examined the hole I had made. I could see I would have dropped further through an incomplete snow bridge into a black hole several metres down. To this day, I can recall its dark details — the stuff of nightmares. I shared the drama with Ralph, the only person nearby, who stared at me and said, 'Gees, you were lucky!' After that, we kept a hand on a sledge or a vehicle as we walked past.

Bunny Fuchs gave me permission to go off with Hal next 'day' to have a look at the nearby geology and glaciology. We left in a whiteout soon after 8 pm and it was tricky skiing through the crevasse belt in the bad light. The crevassing was very complex, with uplifted sections caused by pressure. There were also extraordinary ice pinnacles up to 20 feet high. We got through to the welcome, smooth snow beyond and skied on to the conical east peak, which I visited in March and where I wanted to collect more fossils. Hal had an interesting time, examining the well-displayed Ice Wall at the west edge of the nunataks, which exposed the edge of the inland plateau ice. He concluded that the ice here was stationary, neither advancing nor retreating. Meanwhile, I collected more *Archaeocyathus* fossils from limestone boulders.

Returning to the vehicles, later in the day we helped probe the last section. It seemed doubtful that the vehicles would clear this last belt of crevasses without problems. They simply had to take the best route through bad stretches, with no way of going around them. However, they emerged unscathed and we drove up a long hill beyond the crevasse belt. I was very tired, and the indefatigable Ralph drove the Muskeg. There was talk of driving on to South Ice, only another 30 miles, but we wisely camped around 10 am. Roy and Ralph went off to examine the same conical peak Hal and I had visited earlier, but on the other side. They wanted to find fossils, so I went with them. We drove almost to the summit on this southern side, where the moraine came up much higher. Bunny joined us, and with four pairs of eyes, we found more good fossil specimens. Back at camp, we ate and then slept, after being on the go for 19 hours.

The convoy left at 9.45 pm for the long run to South Ice. This was interrupted soon after, when Bunny's Sno-Cat started boiling, a consequence of leaving the radiator cover on. Bunny was annoyed with himself, but we were all very tired. We drove through more nunataks, which Ken and I had been unable to see in drift conditions on our manhaul trip but we pressed steadily on. The Muskeg galloped on hard sastrugi surfaces at first, but later wallowed in the soft snow.

We reached South Ice at 6 am, on 21 December, just in time to surprise Hannes coming out for a morning weather observation. The trip from Shackleton had taken us four weeks and we were well behind the tentative schedule.

The Americans were soon expected up from Shackleton and Bunny asked us to park 'tidily' as a team. I was fascinated that he was still determined to display regimented routines — not that we were sloppy. It was good to see Hannes and Geoffrey again, and to say hello to our dogs. The dogs looked fit and eager to set off for the Pole.

We had a celebratory party in the hut, all 12 of us. It was crowded, and it felt strange to see so many people after the quietness of our three-man winter. Fuchs must have been relieved to have completed the hazardous journey from Shackleton without any injuries or vehicle loss. We slept in our tents, secure in the knowledge there were no crevasses. We prepared to change back to a normal am–pm day, because the day temperatures had returned to 0°F (-18°C) again and we would be awake when the Americans were due to arrive, about 1 pm local time, on 22 December. We only got four hours sleep, as the twin-engine Dakota arrived earlier than expected.

The plane seemed enormous after our Otter. The six Americans included Finn Ronne (Officer in Charge at Ellsworth Base) and Jim Lassiter, the pilot. Lassiter had also been with Ronne in 1947 at Stonington, when they met Bunny and John Lewis. They brought 12 drums of TAE vehicle fuel from Shackleton on Bunny's request, and other odds and ends. Lassiter was keen to see the station, because he might be using it later for his photo-survey flights. Our visitors seemed very taken by the tunnel warrens and I chatted to Ronne and Lassiter, who were interested in our fossils. I had time to pack all my geological specimens and a kitbag of my surplus gear left at South Ice, to go back to Shackleton. I failed to pack my Bardot pin-up, which must still be there. The Dakota returned to Ellsworth via Shackleton Base, after Ronne had given us reports of their geophysical party's successful 450-mile traverse to the Dufek Massif, which Ronne said was composed of sedimentary rocks.

Ken and I organised the dog food, sledging equipment and our own food, ready for our departure with the dog teams the next day. I had a chance to talk with Geoffrey and Hannes who were up late, writing final letters in the hut.

THE NEW ZEALAND PARTY'S SOUTHERN JOURNEY FROM SCOTT BASE

While Fuchs was negotiating the first leg of the crossing, to reach South Ice, the New Zealand Party had been establishing a vehicle route from Scott Base up onto the Polar Plateau for the crossing party to use after it had progressed past the Pole.

The NZ spring operations in 1957 from Scott Base were to establish a vehicle route up the Skelton Glacier to the site of Plateau Depot, and a route south from there to reach a locality for Depot 700, about 500 miles from the Pole. Hillary's party had the responsibility of establishing fuel and food depots for the main crossing party.

Hillary[3], who describes the New Zealand journeys in books by Fuchs and Hillary, regarded the Skelton Glacier as the crux of the southern journey. South from Plateau Depot, the vehicle route was well to the west of the Trans Antarctic Mountains, which form the edge of the Polar Plateau. These mountains form the major escarpment, which runs south and was first discovered by Scott's *Discovery* expedition (1902–04). Scott also reached and discovered the Polar Plateau, extending west from the source region of the Ferrar and Taylor Glaciers. Both Scott's southern party and Shackleton's *Nimrod* party (1908–09) travelled south across the Ross Ice Shelf from McMurdo Sound, moving past the mountains towards the Pole. Shackleton first discovered the route up the Beardmore Glacier, reaching the Polar Plateau at its head, and sledged to within 180 km of the Pole before turning back. He might have got closer to the Pole if his last pony, Socks, had not been lost in a crevasse on the Beardmore. On his *Terra Nova* expedition (1912–14), Scott followed this Beardmore route and reached the Pole, but perished on the return.

Major glaciers rise near the edge of the Polar Plateau and pour down through the escarpment to feed the Ross Ice Shelf. Hillary's vehicle route had to negotiate the Skelton, reach the plateau at its head and then

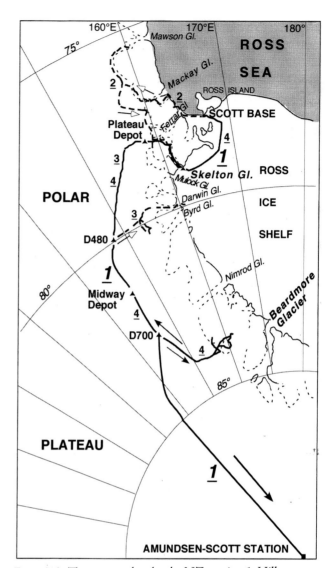

Figure 18 The routes taken by the NZ parties: 1, Hillary; 2, Northern Survey; 3, Darwin Glacier Survey; 4, Southern Survey.

continue south, keeping well to the west away from the heads of the glaciers which flow east through the mountains, to avoid their crevassed source regions. These are huge glaciers and include the Mulock, Darwin, Byrd and Shackleton Glaciers, all south of the Skelton Glacier.

In addition to the vehicle journey to reach the site for D700, the NZ TAE Party had three survey teams, which carried out considerable mountain exploration and mapping. Figure 18 shows the routes of the NZ Parties.

Hillary left Scott Base on 14 October with three Ferguson tractors and a Weasel. His party included Murray Ellis, Peter Mulgrew and Ron Balham, and the vehicles headed for Skelton Depot, established by air late in the previous summer. A sledge encountered the first crevasse on the Ross Ice Shelf, just over five miles from base, and it took several hours to unload and recover it. The next day, soft snow and very slow progress forced them to reduce the total sledge loads by offloading eight drums of fuel, after which they travelled 23 miles. The extensive crevasses were of major concern. They spread out from White Island and Minna Bluff, landmarks well known to the Scott and Shackleton expeditions. Hillary's route swung wide to the east to avoid them. The Weasel had mechanical problems, but was nursed along to reach the Skelton Depot. Jim Bates, who had just flown in, and Murray Ellis spent two days making major repairs, lifting the engine out with a heavy wood bipod and chain. These two men were the party's skilled vehicle engineers.

At Skelton, the vehicle party met the Southern Survey party, Bob Miller and George Marsh. They had flown in on 18 October, with their two dog teams. Bill Cranfield made the first flight and confirmed the depot had not been buried by winter drift. He had to land across the wind, parallel to the sastrugi. The Beaver brought six dogs on each of the first two flights, and on the second flight John Claydon brought a dog-sledge under each wing. He returned with Bates at midnight on the third flight. Unfortunately, Bates brought influenza from McMurdo, which steadily made its way through the group.

The vehicle party traversed up Skelton Glacier and in spite of bad weather eventually reached Plateau Depot after nine days. They found a careful route which avoided the crevassed regions on the glacier. Miller and Marsh had set out to travel with their dogs, planning to keep in touch with the vehicles, but in the bad weather had to make their own way. The vehicles could still travel in wind and bad drift, whereas the dog teams could not.

The Darwin Glacier Survey party, Harry Ayres and Roy Carlyon, were flown in to Plateau Depot with two dog teams. The surface near the original depot site was too rough for landing and later the depot was moved three miles to a more sheltered location. Ayres and Carlyon received the vehicles when they arrived at the end of October, and Miller and Marsh arrived two days later. Plateau Depot was 280 miles from Scott Base, but its latitude was only 10 miles further south. Hillary and Balham flew back to Scott Base, and

Hillary returned to Plateau Depot on 10 November. Two of the vehicle party, Ellis and Mulgrew, had to be evacuated from Plateau Depot to Scott Base because of injuries, and Derek Wright and Ted Gawn were flown in to replace them.

One important role for the Southern Survey dog party was to support the vehicles south from Plateau Depot, and they continued their exploration journey to reach the planned sites for Depots 480 and 700. After reaching D700, they diverted to carry out independent exploration west of Beardmore Glacier. The Darwin Glacier party, Ayres and Carlyon, continued to D480, and then set off east on their survey.

The dog-team parties set off from Plateau Depot on 8 November, with very heavy sledges, and experienced difficult snow conditions. Despite the dogs' eagerness, and even after several days' rest at the Skelton Depot, the teams could not progress until some of their loads had been jettisoned. The vehicles, following, were obliged to pick up these extra loads. The route south is shown on Figure 18.

The vehicle party was first to reach the site for D480, on 25 November. Miller and Carlyon more accurately confirmed its location when they arrived with the dogs two and a half days later. As they said, 'We were lucky to find you'. The Beaver flew in with Claydon shortly afterwards, and he also experienced problems finding the depot, as the six-mile correction to its original coordinates had still to be sent to him.

The Beaver aircraft flew in drums of vehicle fuel to steadily build up D480 and, later, D700. This was an enormous task, with many flights. Claydon recognised that the long flights from Scott Base were hindered by weather changes along the way, and were not fuel-efficient. Because the Beaver could carry slightly heavier loads over shorter distances, Claydon used staging depots near the outflow of the Darwin Glacier for D480, and later, the 'Wigram' Depot near Shackleton Inlet, for D700.

Exploration for the route south continued from D480, when the Southern Survey group, Miller and Marsh, set off on 1 December. The Darwin Glacier Survey party, Ayres and Carlyon, left D480 six days later to explore a difficult route down Darwin Glacier, and reached the Ross Ice Shelf in 45 days.

After the Beaver had finished stocking D480, the vehicles set off on 6 December to follow Miller and

Marsh and their dogs. Ellis had rejoined the team at D480 after recovering from a back injury and Mulgrew also returned, his broken ribs healed after he fell onto a tow bar from the roof of the 'caboose' at Plateau Depot. A new member of the NZ Party, the journalist Doug McKenzie, also joined the tractor group at D480, having arrived in Antarctica only a few days before.

Driving a Ferguson tractor must have been an ordeal. The drivers were exposed behind a simple windshield, very different from a Sno-Cat. The caboose was towed by one of the vehicles, to provide shelter for the resting drivers. It was a light but strong caravan, and was built on a sledge. Made from quarter-inch piping, plywood and heavy canvas it was 11 x 4 feet, and it had two bunks. Forthwith, Bates had constructed a simple heat exchanger for it, using the tractor exhaust. The caboose also contained the radio.

The Weasel performed better than the Ferguson tractors. Bates and Ellis went to great lengths to keep the Weasel going, without adequate spares. However, it was eventually abandoned before they reached the site for D700.

The route crossed many crevasses. Warned by the dog teams, the vehicles diverted further west in some sections, but still had to negotiate dangerous situations. They were roped together when travelling through bad areas, but a number of crevasse incidents required vehicle recoveries. They were forced to probe on foot for a way through in some places, roped together. The vehicle party established Midway Depot, 124 miles south of D480, with food and kerosene and six drums of vehicle fuel.

Miller and Marsh reached a site suitable for D700 (at 82°50S, 146°02'E) with their dogs on 15 December, and a few days later the three Fergusons arrived. The Beaver flew in from the Wigram staging camp and began building up the depot with fuel and other supplies. This was to be the first depot for Fuchs' crossing party after it left the Pole. When the depot was complete, the vehicles set off to confirm the route for the next few hundred miles south. There were some minor changes to the vehicle team with some men exchanged by air, and Hillary's four companions were now Bates, Ellis, Mulgrew and Wright. McKenzie and Gawn returned to Scott Base.

Miller and Marsh left D700 on 19 December with their dog teams, to explore eastwards. Hillary did not have sufficient fuel to establish a depot for them further on, but Cranfield met them with the Beaver, 37 miles out, with supplies, including tobacco for Marsh.

John Claydon and Bill Cranfield had provided the depots very efficiently with the Beaver for Fuchs' crossing party, completing D700 on 20 December. The New Zealand Party had now fulfilled its role in TAE — to establish a vehicle route from Scott Base to D700 and to stock the depots for the crossing party coming from Shackleton.

On the other side of the Pole, Fuchs' crossing party had reached South Ice on 21 December. The vehicles departed late on Christmas Day. A day earlier, Hillary's party left D700 in the three Fergusons to clear all the crevasses ahead and then, if his fuel and vehicles permitted, he was heading for the Pole.

THE CROSSING JOURNEY: SOUTH TO THE POLE

Ken and I were up at 8 am on 23 December 1957. Our role was to lead off with the dogs, acting as scouts for the vehicles, which would follow in a few days. Allan took us into the hut after breakfast, to weigh us and measure our fat thickness for his physiology program. We packed the sledges, making sure we had everything. We were to travel south to check there were no crevasse or other obstacles ahead. We felt sure we had left the last of the mountains at the Whichaways.

The dogs were fresh and excited and we left at 10.45 in a rush (Plate 48). They were almost uncontrollable. It took three others to help me hold my team. Within the first mile, I dropped my wad of letters delivered via Punta Arenas and to retrieve them had to turn my sledge over, as pickets could never have held the eager dogs. Ken also had trouble with his team, and soon changed his two lead dogs. Frequent collapses of hoar layers in the snow crust occurred over the first few miles and his leaders refused to run properly, creating a shambles. Ken moved Nannok and Erik to the rear, leaving Nunatak and Whitenose in front. His dogs now ran better, and in no time we had gone five miles,

48 Setting off with my eager dog team from South Ice. I was following Blaiklock's team. I needed help to control the dogs. Homard, D. Pratt, Fuchs, Stephenson and Lowe. (Photographer not known)

49 Ken Blaiklock building a snow-block cairn for the vehicles to follow our dog-team route.

as measured by our mileage wheel. We stopped, and with a saw and shovel cut snow blocks to build the first six-foot-high cairn with a flag on top, marking the route for the vehicles.

It was an overcast day, warm by Antarctic standards, and I skied beside the sledge, holding onto its end bars. I had no chance of keeping up otherwise. The soft lighting made the sastrugi hard to see and skiing was difficult. I fell over often. Making cairns every five miles (Plate 49), we stopped after 15 miles to erect our tent. We staked out the dogs, fed them, and after a welcome meal ourselves had our first uninterrupted sleep for some days. Next day, we travelled another 15 miles. It was Christmas Eve and we tried to talk with South Ice, only to experience silence, but on our pedal radio we were able to speak very clearly with the four RAF men still at Shackleton, in a happy, festive exchange. On Christmas Day we went through more fields of sastrugi, hard and sharply carved by the wind. They were to provide trouble for the vehicles following and they persisted, virtually to the Pole.

We had had quite a lot of snowfall at South Ice in September, forming a soft, relatively smooth surface. Then the winds returned to start shaping the soft snow into sastrugi. I saw how the previously soft snow began to set, like iron, by maturation and attachment of the adjacent snow grains, with the wind continuing to carve it. The sastrugi were irregular, up to four feet high and with local undercuts. Some undercuts were chisel-sharp, and a few had anvil-shaped ends which would sag as spectacular sculptures. The dogs were not impressed, and tended to take a line straight across a field of sastrugi, as if challenged like mountaineers, and the sledge would often overturn. About this time I had a moving experience with my oldest dog, Joe. He was surly and withdrawn, was known to snap, but always worked hard. He usually ignored my presence. Joe was unlike the other dogs, which were responsive, even affectionate. I like dogs, and perhaps because of our isolation, I became attached to them. They had such distinct personalities, like remembered friends.

As we ran along that morning, over and through the sastrugi, Joe suddenly started howling, obviously in extreme pain, dragged along by his harness. When I stopped the team with an 'Aaaah now' I went to investigate. I found his harness clip had dislodged and closed through one of his back leg sinews. I wondered

what to do, because Ken was well ahead and out of earshot. Though Joe was usually not responsive to my near presence I held him, and with complete trust he allowed me to wrestle with the clip to remove it without flinching. Finally it was done. He had not suffered any wound, and without any further ado let me reattach him to the main trace to resume work. The dogs became our close and trusted companions and colleagues. Many Antarctic travellers have written about their exceptional dogs, and Fuchs has some memorable anecdotes in his books. Under the 1991 Antarctic Protocol, dogs are now banned from Antarctica. Most experienced dog men were heartbroken by the ban. It is recorded that some dogs liked to hunt penguins and there was also concern that they might transfer distemper to seals. But if you found yourself in an increasingly heated argument with your fellow expeditioners at base, you could always go and have a chat with the dogs.

This run south from South Ice ahead of the vehicles involved Ken and me in private exploration, alone with our thoughts. Our responsibility was to recognise any potential problems for the vehicles, especially crevasses. We did not see anything untoward, except the fields of high sastrugi, and crossed mildly undulating country. In retrospect, we were enjoying our independent exploration, and I revelled in this, following Ken's team into the unknown. It was a wonderful privilege, though I didn't fully appreciate it until some years later. At the time, it was simply another part of the journey, which I took for granted, enjoying the journey and the brilliant weather. As I scrutinised the landscape ahead, there was nothing that seemed unusual. As we steadily advanced, I waited for changes in the topography as we very slowly gained altitude. Any changes were subtle, and the scene to east and west remained featureless. This was country no one had seen, even from a plane, and there was always a possibility we might see new nunataks. Earlier in the year the Otter made a short flight beyond South Ice, revealing that the plateau extended south, with no special features. Forty years later, radar satellite images were obtained which show that Recovery Glacier does have a southern tributary, which our air exploration had not reached. Had our route with the dogs been 60 miles further east, we might have encountered more challenges and crevasses, rather than the gently ascending plateau.

The eight vehicles left South Ice around 8 pm on Christmas Day to follow us. The Pole lay 555 miles ahead and the total vehicle load, mainly on sledges, was more than 25 tons. It comprised 44-gallon fuel drums, lubricants, tools and spares, seismic explosives, food and other gear and the vital tents. The South Ice hut had been scrubbed out and tidied, ready for the RAF group to occupy as a staging post on their Otter flight later, across the continent to Scott Base. The crossing party waited there, to listen to the Queen's Christmas Day Broadcast. She was TAE's Patron.

Over the following days, the vehicles followed our route, finding our prominent cairns, which were visible from several miles as 'shining white pillars' in the bright sunshine. For some distance south of South Ice, a series of undulations in the surface occurred, around four miles across with heights of 80 to 280 feet. Fuchs records the worst sastrugi were always on the northern slopes (Plate 50). Persisting coolant leaks in Hal's Weasel delayed its progress and David Pratt stayed with it in Able. Geoffrey and Hannes went ahead in Haywire to set up the next seismic station. The delayed vehicles caught up the next day, after replacing the Weasel's radiator. One of the Sno-Cats lost power, but Roy soon solved this problem and they reached our 55-mile cairn. The vehicles developed a routine — long, slow grinds through either sastrugi fields or soft snow; meteorology and gravity measurements every three hours; periodic drilling for Geoff Pratt's observations including his seismic soundings with explosive charges. There were also vehicle problems to be solved.

The vehicles reached our 100-mile cairn, and caught up with us on 29 December at 83°33'S, around 5800 feet. It was time for the regular vehicle maintenance, and several broken sledge tow bars needed electrical welding. Fuchs notes that the Sno-Cats tended to overheat with the increasing altitude. In a nice piece of serendipitous anticipation, vehicle overheating (in the Antarctic?) was seen as a possibility and David Pratt decided at the last minute to bring spare, larger fans for the Sno-Cats from London. A change from four- to six-blade fans proved helpful in some of the vehicles. The vehicle repairs allowed us to continue ahead with the dogs, and the vehicles followed on 31 December, after long tow-bar repairs.

They left the inefficient Muskeg at this camp. Soon, a sequence of problems held them up — some Weasel difficulties; Hal's rammsonde got stuck at three metres and had to be dug out; one of George's sledges broke a runner, and Allan's Weasel broke a track. There were no more spare tracks and the Weasel had to be abandoned. They went back to get the Muskeg, which was the first vehicle abandoned, because of fuel logistics. It was New Year's Eve, and Bunny did the rounds at midnight with tots of brandy for everyone to celebrate. The group travelled teetotal, and the spirits were, of course, strictly for medicinal purposes.

New Year's Day went well, with 39 miles travelled. The Muskeg could only travel at two or three mph in soft snow and one of its heavy sledges was transferred as a third sledge for the Sno-Cat, County of Kent, which towed it easily. The Muskeg, with one sledge, could then keep up at 5 mph. The next day travel was difficult through unending sastrugi. Fuchs notes how the Sno-Cats handled this better than the slower Weasels, but the rear sledges tended to swing and catch up to ram the vehicle or sledge ahead. By this time, Fuchs hoped to be well up onto the Polar Plateau and expected relatively easier going instead having to negotiate this seemingly endless sastrugi. The Muskeg was again abandoned, just south of 85°S, though still in good working condition. Fuel economies left us better off without it. It was left behind with an empty sledge and a pile of empty fuel drums. I had some affection for Hopalong, and at the last moment I took out one of its perspex side windows, on which I had drawn a kangaroo, and put it in my kit. David Pratt came to hear of my stupidity, and rightly chastised me — what if we had to return for it a second time? It might have become drifted up inside. So I chose not keep my souvenir.

Ken and I blissfully continued with the dogs and I was able to fully appreciate his considerable navigational skill. He always went first and followed a course using his sun-compass. This comprised a horizontal dial with a knob to turn its setting and a thin, central rod, which cast a shadow which had to be kept on a heading, set on the dial. Ken had a set of nicely printed azimuth cards for each day, which had been prepared in London, giving the direction of the sun every 10 minutes or so at various latitudes. The direction changed quite quickly as the sun wheeled around, and the heading had to be periodically adjusted. I was astonished to find our sun compass still had its RGS label tied to it, identifying it as one of Bagnold's. Geologically, I knew something of Bagnold, the desert explorer, his travels across the Sahara and his seminal scientific work, *The Physics of Blown Sand*. Hal was well aware of Bagnold, and that blown sand has some parallels with drift snow. At one point, our central, metal shadow-rod fell out and was lost; Ken immediately took a strand from the whiskbroom we used for sweeping out our tent, a standard sledging item. Improvisation! It was just the right size and he now had many spares.

One flawless day was memorable, and we travelled over some of the long undulations on the vast plateau. Ahead I could see a long hill, and the first striking topography since we left South Ice. When we reached the next point for a cairn, I looked back and there was our track, clearly visible in the sunlight. I could see more than 15 miles. Not only was the track straight, but the three cairns were also in line, thanks to Ken's expert navigation.

At this stage we were the pathfinders for the crossing party. It was a delightful time, by ourselves, pressing on into the mostly featureless landscape, which ran to the horizon in every direction, the skyline forming an unbroken line all around us. There were no crevasses, the undulations on the plateau were unobtrusive, and the sastrugi fields came and went. It was a sweet period in my life but I cannot recall where my thoughts took me. If I tried singing, the dogs would pause to look back, querying the noise. Ken always led with his dog team, and I simply followed. He always knew where we were and where we had to go.

Ken and I had little time on our hands, but we occasionally built a fancy cairn to amuse the vehicle party. With a saw and spade, it was easy to dig out quite large plates of snow, because of a weak layer a foot or so down. These plates made ideal cairn materials and we built one we called 'Snowhenge' (Plate 51). Ken surprised me when he mentioned that he could see one of the vehicles behind. I strained, jealous of his good eyesight, without being able to find it. We had binoculars, and when I sceptically searched the blank scene there was an orange Sno-Cat, many miles behind. It was Haywire, with Geoff and Hannes, stopping for another gravity reading.

The other vehicles also caught up with us later that day. Ken and I were relaxing in our tent when David Pratt strolled past. We passed the time of day and David started scrutinising our nearly empty food box, and saw an unmarked and unopened tin. 'Don't you want this?' 'No,' we said. 'Okay, can you lend me a tin opener?' It proved to be a tin of jam and David asked if he could borrow a spoon. He then proceeded to eat the whole tin, relishing every mouthful and followed with, 'You don't have any more jam, do you?' I was always aware of what I liked to eat. For instance, I enjoyed spoonfuls of butter on everything. This craving seemed to overwhelm other tastes, such my liking for sugar, though we consumed this too. I never lost my enjoyment of pemmican, night after night, and porridge each morning. We ate the traditional ship's biscuits for lunch, spread with butter and Marmite, with thermos cocoa. Frozen, the biscuits were a bit like a rock wafer. Chocolate was a delicacy, as was cocoa after dinner. We ate very well.

As we travelled from Shackleton and then beyond South Ice, we knew of Hillary's and his vehicle party's progress, on the other side of the Pole, many hundreds of miles from us. Each night, when Ken and I camped and prepared our meal, we would listen to the news on our radio, usually New Zealand or BBC world news. The world news was of passing interest, but it usually contained progress reports on TAE, which was coming to be an item of increasing interest, in Britain anyway. We were impressed that, almost every day, there would be a report on the New Zealand Party — how it had been progressing, now having reached and moved on from D700. It was apparently proceeding for the Pole itself. There was seldom any reliable news of Fuchs' party, and any news report seemed uncertain just where we were, let alone how fast we were moving. On one remarkable day, the news discussed three wide-ranging possibilities for our whereabouts, apparently disregarding the correct information supplied from the TAE London office. The circumstances encouraged some in the media to report that a 'race for the Pole' was in progress. Had such a race been declared, Hillary would certainly have won it.

It is interesting to recognise how this contrast in news of the two TAE parties, approaching the Pole from opposite sides, came about. Ed Hillary had an advantage

50 Bunny Fuchs standing on some mild sastrugi.

in relaying progress reports through Scott Base, as radio connection was usually successful. Hillary gave brief, clear, informative reports and it was obvious that he understood the importance of communication with the media and how to maintain his profile. He obviously believed that a nationally sponsored expedition was newsworthy, and perhaps he felt it was expected of him. Bunny Fuchs was a different personality. He distanced himself from publicity, and delayed his communication until there was firm progress and real prospects to report. Periodically, he would compose a careful report for transmission to London, which Ralph Lenton would endeavour to send. Often, this would take several hours, and might not get through until the next day. Ralph had a very strenuous and at times frustrating life.

Where did Ken and I stand? I suspect each of us was probably close to Bunny's philosophy. While we didn't know the full situation, we found ourselves increasingly irritated by the persistent Hillary reports. We welcomed his progress, but not the endless publicity. While we did not know Ed well, and in my case not at all, we were always ready to judge. Others were involved, especially George Lowe, Ed's close friend and best man, who had taken part on the Everest and other expeditions with him. This must have been a difficult time for George. He would have been well aware of the attitudes surrounding him. But there were more dramatic events about to occur for TAE, which Bunny described later as becoming a *cause célèbre*.

From here on, our dogs would be travelling with the vehicles towards the Pole, hard pressed not to delay their progress. The new company excited our gallant animals, but after several days trying to sustain 30 miles each day, they were showing increasing strain and exhaustion.

An ailment, by way of a gastric disorder, had been slowly working through the vehicle party. Perhaps it had been passed on to them when the Americans flew in to South Ice for their visit, just before Christmas.

51 'Snowhenge', a cairn for the vehicles following well behind us to chuckle over.

On the morning of 15 January, as Ken and I left with our dogs, Ken did not feel well. He was soon overwhelmed with vomiting, and George took over his dog team. I rested, relieved that I didn't feel affected. Suddenly, our two teams took an abrupt, uncontrollable left turn, to converge on a spot where one of the vehicles had paused for a call to nature. The dogs were always hungry and at any time were ready to seize on any waste. Their senses were acute, over hundreds of yards. The teams arrived simultaneously, and neither George nor I could control the ensuing collision. Abruptly, we had a quite magnificent dog 'mix-up', with snarling, snapping and fighting animals, their traces tangled and thoroughly intertwined. We bellowed abusive commands and for once resorted to using the whips, until a standstill was achieved and we were not getting bitten further ourselves. We then had

to slowly untangle the mess. It was my first experience of an all-in dog melee, and it was a matter of patiently pacifying and persuading dog after dog to let us unclip its harness, then rearrange the links, keeping the other 17 dogs at bay, snarling. I became aware I was not feeling well either, and by the time David Stratton had helped us with the last unravelling he had to take over my team, leaving me acutely ill, to travel supine in a vehicle. I felt annoyed at having to surrender my dogs. Fortunately Ken and I recovered quite quickly and reclaimed our dogs. So we all continued, vehicles and dogs, for the Pole. George and David must have felt reluctant to hand the dogs back to us.

From here on, the dogs would be travelling with the vehicles towards the Pole, still hard pressed not to delay our progress. They were eventually flown out from the Pole.

5 HILLARY'S DASH FOR THE POLE

By 15–18 December 1957 the NZ Party, with two dog teams and the Ferguson tractor party, had established the site for Depot 700 on the other side of the Pole. By 20 December, the Beaver had deposited the last of the fuel and food planned for Fuchs' crossing party.

The achievements of John Claydon's RNZAF Antarctic Flight for the NZ section of TAE cannot be overemphasised. The Beaver had flown supplies, equipment and personnel, seemingly endlessly, to set up depots at Skelton, Plateau, Cape Roberts, Darwin, D480, Mackay Glacier, Wigram and D700. Over 47 tons of freight was airlifted, involving more than 100 hours flying. Given the challenge of flying in Antarctica, this was a remarkable achievement.

At the time D700 was being completed, Fuchs' vehicles were about to reach South Ice. A distance of 1000 miles still separated the two parties across the Pole. The original planning for the crossing had anticipated that the southern exploration from Plateau Depot towards the Pole would mainly involve the dog teams, with the depots for the crossing party to be put in by the Beaver. Hillary and his men had brought their Fergusons all that distance, importantly confirming the route for vehicles. Now that these vehicles were at Depot 700, the question of what the NZ Ferguson tractor party should do now arose. On Fuchs' original plans, the crossing party had been expecting to reach the Pole by Christmas.

Hillary gives a full account of his journey.[1] Long before he climbed Everest, he had been excited reading the stories of expeditions to Antarctica, especially Shackleton's achievements. Early in the TAE planning, long before sailing from New Zealand, he had raised with the Ross Sea Committee the possibility of his party travelling as far as the Pole.[2] He kept this idea alive although, as he writes, 'obviously neither the Committee nor Bunny Fuchs took me seriously'.

After establishing Scott Base, he began to consider the best use of his resources. Initially, he would have considered ways of using the dog teams to reach the Pole, but he was also keen to evaluate the performance of his tractors. He tested and developed the vehicles, with growing resolve to use them on the journey south. He was originally impressed by their potential when he visited Jotunheimen in Norway, to evaluate vehicle performance with David Pratt and Bob Miller after their return on *Theron* in 1955. He baptised the tractors on the Cape Crozier journey from Scott Base at the end of the 1956–57 summer. Subsequently, Jim Bates and Murray Ellis prepared them for a real test, hauling across the ice shelf in the spring and then up the Skelton Glacier. These events, and then following the dog teams, had brought the three tractors to Depot 700 before Christmas.

After establishing Scott Base, Hillary began to draft plans for the next summer's activities. He refers to his 'bad psychology' in mentioning some of his plans to his Expedition Committee in New Zealand, especially its Executive. He soon experienced opposition to aspects of them, including the view that a trip to the Pole would be 'potentially spoiling Bunny's effort'.[3] His dilemma highlights the classic problems of having a committee in New Zealand, wanting to influence or try to control a forceful field leader. This was compounded by the existence of another committee in distant England, overseeing the entire expedition. The NZ committee advised Hillary to modify his plans, concentrate on laying the depots and then await Fuchs' arrival. Discouraged, Hillary informed his committee he was shelving his plans for the Pole.[4] He even mentioned a new project, namely to use the vehicles from Plateau Depot in a strike west towards the South Geomagnetic Pole. This was likely a smokescreen, and by early summer it had been quietly abandoned for the original Pole idea. The committee documents, cited by Helm and Miller, reveal how events evolved. Hillary never again made the mistake of suggesting a journey to the Pole until he was in position to execute it from D700.[5] I believe that a central facet of Hillary's personality has always been to delight in achieving the unexpected and/or impossible. He was not a fan of exploration with dogs, but wanted to confirm his humble tractor's performance in an exciting new challenge, with the Pole the ultimate pinnacle. A 'push' from D700 had been in gestation in Hillary's mind for over a year. Interestingly, Bates and Ellis, his two mechanics, were not as convinced as was their leader, as they recognised the vehicles were showing significant wear and feared they might not hold out. There were no such reservations from the optimistic Mulgrew.

Having reached D700 and seen it established, Hillary could assure himself he had performed all his TAE obligations. He had established a route for vehicles across the Ross Ice Shelf, up the Skelton Glacier and from Plateau Depot to D700. The NZ TAE had three dog-team parties, well positioned to continue their independent travel and exploration, and John Claydon's very impressive RNZAF team could operate as far as D700. Hillary could justly feel he had done all that had been asked of him.

However, just what other possibilities were there for him? I believe there were six alternatives:

+ Wait at D700 for Fuchs' party. This would have involved about seven weeks. Waiting, even for shorter periods, can be soul-destroying if no projects are to be undertaken.
+ Make a short journey to the east, to support Miller and Marsh's survey exploration with their two dog teams, by establishing a depot 100 miles out. Hillary said he did not have the vehicle fuel to do this and he arranged Beaver flight support for the party.
+ Undertake exploration to the west, to confirm the possible existence of unknown mountains, which are perhaps the source of the heavy, katabatic winds. Mawson had experienced these winds in Adélie Land, west of the Ross Sea. The distance would have been limited; we now know there are no such mountains.
+ Return to Scott Base by air, to await Fuchs' progress and be on standby to assist if the Fuchs party had problems. There were no projects planned from Scott Base.
+ Continue a few hundred miles towards the Pole to confirm there were no further zones of crevasses. There certainly were more crevasses to be negotiated.
+ Continue on to the Pole itself.

Hillary has never been one to wait around with nothing to do, and it was already five days since he had arrived at D700. When the last Beaver freight flight was concluded, he set off south. His four companions were Mulgrew, Ellis, Bates and Wright. The photographer, Derek Wright, had replaced the journalist, Doug McKenzie, who had driven from D480 to D700 but decided not to continue. The day he left D700, Hillary sent a telegram to his NZ Committee advising them of the depot completion and of his intention of travelling further south. Replies ensued, first stating, 'Meanwhile you should not proceed beyond Depot 700', and next, raising various questions, including the necessity for Fuchs' approval as 'Commander in the Field'. The London Committee stated they 'were happy to fall in with any modification of original plans which is agreed between Fuchs and yourself'.

Hillary had also sent a communication to Fuchs, confirming all was in place for the crossing party, as requested, and that he was checking crevasses further south. Was there anything else he could do to help the crossing party? He offered to: 'scrub southward jaunt if vehicles and fuel can be used in any way to expedite your safe crossing either by a further depot or anything else you suggest'.[6]

This almost seems to invite a direction from Fuchs, but Hillary states that he was startled by Fuchs' urgent reply, on 27 December, the day he left South Ice. Fuchs expressed concern over his vehicles and his fuel consumption.

> Am in difficult position of feeling I must accept your offer to clear present crevasse area then establish additional fuel depot at appropriate position from D700 thus abandoning your idea of reaching Pole. Know this will be a great disappointment to you and your companions but the additional depot will enormously strengthen the position of the crossing party which cannot afford at present to deviate from the direct route...[7]

By the time communication was continued, Hillary sent a reply: 'Your message has arrived too late as we are now 240 miles from the Pole with only 10 drums left. Have neither the food nor fuel to sit here and await your arrival.'[8] Radio communication can be uncertain in Antarctica and messages anywhere can sometimes be ignored, as Nelson showed at the Battle of Trafalgar.

Hillary's vehicles continued, cleared the last crevasse belt and continued to the Pole, moving though the 'night', as far as their time was concerned. This made navigation easier with the sun ahead, using the astro compass. They also hoped the surfaces might be better at night. Travelling was strenuous, with two drivers spelled in the caboose while the other three drove. The vehicles struggled, digging down in soft snow and barely able to keep going. They experimented with every vehicle and sledge combination they could think of to overcome this problem, and Hillary records the best arrangement involved the three vehicles connected by strong terylene rope, so that each tractor broke its own trail, achieving the best traction, with the caboose and two sledges attached behind the last tractor.

They entered a region of light wind towards the Pole, which both Amundsen and Scott had noted, with smooth surfaces and very soft snow. Hillary did not want to abandon a vehicle in case they suffered a crevasse collapse. In spite of their concerns that the vehicles were wearing out, Bates and Ellis managed to keep them going. Hillary worried over the inaccuracy of his bubble-sextant navigation as the bubble had been getting larger, either from fluid leakage or evaporation. He found he could not get a more precise position than two to four miles, providing the sun remained visible. There was no leeway with the fuel; if they missed the Pole, the party would have been reduced to manhauling their emergency sledge. This situation inspired the title for his book, *No Latitude for Error*. Eventually, when progress became desperate — six miles in six hours and with fuel shrinking — they jettisoned everything that was surplus, including the sledge. When they were 10 miles from the Pole, Hillary was greatly relieved to see a distant flag. Next morning, the two American leaders, Vernon Houk and Paul Mogesson, drove out in a Weasel from the Pole Station to meet them and offer hospitality. Hillary had only 20 gallons of fuel left; it was a close call. They arrived at the Pole on 4 January 1958.

For the Americans, the sight of Hillary and his team, with their three Ferguson tractors and a caboose, must have seemed bizarre, given the Americans' sophisticated technical and transport facilities. They had Sno-Cats and large D9 tractors at McMurdo. Hillary and his men must have savoured the moment — a wonderfully impossible achievement. Hillary was the only one of the five men who had driven the full 1250-mile journey. Both Ellis and Mulgrew had sustained injuries, were temporarily flown out and therefore missed part of the journey. Bates had not joined the group until Skelton Depot and Wright at D700. The journey had been severe and all lost weight, except the wiry Jim Bates. Hillary, a tall man, had lost 35 pounds (16 kg) to be only 165 pounds (75 kg). Mulgrew told me Hillary had modified his diet, because he had difficulty digesting pemmican, the core of traditional sledging rations. He substituted bacon and powdered egg. The stress must have weighed heavily on him, and the day before reaching the Pole he sent Fuchs a controversial message expressing concern over the lateness of the crossing party, urging him to consider wintering his vehicles at the Pole and return to complete the journey the following summer.

Hillary and three of his team flew back to Scott Base a few days later. Peter Mulgrew remained at the Pole, to provide a radio link with the crossing party. The day after their return, the TAE Otter made a flight across the continent from South Ice via the Pole, arriving at Scott Base on 6 January. The Otter was the first single-engine aeroplane to fly non-stop across Antarctica.

But suddenly, TAE became a *cause célèbre*, and the international press fed on what was seen as a sensational dispute between Hillary and Fuchs.

THE CAUSE CÉLÈBRE

Inadvertently, the message that he sent to Fuchs the day before Hillary reached the Pole was released to the press in Wellington. The circumstances leading to this are described in Helm and Miller.[9] Fuchs replied, and the full texts of the two messages are as follows:

Hillary to Fuchs (2 January, GMT, 1958):

Dear Bunny, I am very concerned about the serious delay in your plans. It's about 1,250 miles from the Pole to Scott Base, much of the travelling north from D700 being somewhat slow and laborious, with rough hard sastrugi. Leaving the Pole late in January, you will head into increasing bad weather and winter temperatures, plus vehicles that are showing signs of strain. Both of my mechanics regard such a late journey as an unjustifiable risk and are not prepared to wait and travel with your party. I agree with their view and think you should seriously consider splitting your journey over two years. You will probably have a major journey in front of you to reach the Pole. Why not winter your vehicles at the Pole, fly out to Scott Base with American aircraft, return to civilisation for the winter and then fly back into the Pole station next November and complete your journey? This plan would enable you to do a far more satisfactory job of your scientific work, and I feel fairly confident that Admiral Dufek would assist with such a flying programme. Personally I feel the need for a break from the plateau after nearly four months of tractor travel, and there's a lot to do. I prefer not to wait at the pole station, but will get evacuated to Scott Base as soon as possible. If you decide to continue on from the Pole, I'll join you at D700. Sorry to strike such a sombre note, but it would be unfortunate if the sterling work you've put into making your route through to South Ice and the Pole should all be wasted by the party foundering somewhere on the 1250 miles to Scott Base. I will go ahead with the stocking of D700, and I will leave at the Pole station full details plus maps of the route from Scott to the Pole.

Fuchs to Hillary, Pole Station (3 January, GMT):

Appreciate your concern, but there can be no question of abandoning journey at this stage. Innumerable reasons make it impracticable to remount the expedition after wintering outside Antarctic. Our vehicles can be, and have operated at minus 60 but I do not expect such temperatures by March. Whiteout and drift will be our chief concern. I understand your mechanics' reluctance to undertake further travel, and in view of your opinion that late season travel is an unjustifiable risk I do not feel able to ask you to join us at D700, in spite of your valuable local knowledge. We will therefore have to wend our way, using the traverse you leave at the Pole. The present field of giant sastrugi has extended 57 miles so far, and continues with ridges up to 4 ft. Are we to expect similar fields north of D700, and approximately how many miles *in toto*? Main damage is to sledge tow bars, which have been electrically welded causing delay. Am shortly abandoning second vehicle as planned, leaving us 4 cats 2 weasels. Max interval seismic stations 30 miles, gravity stations 15 miles, rammsonde once or twice daily, meteorology includes fluxplate and radiation measure-ments. Present position 83°43'S. Altitude 7,000 ft. Bunny.[10]

The media response to this 'scoop' was instantaneous, and a wide range of 'expert' advice was quickly generated. Fuchs' answer was concise and final. He called us together before we set off that morning, told us simply of Hillary's suggestion and of his own decision and reply. He would have discussed it with David Stratton and perhaps with others, but for most of us it was a surprise. My personal reaction was one of disappointment that it had not been discussed.

But how could Fuchs have done anything else? TAE was strapped for money. How would we get out from the Pole, where would we have waited, and what would we have done for nine months?

A few years before he died, Fuchs recorded a video discussion with Charles Swithinbank, for the Scott Polar Research Institute. This contained remarkable recollections and comments, including Hillary's wintering suggestion and Fuchs' response. Fuchs said the group discussed it; as I have said, my recollection is that it was not discussed, but we would clearly have agreed with Fuchs' decision.

The furore was to follow. The media, including the international press, became interested in TAE, especially with the regular Hillary news and the contrasting Fuchs silence. The press had been quick to promote a race to the Pole between Hillary, the heroic conqueror of Everest, and the little-known, publicity-shy Fuchs. This sells newspapers, but this was a non-event as far as the two parties were concerned.

The press reporting of TAE had another interesting side. Antarctica was generally seen as inaccessible, and the official TAE news releases were distributed through *The Times* until Noel Barber (*London Daily Mail*) succeeded in flying to McMurdo with the Americans.[11] He soon managed to visit the Pole Station and succeeded in getting access to the radio messages Fuchs was sending to Hillary via the Pole, every few days. On 16 December, he listened in on a radio contact the Pole made with Fuchs' party, who were at that time negotiating the Ice Wall west of the Shackleton Range. He found he was able to have a conversation with Ralph Lenton, our radio officer. Barber was careful not to seek an interview with Fuchs, but did obtain a scoop about progress and conditions from Ralph, to the delight of his newspaper in London.

This led to a request, perhaps from Admiral Dufek, overall commander of the US Antarctic field program, to the Pole Station Commander to withhold from the press all information sent via the Pole about the expedition's position. He commented: 'It is not my policy to withhold non-classified information from the Press. Request you inform Dr Fuchs and Sir Edmund Hillary not to send information to American stations, which they do not wish to be made available to the Press.'[12] Barber chose to return to McMurdo, but flew back to the Pole Station for Christmas, having become almost an honorary guest there, and stayed on for Hillary's arrival on 4 January. Barber's account of his three months in Antarctica in *The White Desert* is entertaining, though careless over some expedition details.

When Hillary arrived, Barber was the only British reporter among four journalists, and he saw the three tractors meet the Pole Station's Weasel in the distance, which then left them to drive in alone which Barber noted as 'a very pleasing gesture'.[13] As stated previously, shortly before Hillary reached the Pole, his analysis of Fuchs' slow progress led him to suggest to Fuchs postponing the completion of the crossing journey until the next summer. When the exchanged messages were leaked to Barber, he commented, 'Now Fuchs *has* to go on'.[14]

THE CROSSING PARTY REACHES THE POLE

Meanwhile, Ken and I continued with our dogs keeping pace with the vehicles, day by day, with successive runs of 30 miles, strenuous for them. Hal Lister's Weasel was abandoned at 88°S, leaking oil increasingly, having broken four U bolts, and with a terminally ill big-end. The five surviving vehicles, the four Cats and a Weasel, were still hauling 22 tons between them.

We pressed on, and on 17 December were close to 89°S. Two American planes flew over us early that morning, late in their afternoon, and Ralph scrambled to the radio in County of Kent to speak with them. The planes were carrying Admiral Dufek, Ed Hillary, our own John Lewis and, to Bunny's surprise, nine reporters. That night we were only 26 miles from the Pole and had emerged from the troublesome sastrugi.

Our dogs were very tired, even dispirited, and were lean and hungry. Their daily food consisted of a one pound block of dog pemmican. They needed more. In hindsight, it should have been a pound and a half. One of my dogs, a likeable rogue called Bouncer, had a neat way of slipping his harness. About this time, he discovered a box of 'man' pemmican on one of the sledges. Bouncer must have eaten several of the one-pound bars, and had not thought to share any with his mates! We enjoyed an airdrop of fresh food, including a cooked steak. I ate mine immediately, but Ken kept his for later. Unfortunately for Ken, Bouncer found it and ate it before Ken could stop him. Ken's rage was profound.

Geoffrey Pratt was continuing with his seismic soundings and, that night, found the rock surface beneath us had risen abruptly to within about 2000 feet of the surface. It had been much deeper, even to 6000 feet. We started our last day to the Pole, and with David Stratton's navigation, sighted some buildings and radio masts ahead. They looked deceptively close, but we needed to turn east so as to approach along the 24° meridian, at the request of the American glaciologist, who had reserved a sector for a snow accumulation project. A line of flags marked the route.

My dogs were increasingly unhappy and I had difficulty keeping them moving, even though my sledge was now almost empty. They must have felt they had completed a marathon journey. Bouncer was quite reluctant to do much more than walk — indigestion, perhaps? Quite suddenly, the other dogs started acting as if they wanted to eat him. Some concerned dog-lovers picked him up and carried him in their Sno-Cat.

We turned in along the flag line to receive an enthusiastic welcome. It was 19 January 1958. Griff Pugh, a research physiologist, was one of several who were at the Pole to meet us. I certainly knew who he was; he had been on the successful Everest expedition. He had a go at driving my dog team, which he did fluently, using my slip-on skis. Griff had been a British ski Olympian. My dogs seemed to wake up and excitedly ran in, with the moving 'show' to where they could relax (Plate 52). The welcome involved dozens of people, including numerous journalists, in addition to the station personnel. It was a big party, but our dogs were a bit behind, so I missed the historic Fuchs–Hillary welcome handshake (Plate 53).

Hillary must have been dismayed over the recent TAE controversy. Apparently, he had indicated to Dufek that he thought it best not to be at the Pole to meet Fuchs. Dufek may have said that to not be there would be interpreted as a rift between the two men. Noel Barber and Doug McKenzie both refer to this in their books about TAE, describing the social evening on the eve of their flight up to the Pole, when Dufek suggested as Ed was leaving, 'Let's fly up together'.[15] Hillary's Ferguson vehicles created considerable interest among the visitors. A photo shows Peter Mulgrew standing next to the caboose (Plate 54).

The clocks at the Pole Station were starting a new day on NZ time, 20 January, while ours showed it was late the previous day, on GMT. There was a welcoming meal and Fuchs spoke, confirming that there was no question of our not continuing after a few days' rest and the inevitable repairs on the vehicles. Bunny was in his element, wearing clean clothes, red moccasins and a white rollneck sweater. He looked impressively fit, his pointed beared trimmed, and he spoke with impressive dignity. I was thrilled to be there as a member of his team. Eventually, when it was evening, Pole time, our hosts insisted we continue to eat their meals and then sleep in the accommodation they provided. We had mail, which was marvellous, and we read the letters several times. George Lowe gave a whoop of delight to find he had received a final tax notice. It had been a long day, with most of us awake for more than 24 hours, drifting from GMT into

New Zealand time. It all became rather hazy, and I was glad to settle into the large, inflated sleeping tent which had a heater stove. I was enjoying deep sleep in an American sleeping bag on a stretcher bed when the heating went off and we woke in the piercing polar cold. Perhaps our tent would have been more comfortable.

The next few days were also a bit hazy but we had a group photo taken (Plate 55). Topography at the Pole is not very interesting, consisting of a level horizon and a featureless snow plateau in all directions. The sun was at a low elevation above the horizon, and simply moved slowly around at the same height all day, winding around through the meridians, which all extended north. The buildings had low profiles, largely buried by snow. One had a tunnel under it, leading to the entrance to the main station buildings beneath the surface. There was a dome and another instrument building with smaller domes, and some radio masts.

I met and got to know some of the scientists and got everyone's signature. The majority seemed to have European forbears, with few Anglo-Saxon names. Mario Giovannetto, one of the glaciologists, was from Argentina. Passionately, he told me almost unbelievable horror accounts of what had been happening in Buenos Aires under Peron, some of it affecting his own family. Paul Dalrymple was the senior meteorologist, and his work was especially relevant to Hal Lister's research efforts at South Ice. Hal must have felt envious of the extensive American instrumentation. For example, there were numerous anemometers and Dalrymple could measure wind speeds simultaneously at many different heights. Hal had only four such instruments and had to try combining different measurements to complete a speed–height profile.

My expedition clothing intrigued Paul. I admired some of his, and he insisted on giving me a pair of his outdoor gloves, well lined, easily pulled on and off, and with draw straps you could tighten or release with your teeth. The gloves had a band of fur across their leather backs, useful for wiping the ice drip from your nose. Later, Bunny saw me wearing them and asked me where I got them. He responded by defending our equipment, emphasising how carefully designed our gloves were, based on extensive British experience.

52 Some of my dogs near the Pole. Gamle and Joe, of the described dog-clip injury.

53 Admiral George Dufek (US) and Ed Hillary greet Bunny Fuchs on our arrival at the Pole. (Photographer George Lowe)

54 Peter Mulgrew (NZ TAE) standing next to one of Ed Hillary's Ferguson tractors at the Pole, with the green caboose.

While I found the American gloves better than ours, all our other gear had proved to be adequate in many demanding circumstances. Our expedition gloves had a tendency to admit drift snow at the wrists. When you took them off they froze and it was a struggle to get them on again, which was how I experienced wrist and finger frostbite on our Whichaway adventure in March. Seemingly minor details can take on increased significance on a long and testing journey.

It was momentous for us to have reached this historic place. Ken and I had arrived with the only dog teams to reach the Pole since Amundsen's in 1912, 46 years earlier. Scott and his four companions spent two days here, after the profound disappointment of finding the Norwegian's black tent and the letter for his King. Amundsen had left a message for Scott in the black tent, but naturally the tent had long gone before Admiral Dufek landed in 1956 in the first US plane at the Pole. The US planes returned to build the Amundsen-Scott Base in preparation for IGY, and when we arrived the station was already manned for its second year. I confess that in looking around the Pole and its surroundings, I felt no deep sense of place or history, apart from a realisation that the historic South Pole is nothing more than the ultimate point in south latitude. I felt swamped by all the strangers and by the large, busy station with a different style and culture from those to which I was accustomed.

55 The crossing party at the Pole: David Pratt, Hal Lister, Bunny Fuchs, Ralph Lenton, Allan Rogers, Geoffrey Pratt, Ken Blaiklock, David Stratton, Hannes la Grange, George Lowe, Jon Stephenson, Roy Homard.

There was nothing for me at the Pole and I soon felt like a bored tourist. Two flagpoles and a circle of drums marked the Pole itself. We were urged to walk around the circle of drums, to confirm we had walked around the world. We were all presented with a certificate confirming this, even giving the arbitrary time we had taken to do it. I found out about some of the science in progress, and walked part way down into their 'snow-mine', an inclined excavation providing a clean snow supply for their water and a profile for the glaciologists. Their water tank steadily accumulated a sludge along its bottom, which proved to be micrometeorites. These very fine glass spheres result from meteorite impacts somewhere on earth, and fall as dust from the atmosphere. There was a record player with some hundreds of classical LPs. I listened to a few, but found them unable to lift my mood. They had a cinema with several shows each week, but I missed these. There was provision for 'the big eye', their term for insomnia, so that anyone afflicted could watch a movie at virtually any time. The Americans were intrigued by our 'basic', uninsulated vehicles and intrigued that we apparently slept at night on the snow, in tents. One chap marvelled that we did not have a coffee urn going non-stop in the back of a vehicle. How ever did we manage? The Pole Station meals were interesting and different, and the maple syrup on pancakes was delicious. The chef, Chet Segers, had worked at the Waldorf. I was amazed; here he was at the Pole, for a whole year.

The visiting VIPs and journalists set out to return to McMurdo and we watched successive attempts by their Neptune aircraft to take off. At the Pole's altitude, 10,500 feet, take-off needs to be jet-assisted. Sixteen jet-assisted take-off (JATO) bottles were fired in bursts when the aircraft reached its maximum speed along the runway. In the distant roar, the receding aircraft would disappear behind a snow cloud and we watched, waiting to see if it had staggered into the air. Not all the firing circuits functioned properly and the two take-off attempts were unsuccessful, the second after having reduced the load. All very dramatic! More JATO bottles had to be flown up from McMurdo, and the two aircraft finally took off early the next morning, each with half the load of visitors. The logistics for the journalists' visit were considerable, and expensive.

Our vehicle work continued, involving welding of broken tow bars and repairing battery heaters. A welder was set-up on our Sno-Cat, Haywire, which was driven into the Pole Station's workshop. David and Roy worked through several nights to complete the work. Geoffrey also fired off several seismic shots, to obtain his interpretation of ice thickness at this unique locality and compare his results with recent measurements by seismologist Father Daniel Linehan, an American Jesuit. In *Innocents on the Ice*, John Behrendt notes that neither measurement was really satisfactory,[16] and the Russians first achieved definitive results, several years later, on a South Pole traverse led by Andrei Kapitsa. Geoffrey's published result was a thickness of 1990 metres (6529 feet). Kapitsa's result was considerably deeper: 2830 ± 75 metres (John Behrendt, personal communication).

We spent four days at the Pole and left in the late afternoon of 24 January 1958. We noted that Scott had left on 19 January 1912. Scott Base was 1250 miles ahead and Shackleton 900 miles behind.

The dogs were left at the Pole, being too slow to come with us, and the Americans kindly agreed to airlift them back to Scott Base. This proved an expensive enterprise. It took them several flights because of weather, and an emergency landing and retrieval on one flight. They ended up travelling in style in a Neptune, instead of a Dakota. When they reached Scott Base, Hillary decided either that some of them were in such bad shape they were not worth saving, or that feeding all of them was beyond the resources of the base. Sadly, he had a number put down. Later, when Ken and I flew to Scott to get seal meat for them for the winter, about a dozen of our 'special friends' were still alive. I am sure every dog would have recovered, given meals of seal meat.

I learned that one dog stayed on at the Pole, slipping his harness when the dogs were being loaded on the plane for McMurdo. I would have suspected that it was our old rogue, the now well-fed, resourceful Bouncer. However, Doug McKenzie refers to the dog left behind as Beauty. Paul Dalrymple later told me the dog was female and became his close associate. There was already a dog at the station and the station commander decreed that the TAE dog was to be shot. Beauty was a survivor, and eluded a vehicle chase across the Polar Plateau until the pistol's action froze. She came to trust Paul and got into the habit of sleeping in his hut, shared with Mario Giovinetto, rested in Paul's office and visited his field instruments with him. Mario apparently put up with the dog's habit of eating his shower-thongs. When Dalrymple flew out at the end of the winter, he planned to take Beauty with him, but the pilot had his own German Shepherd on the plane and refused Beauty a passage, so the dog spent a second winter at South Pole. Her later adventures are unknown.

The goodwill, generosity and patience of our friendly American hosts at the Pole were impressive. But towards the end of our time there, I sensed we had outstayed our welcome; the station men had busy routines, scientific and otherwise. In the whole course of the TAE expedition, the Americans did a succession of generous favours for us.

The Otter flew non-stop across from South Ice to Scott Base on 6 January, with the four men making up Fuchs' RAF contingent. This pioneering flight is described later in this chapter. An additional stocking of D700 took place on 16 January, when the Otter and Beaver brought eight drums of fuel to the depot for Fuchs' vehicle party.

THE CROSSING JOURNEY: SOUTH POLE TO DEPOT 700

The final section of the crossing route is shown in Figure 19. We left the Pole Station on 24 January 1958, two months after leaving Shackleton. We were still less than halfway on the crossing journey, but we were to follow Hillary's proven tractor route and Fuchs expected to make much faster progress. Winter was approaching, but Fuchs had no concerns that we would experience severe low temperatures, such as below -40°F.

Hillary predicted the weather would get worse in the next few months, with rising winds, drift, and more frequent whiteouts. Fortunately, these conditions did not eventuate. He was to join us at D700 and guide us to Scott Base. Navigation without sun in whiteout, which we occasionally experienced, is a problem, but initially we could still navigate with a compass.

The South Magnetic Pole was still about 1250 miles (2000 km) from us when we left the Pole, but as we travelled north, the compass became progressively weaker

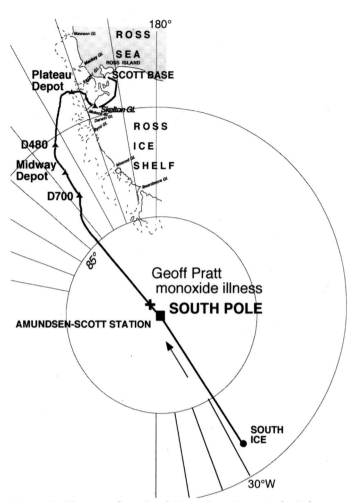

Figure 19 The route from South Ice to Scott Base via the Pole.

and eventually proved hopeless in a moving vehicle.

Without our dogs, Ken Blaiklock and I felt demoted and dislocated, and travelled in the back of the Sno-Cat, County of Kent, driven by Roy Homard and Ralph Lenton. It was not the easiest way to travel, because the back was neither insulated nor heated. We travelled lying down in our sleeping bags. Reading a book was difficult, but we could peer ahead through the windscreen. There were stops, vehicle breakdowns, and the usual crevasses to investigate and some unplanned incidents. Ken and I felt frustrated and, not surprisingly, our thoughts often turned to life after TAE. We started hatching plans for a private expedition and discussed our ideas with Bunny, who was very encouraging. We wrote a carefully worded letter to Admiral Dufek, outlining our ideas for an expedition in the 1958–69 summer, using the TAE dogs. We suggested the Horlick Mountains and asked for American air support to get there from McMurdo. The idea, growing in our minds, was a welcome diversion, and helped keep boredom at bay. The prospect of our own, small-scale expedition excited my imagination, as I'm sure it did with Ken. Although Dufek later replied courteously and encouragingly, American logistic support could not be provided and this scuttled our plans, even though we raised finance in London.

Geoff Pratt's Poisoning

The vehicles progressed 100 miles in three days, and Geoffrey Pratt continued his seismic and gravity measurements. But, on 28 January, about 140 miles from the Pole, he collapsed at the back of his Sno-Cat while preparing for another sounding. He was pink in the face and twitching. Allan Rogers quickly saw he was suffering from carbon monoxide poisoning, and revived him using the medicinal oxygen from a cylinder used in welding. The oxygen we carried would only serve for five hours, and at 10,000 feet his recovery might be slow. It was urgent that either he be evacuated to sea level, or more oxygen be flown in. We were at the extreme range of the Otter, so using it to drop more oxygen cylinders was dangerous. If it were to land, it couldn't take off at this altitude. Fuchs asked Hillary to approach the Americans for help, to which Dufek immediately responded.

Two Neptune aircraft left McMurdo with oxygen cylinders. Meanwhile, Geoffrey was made comfortable in the back of a Cat, but wanted someone to complete his geophysical measurements. The vehicles travelled on, awaiting the arrival of the Neptunes, which reached us after we had travelled 10 miles. The weather had changed to completely overcast. The US Navy pilots, Captain Coley and Lieutenant Cook, flew straight to us — fine navigation, guided by our Sarah beacon — and then decreased altitude to circle us, below low cloud. On board was Dr Griff Pugh of the British Medical Council. He was undertaking a summer research program with the Americans, and had previously specialised in monoxide poisoning. Pugh and Rogers discussed the state of the patient over the radio, and the planes then dropped two large oxygen cylinders by parachute, with facemasks. Geoffrey was given oxygen as he lay in the back of a Sno-Cat and recovered quickly. He was able to resume his research two days later. In the meantime, Rogers, Lowe and Lister undertook all his measurements. The monoxide, which had affected Geoffrey in the driving cabin, came from a slow exhaust leak into the heating system.

Our last remaining Weasel, Wrack and Ruin, had engine trouble, involving frequent vapour locks, and was towed to the next campsite. It was repairable, but was abandoned near 87°S. It was no longer needed, given the reduced loads, and its stores were transferred to the remaining vehicles. Each abandoned vehicle had a fine tool set, which some of us could not resist trying to add to our personal gear. David and Roy got wise to this, and took to burying the tools to avoid carrying the extra weight. On the last day of January, the vehicles traversed 70 miles, a record run, and Fuchs noted that for the first time it was possible to use top gear on much easier surfaces. However, a series of mechanical problems developed with the Sno-Cats, and tested the skills and patience of David and Roy in carrying out repairs to pontoon bearings and loose vehicle tracks.

In spite of sastrugi, the fuel consumption was improving on the harder surfaces, and fuel was no longer a worry for the party. On 5 February, Fuchs believed he had passed the crevasse belt reported by Hillary, but around 8 pm we reached a crevasse belt which continued for several miles. We camped and next morning, and after a long search for better ground, crossed the first, wide crevasse.

Some of these crevasses were the largest on the whole journey. They had broad, sunken bridges and remarkable parallel sides, which seemed to extend beyond the horizon. We followed one for several miles and its appearance did not change. Probing of the edges did not reveal any sinister, concealed canyons, and a crossing point for the first crevasse was finally chosen, where hard sastrugi ridges led across the near edge. I watched from a distance as Fuchs drove across and was struck by the width of the depression he was negotiating — considerably more than the length of the Cat and its sledges. Fuchs refers to widths up to 75 feet and I could see that if the whole bridge collapsed, everything would drop in. Fortunately, nothing happened! Twenty-five miles further on, a small crevasse gave trouble, which resulted in Rock 'n Roll cracking its large, cast-aluminium rear steering platform. Roy and Ralph spent several hours strengthening it with timber and rope. Another of the Cats, Able, broke a steering arm pin and a new one had to be fitted, so two Cats went on ahead. This small, troublesome crevasse proved to be part of another field of parallel crevasses with thin bridges, and was judged impossible to cross. Fuchs decided to follow the edge of the crevasse field towards the south-east, hoping to find where Hillary's tractors had got through and marked the way with snow cairns. He followed the first crevasse for six miles without finding Hillary's cairns. Next morning they found that the bridges there were stronger. Making use of drift ridges, the vehicles crossed successive crevasses safely, leaving flags marking the way for us to follow, still well behind. Fuchs records having to cross 19 crevasses. Eventually, the vehicles all arrived at D700 late on 7 February, having travelled the 521 miles from the Pole in 15 days. This was the same time it had taken Hillary with his tractors.

Hillary was to join us here, which he did in the Beaver two days later. Fuchs records that 405 gallons of fuel were pumped into the vehicle tanks, and the empty drums on the sledges were refilled. One of my recollections at D700 was Fuchs' silent fury when he scrutinised the fuel drums in the depot, established by many Beaver flights. There were some dark olive green drums, which were not our usual BP drums. Bunny said that on no account was fuel from the American olive green drums to be used. Presumably, they are still at the depot. They must have been put in on the last joint Otter–Beaver flight. This was one of the few occasions I saw Bunny angry. I have mentioned previously that he wanted to avoid seeking assistance from the US. I do not know the background for this — perhaps it stemmed from the time when he was working hard to get the expedition started and encountered opposition to his plans for a crossing expedition. At that time, someone suggested that he should 'Leave a crossing to the Americans'.

We took on new food boxes, including many extras at D700, with chocolate, dates and raisins, which were most welcome.

OTHER TAE ACTIVITIES

The Otter Flight Across the Continent

The four-man RAF group saw us off from Shackleton, and as we journeyed up to South Ice, provided regular support during the vehicles' slow progress through the crevassed sections. Their flight across the continent is well described in Fuchs and Hillary's *The Crossing of Antarctica*, and a summary account is included here. It was a noteworthy achievement in a single-engine aircraft, and not without drama.

The group had first to make arrangements for the Auster to be shipped back to England on *Tottan*, the Royal Society's supply vessel, due to revisit Halley Bay later in the summer. The Otter and Auster flew to Halley Bay, with Peter Weston and two Halley men, Ivor Beney and Fred Morris, who had helped at Shackleton and South Ice during the last weeks of preparation for the crossing journey. Taffy Williams stayed behind alone at Shackleton, to maintain radio contacts. At Halley Bay, the RAF men spent four days dismantling the Auster for shipment, and crating all the equipment and records to be taken to England, including my geological collections. They flew back to Shackleton in the Otter on 14 December and continued with the preparations necessary to close down the base. Shackleton Base, first occupied by two of the Advance Party in August 1956, had been a comfortable home for the expedition.

The four RAF men were also preparing the Otter for its long flight to Scott Base. The work of closing down Shackleton was considerable — it needed to be left clean and secure, for possible reoccupation should the crossing party be forced back.

The Otter would fly, unsupported, from South Ice, via the Pole, to Scott Base. There was little room for emergency: the plane could not seek assistance at the only occupied station on the route, the American Pole Station, because it would be unable to take off again on account of the altitude. Peter Weston thoroughly overhauled the Otter and fitted an auxiliary fuel tank inside. This provided a total of 356 gallons, doubling the range of the plane to 1600 miles. The flying distance from South Ice to Scott Base was somewhat more than 1400 miles. Good navigation, good weather and flying conditions were therefore vital. The plane's payload was only one ton, and the four men all had to wear relatively heavy clothing. The plane also had to carry emergency gear — tents, survival rations, cooking equipment and fuel. They set out to minimise packaging by using plastic bags, and everything was carefully weighed.

They waited to take off until the crossing party had left South Ice and travelled 50 miles. They passed their first test, getting off the ground at Shackleton, on 27 December. It was a fine day, but they needed 300 yards to take off in warm conditions, with little wind and a tacky surface. The three-hour flight to South Ice was completed without incident and, on landing, the gear was unloaded for staying at South Ice. The base had been left clean and prepared by the crossing party two days before.

Taffy Williams kept in contact with the vehicle party ahead and with the Pole, Scott Base and Halley Bay, to help the pilots choose a suitable day for the long flight by coordinating all the reported weather conditions ahead. On the 28th, conditions were bad. The 29th appeared to be better, but with some patches of cloud expected at the Pole and thin cloud at McMurdo. Not ideal, but they decided to leave, as planned, in the late evening so as to optimise the position of the sun for navigation. Gordon Haslop got the plane off the ground with two bounces around 10.30 pm. The sun would remain ahead during the night, above the horizon.

The first hour went well and they flew within two miles of the vehicles, confirming their navigational accuracy. The vehicle party had retired early after a long day, and Taffy could not raise Ralph Lenton. By early morning, conditions began to worsen, with some cloud thickening ahead. Fuchs had hoped they would be able to comment on his ground route ahead, specifically to identify mountains, if any, and crevasse areas. By 2 am, at 87°40′S, they were flying in thick cloud, with rime ice forming along the aircraft's leading edges. Their altitude was around 10,000 feet and the plane could not maintain this height. Reluctantly, they had to turn back for South Ice, having covered around 400 miles.

They now had a serious problem in finding South Ice again. Lewis took his turn as pilot. Perhaps they might later be able to see the Whichaway and Shackleton Mountains well off, to guide them. Before

3 am the plane emerged from the cloud and two hours later they were jubilant to see the vehicle camp, still sleeping. But three hours after turning back, they could see more thick cloud ahead, which extended down to the surface. Once they entered this cloud, they would be flying blind. They circled, deciding what best to do. Suddenly, and luckily, they saw vehicle tracks below and quickly dropped altitude to follow them, only 10 feet above the ground. 'Flying by Bradshaw', a reference to the British Railway guide, Lewis followed the tracks for 40 miles back to South Ice, where they landed in 100-yard visibility. They remembered that the vehicles had turned sharply on leaving the station, and located this spot.

So they were back where they started, with a significant amount of their fuel spent. Bad weather followed, and they saw in the New Year with the weather getting worse. Over the next three days high winds continued, but on 4 January they refuelled and Weston carried out his aircraft checks. The Otter was 25 gallons short, about an hour's flying, and so no safety margin existed to reach Scott Base. Four 40-gallon drums of fuel had been left at Shackleton, the last of the 9000 gallons brought down on *Magga Dan*, but retrieving these with the Otter would only make its situation worse. Our American friends at Ellsworth Station offered to solve this dilemma. Jim Lassiter said he could call at Shackleton and bring our fuel up in his Dakota, which he did on 6 January, and the Otter's tanks were filled.

The weather cleared and they prepared to leave, checking conditions with the vehicle party and the Pole. The plane took off again in a light breeze just before midnight. A following wind gave them some assistance and they flew over the vehicle camp, again

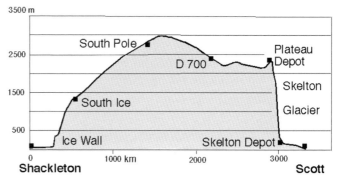

Figure 20 The TAE route. The height profile from Shackleton to Scott Base, via the South Pole, is from TAE's survey.

sleeping. At 4 am they flew over the Pole Station, and reset their course to follow Scott's final, tragic march down the Beardmore Glacier. They then crossed the Ross Ice Shelf to Scott Base. Everything went well and several American planes met them as they prepared to land.

The flight from South Ice had taken 11 hours and covered a distance of 1430 miles. Taffy had ordered some 'very cold beer', which was ready for them at Scott Base. The Americans had previously flown across the continent, to the Weddell Sea and back from the Ross Sea, but their explorations had been in four-engine aircraft. Flying a single-engine aircraft is inherently more dangerous. The Otter route was from South Ice to the Pole (Figure 19), then down the Beardmore Glacier to Scott Base (Figure 18).

John Lewis sold the Otter to the Americans after a party at McMurdo.

New Zealand Survey Exploration: Journeys From Scott Base

During the 1957–58 summer, three different NZ dog team parties undertook new mountain exploration and mapping. These were known as the Northern Survey, the Darwin Glacier Survey and the Southern Survey. These surveys are described in detail in Helm and Miller's 1964 book.[17] All three were significant achievements.

Figure 18 shows the three parties' routes.

THE LAST CROSSING LEG — D700 to SCOTT BASE

Hillary arrived at D700 with John Claydon and John Wright, one of Ed's Pole party tractor drivers, in the Beaver. They had been forced by the cloud to fly across the mountains via a new route up the Barne Glacier, a six-hour flight from Scott Base. Claydon and Wright refuelled, but had to tie the aircraft down, camp and wait for better weather next morning before returning.

Ed acted as our guide from here to Scott Base, and for parts of the way we could follow his vehicle tracks. Crevasses had to be cleared within 10 miles of D700, but in spite of our seeking a better route around them, Able broke a rear spring, which was quickly replaced.

But on 11 February, heading for Midway Depot, the same vehicle fractured a weld of its main steering crossbar, and County of Kent with Roy and Ralph went back with the spare they were carrying. David Pratt urged the leading vehicles to continue to Midway Depot while they completed the repairs. However, Able's main transmission box then broke, only five miles further on. So Ken and I travelled the last, long stretch in the back of County of Kent with Roy and Ralph, in deepening, gloomy light. Visibility was poor, with drift snow snaking in tendrils across the surface, and I was bemused to know how Roy could somehow sense the occasionally indistinct vehicle tracks ahead. We arrived, and I remarked to my vehicle companions how weird I had found the landscapes ahead. Perhaps it was the strange light and unusual patterns of snow mounds, and we agreed it reminded us of the surface of the moon. Fuchs celebrated a birthday quietly on 11 February and I was amazed to learn it really was his 50th.

Beyond Midway Depot, the next depot, D480, was only another 80 miles. In better visibility, we regained and followed the tracks of the tractors. However, Rock 'n Roll's steering failed, and new steering rod welding was needed. On inspection of the other vehicles, Haywire was seen to be in imminent danger of similar failure. The special terylene tent was erected for Roy and David to undertake the welding under shelter from a brisk breeze. The portable electric welder had to be fixed each time to David Pratt's Sno-Cat gearbox and driven by big belts, which kept stretching. David Stratton and I helped by holding blowtorches to assist in pre-heating and then the slow cooling of the welds. Roy and David's skill and improvisation in carrying out this long job in a temperature of -38°F (-39°C) astonished me.

After D480, complete whiteout prevented sun compass navigation, and the magnetic compass was responding too weakly for use in a moving vehicle. However, by placing a compass on the snow surface, it would very slowly oscillate and finally settle. Flags were laid out by skiers to mark the route ahead, and then used to maintain a straight driveline. From then on, the lead vehicle driver had to navigate by looking backwards. Ed was tall enough to stand in the escape hatch, look backwards, and call 'left' or 'right' to his driver to maintain a visual line. Fuchs notes that the 15 miles travelled was not enough. Next day, in continuing whiteout, David Stratton developed another modification by looking back out of the open door and steering behind his back, with his passenger using the accelerator. It was strenuous driving, gripping the window frame to avoid falling out, and the lead driver was relieved every two hours. In this way, 42 miles were covered.

The visibility varied until Plateau Depot was reached. Here, John Lewis and John Claydon arrived from Scott Base with the Otter and Beaver. Ken and I flew back to Scott with them, to prepare seal meat for our dogs through the winter, so we missed the last stages down the Skelton Glacier and across the Ross Shelf.

Our flight down was spectacular, and I felt envious of the NZ geologists, Bernie Gunn and Guy Warren, and the expanse of dramatic scenery and rock exposure in the remarkable ice-free Western Mountain Dry Valleys.

Ken and I were made welcome at Scott Base and enjoyed more mail. It felt strange to sleep on a bed. Harvesting about 60 seals was a bloody and unenviable task, and we worked hard for about a week. We met Bob Miller and George Marsh when they returned from their epic Southern Survey journey. Over a meal, we talked into the night about our different parties and their achievements. Ken knew George well from FIDS days and I regretted I did not have a tape recorder. The two were frank about happenings in the NZ Party, and I was somewhat shocked to hear very strong remarks about their leader. I have remained very impressed by what the New Zealand party achieved, on all fronts, about which Doug McKenzie has thoughtful comments in his book, *Opposite Poles*.[18] Some New Zealand members also felt, like many of us from Shackleton, that there were, in effect, three expeditions — the TAE Crossing, the NZ TAE, and Hillary's Expedition to the Pole.

One fine evening, I had the opportunity to ski out from Scott Base, to look briefly at some of the historic surroundings. The light was wonderful and I had good views of Mount Erebus (Plate 56). There was also Castle Rock, frequently mentioned by the Scott expeditions. I was able to ski up to it and then climb on top, which kindled memories of the polar expeditions 40 years earlier. I had a wonderful view across McMurdo Sound, and was impressed by the folds in the edge of the Ross Ice Shelf (Plate 57). I could see the *Discovery* hut, but did not try to visit it. I had yet to develop a true appreciation of the historic significance of the early exploration here: Scott 1902, Shackleton 1908, Scott 1912 and then Shackleton's Ross Sea party, 1914–16. Today, the hut is well preserved.

David Burke was an Australian journalist at McMurdo. Later, he also found he had been bitten by Antarctica and wrote a gripping account of flying there.[19] David tapped into my more dramatic TAE recollections from our epic journey across the continent. While there weren't many, he was delighted to have me share them. He was probably surprised with my reply when he said to me, 'It must have been an unforgettable experience'. My response was that this hadn't really been my feeling at the time. Only later, with the perspective of distance, did I see the experience as unforgettable. The adventure was close to what I had hoped it would be like, and all I wanted was for it to go on, indefinitely.

The vehicles had an adventurous journey down the Skelton Glacier.[20] Hillary's guidance in avoiding the severe crevasse belts was vital down this tortuous route. Occasionally, he lost the way owing to a combination of characteristic bad weather in some sections, with katabatic winds, drift snow and the guiding mountains invisible. On 1 March, just as they were leaving camp, an American Otter flew towards them and circled. In recognition, Fuchs wrote, 'We fired a flare as a gesture of *joie de vivre*'.[21] The Americans took this to mean something was needed and came in to land. Fuchs gave a signal to David Stratton to stop, and the following Cat drove into the back of Fuchs' sledges and started to climb over them. There was little damage, but a box containing hundreds of detonators was splintered. Fortunately none exploded.

The vehicle convoy finally rolled in to Scott Base. The whole journey covered 2158 miles (3473 km), taking 99 days from Shackleton. Fuchs quietly observed that this was close to his estimate of 100 days for the journey. The elevation profile along the TAE route in Figure 20 shows how much of the journey involved the cold, elevated Polar Plateau.

Fuchs, in *The Crossing of Antarctica*, describes the enthusiastic welcome on reaching Scott Base.[22]

56 Mount Erebus and Castle Rock from near Scott Base.

Numerous vehicles came out to meet them, followed by a ceremony featuring a musical tribute from the 'McMurdo band', which included 'God Save the Queen'. The band had been formed the night before. Fuchs records that they apparently 'collected everyone who thought they could play an instrument. The edict went forth, "It doesn't matter if you can play — but you gotta be able to play loud"'.

There was a celebration that afternoon at Scott Base, and David Stratton read out a large number of congratulatory telegrams. To climax this, John Lewis read a communication from the Queen, conferring a knighthood on Fuchs. The Savoy Hotel had consigned a generous tribute in the form of champagne, caviar and biscuits. I was new to champagne and found it disappointing. My only other recollection is that the caviar and biscuits did not last much longer than an initial taste, doubtless as a consequence of the considerable number of expeditioners and visitors. The Savoy provided us a touch of class for the celebration.

We had a few more days before we sailed for New Zealand. David Burke showed me around McMurdo, where I learnt to distinguish between two American beers, one of which 'flocculated' when it was frozen

57 From Castle Rock. A view of the waves in the Ross Ice Shelf.

58 My homemade Australian flag on the back of my dog sledge, approaching the Pole. I am enjoying my lunchtime thermos cocoa. (Photograph by George Lowe)

and retained this disfiguring appearance when thawed. David took me to a 'night club' style bar, and I was surprised to recognise how different the Americans were. They enjoyed themselves differently from us, regardless of their special Antarctic surroundings. It may be that most did not have any opportunity for travelling in the exceptional Antarctic environment, so we lacked this common experience as a basis for fraternising.

Of much greater importance to me was my flag. At Shackleton, before we set out on the crossing, I became aware that the Expedition did not have an Australian flag. We had British, New Zealand, South African flags, and even Bruce's flag from the Scottish Geographical Society (from his 1904 Scotia Expedition), and various other flags. I was concerned about this and, in a moment of inspiration, decided to make an Australian flag. Using a white bed sheet and paint from the store, I sketched the design from a small flag reproduced in an encyclopaedia. My flag fluttered its way to the pole on my dog sledge (Plate 58), and then on a convoy sledge to reach McMurdo. It had faded slightly in the Antarctic sun and its edges were shredding. It was flown on its pole on a vehicle sledge after the convoy reached McMurdo. Then, one morning, it was gone. An enthusiastic American must have judged it to be finished with and unwanted, and therefore a suitable souvenir. He had not reckoned with David Burke, who hunted it down at McMurdo after we sailed for New Zealand, and returned it to me in Australia. David wrote a nice story about his search for this bedraggled flag for his Sydney newspaper. To my enormous satisfaction, it is now in the Tasmanian Museum in Hobart.

We embarked on *Endeavour* on 5 March 1958. The nearby American base at McMurdo, a reminder of civilisation, felt far enough away and did not spoil the impression of leaving an untamed wilderness. The McMurdo scene is haunting — the *Discovery* hut, Mount Erebus and the historic surroundings. The memorial crosses to Seaman George Thomas Vince, lost on Scott's first expedition, and the Scott polar party are there, high on the hill,

Endeavour slowly eased away from the ice, with penguins to see us off. It was very cold, and the sea was on the point of freezing. Our parting view was across McMurdo Sound to the distant mountains. It seemed fitting that, after such a remarkable journey, we were leaving the continent at such an historic place. I left Antarctica reluctantly.

6 AFTER TAE

For many of us, our lives changed direction after TAE.

Fuchs has described the enthusiastic receptions when his expedition returned to England in 1958.[1] The crossing party docked at Southampton, having cruised from New Zealand on MV *Rangitoto*. I had been given leave to first go home to Brisbane, almost missing my RNZAF free flight to Melbourne from Auckland. I went home and later visited a beach to surf at Mooloolaba, where my young nieces were amused by my 'Antarctic tan' — I looked bleached and did my best to develop a normal complexion quickly, without sunburn. In those days in Australia, a 'normal complexion' was a suntan. The flight to London by Constellation took three days, due to engine trouble, but Eleanor Honnywill met me and got me to Southampton in time for the ship's arrival.

The red carpet was rolled out in style for us. We were given a civic reception in the Southampton Town Hall and travelled by train to London, where Sir Alec Douglas Home, the Commonwealth Secretary and future Prime Minister, welcomed us. Then we all travelled in an open car convoy slowly through London, to a press conference at the Royal Geographical Society. The expedition's four Commonwealth representatives were in the leading car, a vintage Rolls, so I enjoyed a place with Fuchs (UK), George Lowe (NZ) and Hannes la Grange (South Africa); we waved in royal fashion, which as a 'colonial' I found a somewhat incongruous experience.

Two days later we went to Buckingham Palace, where Fuchs received his knighthood from Queen Elizabeth and we were invested with the Polar Medal. We were then introduced to the Queen. Fuchs mentioned that Ken Blaiklock and I were planning an expedition later in the year, and the Queen quickly laughed, saying, 'Fancy wanting to go back down there again'. Later, we heard that the Queen had named one of her racing horses Snocat. Unfortunately, it did not enjoy conspicuous success.

Fuchs and David Stratton presented the first lecture on the expedition, at the Royal Geographical Society and Fuchs was presented with the Society's Special Gold Medal. Afterwards, there was a reception, and I met some members of Gino Watkin's and John Rymill's historic Greenland and Antarctic Peninsula expeditions. The chairman of the TAE expedition scientific committee, Professor H.H. Read, my PhD supervisor at Imperial College, told me someone had asked to meet me. This was Clement Atlee, the senior Labour politician and former PM. Gimlet-eyed; he was brief, asking if I had found any useful mineral deposits. I spluttered that I had not, to which he instantly responded, 'Thank goodness!' Later I was introduced to Princess Margaret, an attractive, vivacious young woman of my age. I felt obliged to try to say something interesting, and launched into an explanation about finding fossils and coal seams. Shortly, after sensing what I took to be a less than excited response, I found myself expanding into the topic of continental drift. That seemed to hit the mark, and she interrupted me, with raised eyebrows,

'You don't really believe that stuff, do you'? It was hardly the moment to digress into scientific evidence and I became aware others were behind me, queued up to be introduced.

Bunny Fuchs and Ed Hilary soon faced the demanding task of writing the official book on the expedition. Fuchs had enjoyed the relaxing cruise home to England with his wife, only to face a fortnight of hectic engagements. Then Cassell, the book publishers, pressed them to keep to their tight deadline. *The Crossing of Antarctica* must have been written in about eight weeks. Fuchs worked continuously from his home in Cambridge and, as he wrote, Eleanor Honnywill, the TAE office secretary, typed. As the chapters were finished, they were sent down by train and handed to a Cassell employee at Waterloo. Fuchs wrote fluently and easily, but found the pressure severe. When the proofs were returned, he found there was little chance for revision. Ed Hillary wrote four chapters, which were sent by air from New Zealand. The whole account had to be coordinated, and the maps completed. A younger member of the Cassell family selected photographs, and I was delighted to write captions for a number of my photos which were included, including the dust jacket and the frontispiece. The book is a reliable record; when I re-read it, I find it to be a modestly gripping account of the expedition. British Petroleum had supported the expedition very generously, providing our fuel and lubricants, and made a film from George Lowe's movie coverage, also called *The Crossing of Antarctica*. As stated previously, Derek Williams of BP had made a movie from his work on *Theron*, called *Foothold on Antarctica*. I attended *Foothold*'s release in 1956 and met the composer of its fine music, Humphrey Searle. Years later, I discovered he was an authority on the music of Franz Liszt, one of my favourite composers.

I unpacked my Antarctic rocks and began studying them at Imperial College, but I found it very difficult to settle into research mode. It was to take me many years to complete my geology monograph, during which time I was studying in London, Birmingham, Brisbane, Lahore, London again, Leeds and, finally, Townsville. In London, I was distracted by the plans Ken Blaiklock and I pursued for our own modest expedition. Our plan was to return to Antarctica, and use our dogs and equipment in a four-man survey/geology trip into the Horlick Mountains. We were awarded a generous grant by the Everest Foundation, and Ken held their cheque for several months. Then we received advice from Admiral Dufek informing us, with regret, that his Antarctic budget had been reduced and his operation could not fly us to the Horlicks from McMurdo. I found this decision impossible to accept — I felt we were such a strong team — and I invested much energy trying to salvage our plan. I met a sequence of very interesting Americans, hoping to influence them to ask Dufek to change his decision. Meanwhile, Ken and I shared a flat in Chelsea and got on with our lives. We had some enjoyable parties, comparing notes on the Himalayas and Antarctica. The first was held at our flat with the blessing of our landlady, Lady Stubbs. When I introduced Geoff Bratt, one of my extroverted Australian climbing friends, to her as 'Lady Stubbs', he fortunately restrained himself from responding, 'Hi, I'm Lord Muck'. A range of friends came to the next party, at out next, basement residence and our exuberant friends painted one of those historic plaques on the outside wall, 'KB and JS, Antarctic explorers, live here'. Later that night, Rainer Goldsmith prepared a poster which read, 'AUSTRALIANS — GO HOME'. His fellow medico, my Australian friend Grahame Budd, instantly added 'BY QANTAS'. A little colonial one-upmanship, all in good fun.

Ken Blaiklock soon realised our Horlick expedition plans were dead and returned our Everest Foundation grant. He was invited to return to Antarctica with the new Belgian Expedition, later in 1958. I remained unable to settle into my research and moved to Leeds to work in Ray Adie's FIDS geology centre. Later I asked Fuchs if I could return to Brisbane to work at the University of Queensland with Professor Dorothy Hill, and he agreed. Before we left, Ken and I travelled down to Kent to see our TAE dogs, which had been brought back and were in quarantine. They had new work ahead of them, in mountain rescue in Norway. They were in splendid condition, seemingly much bigger, and with long, clean coats. They were such handsome huskies and knew us well, but seemed puzzled we were not taking them for a run.

THE BOOKS ABOUT TAE

The official account by Fuchs and Hillary, *The Crossing of Antarctica*, appeared in 1958. Fuchs published *Antarctic Adventure* in 1959, written especially for younger readers. *The Crossing* was published in several languages.

There have been several books about the expedition. These include Noel Barber's *The White Desert* (1958); *Because it is There* by George Lowe (1959, about Everest and TAE); and *Opposite Poles* by Douglas McKenzie (1963). Arthur Helm and Bob Miller wrote *Antarctica: The Story of the New Zealand Party of the Trans-Antarctic Expedition* in 1964. This book describes all aspects of their outstanding exploration work, some of which is not well known. John Claydon wrote an official account of the NZ expedition, giving details of the RNZAF flight division's remarkable work.

Ed Hillary published *No Latitude for Error* in 1961, an exciting and personal account of his South Pole journey. I was startled to read a perceptive review by Geoffrey Dutton, titled 'The Hero as Egoist'. He says:

> When Hillary is boss, amongst his New Zealanders, there is no trouble. He just does not seem to be the man for a Number Two … there is plenty of humour and good fellowship. It is fitting that Hillary should be at his best on Everest and at the Pole, where there is a cold ruthlessness in the elements that calls to the blizzard at the hero's heart.[2]

Hillary's book has some uncomplimentary observations about Fuchs, and it seems that Ed never understood him. In this book I have tried to record just where Hillary found himself on TAE and how he came to make his impressive tractor journey to reach the Pole. In his long career, Hillary enjoyed a succession of remarkable achievements, culminating in his sustained work for education and health in Nepal. He was deeply loved by all Sherpas, and revered by his fellow New Zealanders. It is said he was the only living New Zealander featured on an NZ currency note. Sir Edmund Hillary died in New Zealand on 12 January 2008, aged 88.

In relation to his journey to the Pole, it may be that Hillary had hoped and planned privately to achieve this for some time, once he had been appointed leader of the New Zealand Party. Soon after arriving in Antarctica, he realised that his Ross Sea Committee, especially the chairman, was likely to oppose any South Pole plans unless they were subsidiary or complementary to the main TAE crossing. It is understandable that he judged it prudent to postpone any announcement of a journey to the Pole until a more propitious moment, and even to offer some alternatives, albeit as a smokescreen. An exploration west of the Polar Plateau was an example of such an alternative. Hillary was a very determined individual, and if he wanted to fulfil his plan for the Pole I can appreciate why he had to follow a private course to achieve it. It was very much an individual ambition and open to misinterpretation. The delays experienced by Fuchs' crossing party made Hillary's Pole venture possible, and the success of his NZ tractor party was brilliant. At the time, I think most of us on the crossing party felt it was underhand.

Hillary described his adventurous life in his 1999 autobiography, *View From the Summit*. Sections of this book further describe his recollections of TAE, and he speaks frankly of some expedition decisions, which he seems to have resented. The book recalls unhappy memories of other episodes and personalities in his life. He wrote some uncomplimentary things about Fuchs, by then deceased. Some of his TAE comments need to be questioned, to put the record straight.

Fuchs and Hillary first met in late 1953, after George Lowe had been appointed photographer on TAE. Hillary writes he was curious as to why Fuchs was discussing the expedition plans with him, until Fuchs indicated he hoped New Zealand would back a McMurdo Sound support base and mentioned the estimated total cost of the expedition. Then, Hillary says, he realised why he was at the meeting, namely to help secure New Zealand's involvement. Hillary implies Fuchs wanted him for his financial influence. My understanding of Bunny Fuchs is that I don't believe that to be the full story; there would have been many other reasons why he wanted Hillary on the expedition, including his ability to find a route up onto the Polar Plateau and to see that the essential depots were put in place for the crossing party. Certainly, Hillary would be an influential figure for promoting the critical role in TAE that New Zealand was to be invited to play. The New Zealand government did confirm its participation in 1955 and Hillary was invited to lead the party, he says, ahead of a 'respected naval commander'.

The plans were made for the Advance Party to go to the Weddell Sea. In *View From the Summit*, Hillary sounds slighted that Fuchs' crossing party was to have three Sno-Cats and other vehicles, whereas the NZ Party would have three modified Ferguson tractors. Fuchs ended up with four Snow-Cats and Hillary with five Fergusons. In his autobiography, Hillary records feeling 'grave doubts about how effectively he and I would work together. He was clearly very rigid in his views and plans and would carry them through to a very determined conclusion. I, on the other hand, was far more likely to change a programme if a better alternative presented itself.'[3]

Hillary believed the program envisaged for the New Zealand Party was less than challenging. However, the plans were evolving, and the NZ role expanded considerably, especially through Hillary's strong promotion. It must have been an interesting situation, and Hillary 'wrote thoughtfully to the Ross Sea Committee', observing that his NZ Party could travel as far as the Pole.[4] He felt that neither the Ross Sea Committee nor Fuchs took him seriously. This is fair comment by Hillary, but it was still early in TAE's planning.

Fuchs invited Hillary, Bob Miller (second-in-command) and John Claydon (senior pilot) to take part in establishing Shackleton Base on the Weddell Sea, with *Theron*. Bunny and Ed shared a small cabin, but Hillary found himself concluding that Bunny arranged this 'to keep a close eye on him'.[5] Fuchs held frequent executive meetings as the cruise progressed, but Hillary records he was never invited to attend though Miller and Claydon were. This is bizarre, as Fuchs would readily have had Hillary along if he had raised it.

Hillary expresses concern over the approach route Fuchs chose to enter the Weddell Sea, rather than the 'traditional' way through the pack-ice on the eastern side to enter the open channels, which usually exist along the coast.[6] However, two points are noteworthy here. First, there wasn't much of a tradition. Weddell himself and Filchner took quite different routes and Bruce (1906) was the first to find the coastal pathway.

The Argentines, in *San Martin*, did not follow it until early 1955. Shackleton had difficulty getting in via that route in 1914. Secondly, an important influence in Fuchs' Weddell Sea plans must have been Sir James Wordie, chief scientist with Shackleton on *Endeavour*. Wordie wrote the first analysis of the Weddell Sea drift and was a long-time associate of Fuchs. He was also Fuchs' Cambridge research supervisor and his mentor for TAE. According to Hillary, Fuchs had an 'unusual plan', to try to enter the pack-ice in the area where two hypothetical eddies join.[7] This seems a quaint and novel suggestion. Perhaps Hillary misunderstood a chance remark about a desirable route.

Hillary reflects on the speed of unloading at Shackleton and resolved to load his ship, *Endeavour*, for McMurdo, differently. His observations were sound. But loading a ship under time constraints, in such a way to access them in the sequence you will need them, is usually confounded by unanticipated problems. Hillary's criticisms of *Theron*'s loading arrangements may seem fair; he learnt from them and set out to do better on *Endeavour*. He suggests that *Theron* could have stayed several days longer at Shackleton, and this would have avoided having to put the stores in a temporary depot on the fast ice, some of which was later lost. Hillary states, 'I was one of the few who realised how dangerous this was.'[8] But it was already very late in the season, and the situation had parallels with those facing *Deutschland* and *Endurance* 40 years before, which became beset. It is easy to reflect, with the benefit of hindsight, on what 'might have been' for the TAE Advance Party.

However, what if *Theron* had failed to reach Shackleton, or had become beset in the ice, to drift north through the winter? What then, TAE? Hillary writes further, confirming his poor assessment of Fuchs' organisation and execution, 'I could hardly believe how amateurish and disorganised the expedition had been.'[9]

In the course of the expedition, Hillary had made a number of requests of the Americans, and Admiral Dufek was consistently generous to the New Zealand Party. It may be that Hillary saw his party's place differently from Fuchs, as a separate expedition rather than as an essential part of TAE. When Fuchs asked Hillary to request Dufek's help to fly out the crossing party dogs, Ed recalls he was 'decidedly uncomfortable about asking the Admiral to do this'.[10] As Fuchs travelled north from the Pole, Geoffrey Pratt collapsed from carbon monoxide poisoning and Hillary arranged for an American rescue flight to bring in more oxygen bottles for Pratt's recovery. Hillary found it 'slightly ironic that Bunny who had often expressed his determination not to accept any assistance from the Americans was now calling on them whenever a problem arose — incidentally using me as an intermediary'.[11]

In relation to a medical emergency, this statement by Hillary ignores the fact there has always been an automatic international response, from every nation, in cases of polar or southern ocean emergency.

Ken Blaiklock and I were upset to learn Hillary had put down our dogs at Scott Base, where the Americans had flown them. The story from Ed was that our dogs created a problem, because of a quarantine embargo on their being taken out through New Zealand. He found it extremely upsetting, having to get Harry Ayres' help to put down the dogs.[12] When Ken Blaiklock and I reached Scott Base to provide winter food for them, most of our dogs were still alive, but we were dismayed to find that some had been put down. Ed judged them to be in such pitiful condition they had to be destroyed. Almost certainly, to judge from many previous situations in the British Antarctic Survey, the dogs would all have recovered their strength. Unfortunately, Ed had no understanding of dogs.

After joining Fuchs crossing party at D700, Hillary writes: 'Then began one of the most bemusing three weeks of my life. It was like going back into the Weddell Sea again. I was no longer the leader of a large expedition. I shared a tent with Bunny but wasn't a decision-maker any more — unless we were lost or passing through crevasse areas.'[13]

Ed became an occasional guide, and after the first day says

> I rarely sat up front on the Polar Plateau. For day after day I lay in my sleeping bags in the gloomy uninsulated freezing back of the Sno-Cat, unable to see anything or even know what was happening, until they lost the tracks again or came to another crevasse area when I was called out of the darkness, put on some skis and went forward to make some decisions. But once the problem had been solved, there was no room for me in the front cabin and I crawled back into my cold dark home. I very much doubt if Bunny realised how miserable I felt.[14]

Hillary, the man of action, must have found the journey boring and uncomfortable. Ken Blaiklock and I travelled this way, in the back of Roy Homard's Sno-Cat, most of the way from the Pole to Plateau Depot. Our own 'dark home' was frigid, but we managed to read by holding the book with one gloved hand, could talk to Roy and Ralph, and peer forward through the front windscreen to watch what was at times an enchanting, half-lit, mysterious scene.

Ed guided the convoy carefully and skilfully through many of the crevasse zones. He also had a leading part in again finding the correct route down the Skelton Glacier, below the Portal. Later in his book he writes: 'I felt proud of my efforts but, strangely enough, I can't remember a single soul saying a complimentary word. Maybe they had no idea of what we had just done — that's the kindest thing to believe anyway.'[15]

The crossing party did appreciate his contribution as guide, in taking us back to Scott Base along his route. In my experience such contributions tend to be taken for granted amongst a team like ours, and I suspect Ed was expecting kudos from a group that was not used to complimenting a team member for what they perceived as their role. This may have been a factor at the core of Hillary's disenchantments, apart from being deprived of a decision-making role.

> As for my recommendation that Bunny should stop his journey for the winter at the South Pole — well, he proved me wrong! I had not known that the crossing party would be able to follow my tracks so easily for seventy-five percent of the way — and I don't believe Bunny did either — that was a great bonus for him. And so was my guidance down the complex Skelton Glacier. Without these two factors the crossing party would have spent an extra winter at Scott Base. It had been close, very close![16]

While this is interesting speculation, I do not believe that we simply followed Hillary's tracks for 75 percent of the way. Certainly, we knew where we had to go, but commonly lost the tracks on the way to D700. Also, some of the crevasse routes were incomplete and on the way to Plateau Depot we were not always able to follow his vehicle tracks. In places they were not evident, and we were in a hurry.

The New Zealand TAE party made an essential contribution to the success of the crossing. Of central importance was their role in finding a vehicle route from Scott Base onto the Polar Plateau, and the Beaver establishing the fuel depots at Plateau, D480 and D700. As part of TAE, the NZ TAE achieved other, significant contributions to Antarctic exploration and research contributions, more important than the tractor journey to the Pole. Hillary's leadership was vital, and the winter and the whole year's operations from Scott Base must have been an exciting time. His party's journey to the Pole and the TAE traverse of the continent were both outstanding achievements. Subsequent crossings of Antarctica have been just as extraordinary and are outlined in a separate chapter.

Ed Hillary's career continued after TAE, and included his term as NZ Ambassador in India. He has major contributions in a succession of remarkable achievements. As stated previously, the summit of all these was his invaluable work for education and health in Nepal.

OUR LIVES AFTER TAE

While we were travelling across the Polar Plateau, I had the opportunity to take photographs of most of the crossing party. I have reproduced the photos here to show relaxed images of these men, and I regret I did not take more. A recent photo, taken at a TAE reunion in the UK in 2007, shows our survivors (Plate 59).

The following are brief sketches of the TAE crossing party and their later careers. Unfortunately, I am unable to describe the New Zealand Party members.

Vivian 'Bunny' Fuchs (Plates 60 and 61)

The origin of his nickname is interesting. His son, Peter, provided me with the following: 'He was at a Prep School, a private school for 8–13 year olds, in Kent. Returning to visit sometime after he left the school he was entertaining the Headmaster and his family with his party trick of the time. That was walking on his hands. To keep his balance his legs from the knees down would be hanging past his head, looking like very large rabbit ears. Thus Bunny came to be so called. This story is told in the Headmaster's daughter's book written by her a few years ago when she was over 80 plus. Even more strange is the fact that when going through some old family movies I found a passage showing him walking on his hands!'

59 Reunion group near Derby, 26 August 2007. From left: Ken Blaiklock, Derek Williams (BP photographer), Rainer Goldsmith, Jon Stephenson, Hal Lister, George Lowe, Roy Homard, David Pratt and Richard Brooke (NZ TAE).

60 Bunny Fuchs and Ed Hillary in their tent, preparing their evening meal, not far from Plateau Depot, February 1958.

61 Sir Vivian Fuchs with Jon Stephenson at Scott Base, at the conclusion of the crossing journey. (Photographer unknown)

Bunny resumed his position as Director of the Falkland Island Dependency Scientific Bureau (FIDScBureau) at the beginning of 1959, taking over from Sir Raymond Priestley who had acted in his absence. FIDS was renamed the British Antarctic Survey (BAS) in 1961. Fuchs continued as Scientific Director until 1973 when he retired, aged 66.

Fuchs visited different Antarctic bases on a number of summer supply cruises. The Halley Bay buildings had been replaced in 1967 because the original base had been progressively buried by snow accumulation. He was at Halley again in 1971 and in 1972–73, when he revisited Shackleton Base. Surprisingly, the roof was still showing above the snow; constant southerly winds had prevented accumulation. He was able to get inside and says he felt an unusual sense of 'coming home'. In 1986, the Filchner Ice Shelf calved and the 30-year-old building at Shackleton was carried away into the Weddell Sea with the iceberg.[17]

After he retired, Fuchs took on many other activities. He remarked that retirement made little difference to his way of life. He had been President of the International Glaciological Society from 1963 to 1966. Once retired, he was elected president of other distinguished scientific bodies, including the British Association for the Advancement of Science (1972), helping to enliven it from a moribund state; the Royal Geographical Society (1982–84); and the Young Explorer's Trust (closely linked with the RGS).

In 1974 he was elected a Fellow of the Royal Society, which, he records, 'exceptionally allows those not qualified by Science to become Fellows'. As FIDS Director, he had served ex officio as a member of the Royal Society's National Committee for Antarctic Research and continued for several years. After serving as President of the RGS, the society nominated him as its representative on the Royal Society National Committee for Antarctic Research.

Fuchs was a guest at the opening of a new Polar Wing of the Canterbury Museum in Christchurch in 1977. In 1979 he opened the new airport at Stanley in the Falklands, which replaced the temporary Argentine airstrip, and ironically he landed in an Argentine plane. The airstrip was used three years later by the Argentine's invading force in the Falklands War, and survived bombing attempts by the RAF.

He was adviser to the Trans-Globe Expedition and met Sir Ranulph Fiennes' Antarctic crossing party when they reached Auckland in 1981. He subsequently saw them off from Los Angeles on their Arctic leg. The next year he was invited to the Institute for International Studies at the University of Chile to help in shaping the country's Antarctic Resources Policy and visited George Lowe there, then headmaster of the English Grange School. He was given the Freedom of the City of London in 1983.

Fuchs wrote fluently and in 1982 published *Of Ice and Men*, a history of BAS, and his autobiography, *A Time to Speak*, in 1990. Later, when we had the opportunity to read this autobiography, the TAE men were surprised that he had told us very little of his other adventures.

Bunny and his wife Joyce celebrated their golden wedding anniversary in 1983. He suffered a stroke in 1985 and three years later Joyce had a heart attack. She died in 1990.

In 1990, when asked what gave him the greatest satisfaction — adventure, comradeship or discovery. He observed that, in the world of exploration, they are indivisible. He was also asked, he says, more and more frequently, what is there left to discover. He believed the reality of exploration today is scientific study of a region about which little is known, ranging from reconnaissance study to attempting the most detailed work.

What was Bunny really like? He was quite tall, thick-set and a particularly strong person, with unusually powerful hands. He was a fine looking man, with arresting, wonderfully expressive eyebrows. Fuchs had great presence and dignity, and when he spoke, people listened. I will never forget his presentation when TAE reached the Pole. The many journalists closely attended his story and analysis of the expedition's position for completing the crossing. I was surprised how fit he looked, and how well-groomed he was after our arduous journey.

Usually, he was very enthusiastic about anyone's expedition plans, though probably most single minded in supporting survey and geology. It is said he declined to support psychology projects in Antarctica, possibly feeling he knew enough about people and how to best lead expeditions. He was an arresting lecturer, somewhat embarrassed by appreciative applause and awards. I recall his first lecture presentation on our return, with David Stratton, when he carefully acknowledged the contributions of all the members of the expedition, as if we had really done the important things. There was never any posture with Fuchs, or sham. At a private social evening before *Magga Dan* sailed, people were dancing, but he was not. With a grin and his raised eyebrows, he quietly said to me, 'Not my line of country'. He also admitted he was not musical, and I suspect he might even have found music somewhat painful and distracting. He certainly rationed performance of LPs at Shackleton Base, though George Lowe told me he could listen privately in his photo laboratory.

Fuchs was athletic, played squash regularly and enthusiastically challenged anyone on the TAE supply vessels to arm-wrestle with him. He could do most things, and reading the account of his long safari across Africa with Joyce, I was impressed by his mechanical competence. Later, I felt curious whether he ever felt tempted to take part in repairing the vehicles on the crossing journey: Roy and David said not, as he left this as their special domain.

I found there was a complete sincerity about Fuchs and he was very generous and encouraging to me. While forceful and reasoned, he never sounded dogmatic. His determination and optimism were Shackleton-like. When the second Antarctic Conference was taking place in relation to a new Antarctic protocol, with considerable international disagreement and discord, I wrote to him expressing my enthusiasm when an unexpected, influential alliance arose between Australia and France opposing mineral exploration. This led to a compromise agreement at the Antarctic Conference. Fuchs' comment on this was interesting. He was strong in his response but expressed the view that, at this early stage, it was best not to try to solve every problem via a comprehensive agreement. It would be better to be patient. Sadly, one clause banned dogs in Antarctica.

The concerted opposition to Fuchs' TAE plans has been described earlier, coming from at least three different directions. I am impressed how he quietly persevered, and how in the end his opponents eventually came to help TAE, as members of expedition committees. Ken Blaiklock told me in 2004 that Bunny once said to him, 'Never get an opponent into a corner from which he cannot escape'. Ken found

him remarkably adroit in persuasive argument against opposition.

He had a strange aversion to receiving help from the Americans, referred to previously. Perhaps it was a consequence of the early opposition he experienced to his TAE plans, and a suggestion that crossing Antarctica should be left to the Americans. He did not hesitate to seek American assistance at various stages, and later gave BAS assistance to several nations, including Argentina and Chile. Fuchs might have been dismayed if he had known just how much other assistance TAE actually received from the generous US.

Fuchs died, after suffering declining health, on 11 November 1999, aged 91. I was shaken to hear of his death; it was as if my own father had died

Most of the TAE party got on with their lives and careers. I found myself accepted into a remarkable group of fine men. With deep dismay, I have seen death take its toll among so many of my 'Antarctic brothers'. Here are brief notes on how some of them fared after TAE.

David Stratton (Plate 62)

David joined British Petroleum and was their aviation manager for Scandinavia. Before TAE, he had learnt to fly a plane and it was said he had yet to learn to drive a car. But he was well versed in handling dogs after several years with FIDS at Hope Bay on the peninsula, with Ken Blaiklock and George Marsh. He acquired skills in driving a Sno-Cat as Bunny's

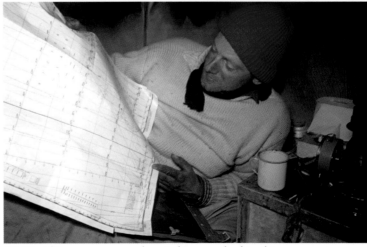

62 David Stratton, survey, alone in his tent, checking his map.

co-driver. After our return, he was awarded the Back Grant from the Royal Geographical Society in 1959.

He was general manger of BP (Belgium) for three years and later was marketing manager for South Europe and North Africa, and his career was moving away from his original zest for exploration.

Then, abruptly, he contracted poliomyelitis during a visit to the Middle East to climb Mount Ararat. For David, the complete paralysis which resulted must have been extremely distressing. He died on 22 May 1972.

Ken Blaiklock (Plate 62)

Ken joined the Expedition Antarctique Belge in 1958 and he spent two Antarctic seasons with them, involving dog-team travel and mountain exploration in the magnificent Sor Rondane Mountains. By then, his remarkable Antarctic experience had involved eight winters.

His Antarctic career began at Stonington Island (Base E) with Bunny Fuchs and later at Hope Bay (Base D) with David Stratton and George Marsh. He was on MV *Norsel* in 1955, establishing two new bases for BAS when he heard of the TAE plans.

On TAE, Ken was capable to doing anything, quite aside from his meticulous surveying. He was knowledgeable about all things relevant to expedition work, but seldom spoke much about his own achievements and experiences. When he did, it was with quiet understatement. After returning from his time with the Belgians, he somehow managed to find time to complete his formal surveying qualifications.

63 Ken Blaiklock, surveyor, at South Ice, making a map of the new Pensacola Mountains from American air photos.

From 1963 to 1965, he worked with the Middlesex County Council Rivers Section Hydrology, in survey and meteorology. He took part in summer work with BAS in 1965 on the Adelaide Islands in the Antarctic Peninsula. He then started an important association with Decca, working with them for two decades. This involved survey for offshore hydrographic work for hydrocarbon exploration companies in a variety of places — Nigeria, Saudi Arabia, Singapore and the North Sea. From 1975 he was chief surveyor on their operations in the Great Yarmouth region, the hub of North Sea Gas. He oversaw the accurate positioning of offshore exploration facilities, including the critical drilling platforms.

In 1968, BAS had an opportunity to coordinate with the Americans on survey and geological work in the Shackleton Range. The US provided the air logistics to fly a small group into the mountains. Ken accepted the opportunity to lead this group, which included Peter Clarkson from BAS. He was able to continue the work he had started in the Shackletons with David Stratton on TAE, this time using more accurate tellurometric methods.

From 1986 he ran his own hydrography consultancy for 10 years, continuing to undertake specialised work for the hydrocarbon industry in the North Sea, primarily as a freelance.

In his 'retirement', he worked with Bernard Stonehouse during three Antarctic summers, studying the effects of tourism on Antarctica, especially on the peninsula.

Ken was awarded the Polar Medal with three bars, 1951–58, the Cuthbert Peek Award in 1957 from the Royal Geographical Society, the Bruce Memorial Prize in 1958 from the Scottish Geographical Society, the Chevalier de la Couronne in 1961 from the Belgian Government, and the OBE in 1970.

Hannes la Grange (Plate 64)

Hannes resumed his work in the South African Weather Bureau and also completed his degree studies in physical geography and zoology at the University of Pretoria in 1962. He was appointed leader of the first South African National Antarctic Expedition in 1959 at their SANAE Station, and undertook a six-week dog sledge journey into the previously unknown region to the south.

Two years after his return from SANAE, he resigned from the weather bureau and joined the South African Council for the Development of Natural Resources. He moved from meteorology into town and regional planning, completing an MSc dissertation in this field. He was appointed Director of Town and Regional Planning for the Orange Free State, until his retirement in 1987, and completed a PhD in town and regional planning that year. La Grange died suddenly in 1999.

Hannes' perseverance and tenacity are highlighted in his *Polar Record* obituary,[18] which refers to his prolific, meticulous and wide-ranging publications.

64 Hannes la Grange, met man, and Geoffrey Pratt, geophysicist, eating dinner.

Geoffrey Pratt (Plate 64)

After TAE Geoffrey resumed his geophysical work with British Petroleum. This would have involved extensive travel in order to carry out geophysical work in distant places, an activity for which he expressed enthusiasm. Geoffrey was one who quietly added curry powder to his food because it wasn't hot enough for his taste. It was Geoffrey who survived carbon monoxide poisoning on the plateau between the South Pole and D700. He was a cheerful, self-contained person who always seemed to be confronted with some new scientific conundrum. I was sad to learn that this gentle bear on our party had died, still relatively young, and have not been able to obtain any details about his later career.

Roy Homard (Plates 64 and 65)

After his significant contributions to the success of TAE, Roy returned to REME, the Royal Electrical and Mechanical Engineers. He continued his distinguished career as an expert in a variety of fields, writing a range of REME repair manuals, serving as assistant adjutant, and giving lectures for officers, administration and management. He was appointed as the Brigadier's Staff Officer in Project Liaison, for rebuilding the barracks, and for major works, services and equipment in the School of Electrical and Mechanical Engineering at Bordon in Hampshire.

From 1972 he was with Marconi-Elliott Avionics, and then lectured in the Technical College at Woolwich. Roy joined the Civil Service in 1973, at the Royal School of Military Engineering Workshop in Rochester. From 1977 he was with the Ministry of Defence in London, as a procurement executive for the Engineering Branch. He was involved with project engineering, writing technical specifications, and managing procurement and design of major equipment for the Ministry of Defence. He retired in 1985.

Since then, Roy has followed a range of hobbies, among which is growing an expansive wild garden at his home in Kent, which produces fruit and vegetables. Roy found ways of growing mistletoe for charity, and worked as a HANDS volunteer assisting the underprivileged. He was presented with a Gold award for his environmental sensitivity.

65 Ralph Lenton with Roy Homard have just finished their evening meal. Ralph is wearing an array of safety pins for torn garment repair and other uses.

66 Roy Homard, vehicle engineer, next to his Sno-Cat, County of Kent.

67 Ralph Lenton, carpenter and radio man.

In recent years in his extensive home garden, Roy has gradually befriended several very cautious foxes. He has even enticed one vixen to eat from his hand, and has made friends with her two cubs. He was known for his success in making friends with penguins on the *Theron* voyage to Shackleton.

Ralph Lenton (Plates 65 and 67)

In World War II, Ralph was apprenticed as a carpenter and then enlisted in the Fleet Air Arm, where he trained in radio and navigation, and developed his interest in ham radio. In 1947 he signed up with the British Antarctic Survey and served four winters in Antarctica. He used his skills as a carpenter in building several bases and improving the buildings at others. His work was recognised through the award of an MBE at the age of 33. Ralph worked for the Arctic Institute of North America from 1979 until 1989, when medical problems forced him to retire. His unstinting generosity and understanding were spontaneous.

Ralph was very knowledgeable, and a key person in

the Arctic Institute. He amused me on one occasion in describing the reaction when he first telephoned the UK to crystallise some expedition arrangement — such an extravagance was scarcely familiar in UK at the time. He helped organise expeditions with the Institute to many different places — the Yukon, Greenland, Arctic ice islands, as well as Antarctica and he led one of the Greenland expeditions. He also spent several summers in Turkey, involved in a project looking for Noah's Ark.

One of the most memorable, unassuming people I have known, Ralph was respected and loved by everyone who came to know him. He died in 1986. One of his sons, Anthony, had spent two summers working at the US Pole Station, Amundsen-Scott. He took his father's ashes back to scatter them there, an appropriate resting place.

Hal Lister (Plates 26 and 68)

After TAE, Hal resumed his academic career in the Geography Department at the University of Newcastle-upon-Tyne and was awarded the Bruce

Memorial Prize by the Scottish Geographical Society in 1958. He sustained his interest in ice exploration and glaciology, and fostered enthusiasm among younger colleagues. He continued to maintain a wonderfully fresh enthusiasm for everything, especially relating to anything relating to ice.

Hal helped organise a succession of scientific expeditions to remote places around the world, ranging from high altitude areas in Afghanistan to Greenland and the Arctic, including ice islands. In 2005, Hal published recollections of his younger years in *Malham — Our Shangri-La*, and in *Ice — High and Low* he has described some of his diverse ice research and exploration.

A master at designing original gadgets and in improvisation, Hal could fabricate whatever he needed. I was fascinated to visit him in his retirement, and find he had a well-equipped workshop behind his home at Oxenholme near the Lake District. He was still making things.

Hal successfully took up painting later in life. The RGS accepted the donation of a number of his paintings, and he was delighted when he learnt their sale helped augment the Lord Edward Shackleton Memorial Fund by several hundred pounds.

George Lowe (Plate 68)

George came to TAE with an impressive record of achievement, on Everest and elsewhere. He was the official photographer with TAE and also its key mountaineering adviser. A schoolteacher, George brought a fresh approach to issues, and was not slow to question some of TAE's tactics and decisions. George was ebullient and could be delightfully irascible, but was always competent. As the only New Zealander in the crossing party, the situation in which his close friend, Hillary, was being criticised must have been difficult for him. Perhaps sharing a tent with the non-judgmental Hal Lister helped ease the situation.

After TAE, George joined the staff at Repton, an English public school, and spent four years there teaching 17-year-olds who were entering family business rather than preparing for university. He explored and climbed in North Greenland with John Hunt's expedition (1960) and was a member of the 'Yeti' expedition in Nepal with Ed Hillary. He helped to establish the Silver Hut, for high-altitude

68 George Lowe, photographer, with Hal Lister, glaciologist, preparing a hot drink.

winter physiological research (1960–61). His further mountain adventures included crossing the length of Greece with John Hunt and others (1961), and expeditions to the Russian Pamirs (1962) and Ethiopia (1963).

George then spent 10 years in Chile. He was two years deputy and subsequently became headmaster of the Grange School in Santiago. This is an all-age bilingual (English/Spanish) private school, whose enrolment exceeded 2000 students when it absorbed a leading girl's school. George was present in Chile during the country's difficult political years, including the coup against Allende by Pinochet and the generals. He returned to UK in late 1973, as one of Her Majesty's Inspectors of Schools, until he retired in 1984.

George had been with Ed Hillary when the Sherpas approached Ed and asked, 'Can you help us?' which led to the formation of the Himalayan Trust. Since 1989 George has been chairman of the Sir Edmund Hillary Himalayan Trust in the UK. His work has been recognised by several awards, including an OBE and CNZM. He received the Cuthbert Peek Award of the Royal Geographical Society in 1958 for mapping and exploration in the Himalayas and in the Antarctic. He now lives in Derbyshire in the UK.

David Pratt (Plates 69 and 70)

After TAE, I had difficulty keeping track of David's movements. He completed his PhD research at Imperial College, on technical aspects of travelling with snow vehicles (Appendix V).

69 David Pratt and Allan Rogers, doctor, are enjoying a hot drink.

David visited the Commonwealth Development Corporation headquarters in London, to see if they had something challenging which might suit his interests and energies. When he discovered that they had no engineering department he persuaded the Financial Controller to hire him for a year. He established an engineering department and became controller of engineering, was responsible for purchasing and marketing and was a founding member of the Executive Committee. He remained with the corporation, in executive positions, for more than 28 years.

The pressure in his job was intense, involving up to four months a year working in more than 50 countries. David describes the work as challenging and enjoyable. He found the logistics to be rather like those needed for an expedition, for example building a palm oil factory in the Solomons, or expanding a Caribbean electricity scheme. The projects were all in tropical

70 David Pratt, vehicle engineer.

Third World countries and usually involved available technology, but some required higher technology, such as one involving a modern sugar refinery.

David Pratt has sustained his passions for flying and gliding and now lives in London.

Allan Rogers (Plate 69)

After TAE, Allan returned to Bristol and resumed his teaching and research position at the university. Allan and I shared a tent on the vehicle journey from Shackleton to South Ice and we were easily able to coordinate our tenting routines. At Shackleton, he documented everyone's daily dress routines, in addition to his physiological research, using IMP (integrating motor pneumatachograph) instrumentation to measure the energy balance of volunteers, when working strenuously and when asleep. These complicated instruments tested Allan's ingenuity and technical expertise to keep them working.

Allan was very skilful with his hands and loved electronics. He published his expedition research findings, though his IMP results were corrupted by contamination of the breath samples from his subjects, which he brought home in sealed ampoules. He later conducted other physiological research, including work on infants' blood pressure. He died in 1990, aged 72.

John Lewis

John was our senior pilot and resumed his career with the RAF after TAE. This involved postings in South-East Asia and Berlin. His command of a transport squadron included a flight over the North Pole. He liked to describe himself, self-deprecatingly, as 'driver — airframe'. On TAE he was the senior pilot on the Otter flight across the continent.

A great conversationalist, John had an endless store of fascinating anecdotes. His stories all seemed to be based on his many and varied experiences. John was an ebullient and optimistic character with an ever-present sense of humour. He died in 1990, aged 67.

Gordon Haslop

Gordon, a New Zealander, was our second pilot on TAE. He was a skilled flier and distinguished himself on many occasions in the course of the expedition. He had some hair-raising encounters on the expedition, and became a master at landing in heavy drift at South Ice. On one occasion, returning to Shackleton with Ken Blaiklock, he tried to descend through 'cloud', which proved to be the ground surface. As noted previously, this locality was later called Touch Down Hills. At the end of the winter, Gordon and Allan Rogers spent 11 days bivouacking in a covered trench awaiting help, having flown past Halley Bay on a mercy flight. He was co-pilot to John Lewis on the flight across the continent and after returning from TAE continued in the RAF. Gordon was killed in a vehicle accident in Singapore in 1961, an unfortunate and ironic fate, given the constant level of risk he faced flying in Antarctica.

Peter Weston

Peter's role was to maintain the two TAE aircraft, and he was a team member on the Otter Flight across the continent. His work was always meticulous, despite difficult circumstances, such as repairing the Auster rudder on the rolling and pitching bow workshop on *Magga Dan*. With the air filled with drying paint smells, Peter would withdraw, be sick, and then return.

Peter was a member of the Norwegian-British-Swedish Expedition in 1949–52, which he scarcely ever mentioned. A self-contained person, inclined to silence, and he was well-informed about Egyptology, one of his great interests. Peter set high cooking standards at Shackleton, which Hal Lister says embarrassed him when it was his turn to cook. After our return, Peter returned to his work in the RAF but I lost contact with him. He died suddenly in 1994.

Ellis 'Taffy' Williams

Taffy Williams, was the colourful RAF radioman on TAE. He was very experienced, having spent the first winter at Shackleton with the Advance Party. Some of the delightful stories about Taffy are related earlier. He came up to South Ice to install our radio and later I enjoyed his company on the Shackleton Range geological traverse with a dog team. Neither of us was experienced in driving dogs but Taffy seemed to enjoy the break from his role as a busy radio operator and kept an eye on the dogs while I looked at my rocks. He handled much of the radio traffic at Shackleton and enjoyed 'telling the world of our privations'. Taffy was the radio operator on the Otter flight from South Ice to Scott Base.

I also lost contact with Taffy after TAE. He died around 2000.

Rainer Goldsmith

After returning from TAE, Rainer pursued an active career in physiological research and teaching. He joined the Division of Human Physiology of the Medical Research Council (MRC) and worked on problems of working in heat and in cold for the next 15 years.

He returned to Antarctica twice. On Deepfreeze V (1960), he took part in Operation Snuffles, seeking to isolate a virus causing the common cold. He also took an opportunity to work on temperature regulation in penguins. He was with Sir Raymond Priestley, a member of the Northern Party on Scott's last expedition, when Priestley revisited the hut at Cape Adare, 50 years later. As they entered the hut Priestley pointed to a tumble down bunk and exclaimed, 'That is where I slept'.

Goldsmith's second Antarctic return visit was with the International Biomedical Expedition to the Antarctic in 1980, to Dumont d'Urville and Adelie Land. They studied the effects of cold on men who were deliberately exposed to uncomfortable conditions, driving skidoos and sleeping in polar tents. The subjects were examined beforehand in the lab at Sydney University, with daily tests of their response to heat and cold, and of psychological performance. These tests were repeated three to four months later as soon as the men returned from Antarctica. The party comprised a random group of men from five nations — the UK, France, Australia, New Zealand and Argentina. Himself a subject, Goldsmith reflects that the most interesting findings were on the influence of social and psychological factors.

Rainer also worked in Aden with the MRC, on an experiment examining differences in performance among soldiers, one group acclimatised and the other not acclimatised to heat. He was also seconded to the International Labour Organisation of the UN to advise on working in the heat of India, Ceylon, and Taiwan.

Leaving the MRC, Goldsmith commenced an academic teaching career in human physiology at Aberdeen University. He subsequently accepted a position as foundation senior lecturer in physiology at the new Medical School at the University of Nottingham. He describes this as among his most exciting times as an academic, helping to plan the first new UK medical school in the 20th century. This involved coordinating new information from several other UK medical schools and from Canada on teaching and learning.

He accepted a Chair at Chelsea College, University of London, and ran the Department of Physiology there for some years, seeking to develop an innovative curriculum, teaching methods and assessment. Later, he moved to the Department of Human Sciences at the University of Loughborough for 10 happy years, capped by running an MSc program in research for medical professionals. Rainer served for over 10 years as editor for two major scientific journals, *Ergonomics* and the *European Journal of Applied Physiology*,

Rainer retired to live near Derby. He revels in gardening, and is an expert photographer. I was intrigued to read the dedication Vivian Fuchs wrote in his copy of *The Crossing of Antarctica*: 'To a young man who could always see a better way to do something'. This was an insightful and prophetic comment about Rainer.

A Concluding Comment

At the time of TAE, I counted myself fortunate to be associated with such an outstanding group of individuals. They were all refreshingly different.

The tyranny of distance, given that I live in Australia, limited my contact to the occasional reunion in England.

It is not surprising, given the talented cast of TAE, that it was such a generally harmonious and successful expedition.

7 THEN AND NOW

Since 1958, there has been comprehensive exploration and extensive scientific work in the Antarctic region. The Antarctic has also seen the development of tourist cruises, especially to the Antarctic Peninsula.

Set against this scenario, half a century later, it is interesting to place TAE in context and outline some of the discoveries. What changes have occurred and what significance has TAE relative to recent exploration and science?

SCIENCE AND EXPLORATION

Scientific discovery has flourished in all fields, stimulated by the International Geophysical Year, 1957–58. At the time, I felt annoyed that geological exploration was not included, but since IGY this omission has been properly addressed and amazing advances have been made in mapping and investigating the geology of the whole continent.

The comprehensive exploration of Antarctica's mountains and glaciers has proceeded. Landsat satellite imagery was acquired, though its orbits were restricted to north of 80°S. This technology has stimulated further exploration in Antarctica. Then, in 1999, special satellite orbits were developed for synthetic aperture radar (SAR) imagery to survey even the most remote corners of the continent.[1] SAR provides images with special advantages for surveying ice terrain.

Ice thickness measurements have changed from seismic sounding on ground traverses to efficient airborne radar penetration, generating continuous ice thickness profiles of the most remote regions, for example, across the Polar Plateau. Numerous subglacial lakes, of presumed fresh water, have been found under some areas of the East Antarctic Ice Sheet, the first discovered in the Vostok region. Deep drilling has profiled the depths of the ice sheet in a number of places, to disclose variations in temperature and atmospheric composition. Bubbles of air are preserved in the deep ice, and analysis of their composition reveals critical data, including levels of atmospheric methane and carbon dioxide, over many hundreds of thousands of years. Such evidence is critical in trying to place climate change in a long-term perspective. The Antarctic Peninsula has been getting warmer, but much of East Antarctica, which accounts for 85 percent of the ice in Antarctica, has been getting colder. Antarctic weather conditions, even in summer, are still severe, and visits to the continent demand a comprehensive understanding of this extreme environment.

The greatest differences which have influenced Antarctic projects since about the time of TAE have involved a clearer appreciation of what is possible. The realisation that, with careful planning, even small expeditions can be successful has revolutionised Antarctic exploration. The frequency of visits by small sailing boats to some parts of the continent has increased. Considerable hazards remain, and though there have been some disasters, most have been successful, even coping with capsize and dismasting. Visits by small aircraft to the continent have also become more familiar through media coverage, though some have been judged as irresponsible.

Remarkable surface journeys have been accomplished, beyond what was considered possible in the 1950s. The changing nature of Antarctic crossings since 1958 demonstrates just how far our understanding of human capability in Antarctica has progressed. TAE, compared with some of the ultra-small expeditions in recent decades, was an enormous and logistically complex undertaking.

EQUIPMENT, FACILITIES AND SCIENTIFIC PERSPECTIVES

A generally held perception is that much improvement has taken place in clothing and personal comfort under cold conditions, compared to the earlier, primitive clothing. Although the equipment we had on TAE may now seem bulky and old-fashioned, I consider we enjoyed good, sensible clothing, far superior to what was available for the heroic era expeditions of Scott, Mawson and Shackleton. I have mentioned that some of our equipment could have been improved, such as our outer gloves and our sleeping mats. Since 1958, clothing has indeed improved, especially in the fabrics used, but other changes in Antarctic exploration have been dramatic.

Major changes have involved access, transport and communication, and the support available in emergency. International coordination and cooperation have been noteworthy and communication is much more dependable. At times, our radios failed to get through, in spite of the skill and persistence of our technicians. Today, travelling parties can keep a better eye on changing weather through regional forecasts. A crossing party can report its progress each day through a satellite transmitter and use a satellite phone with clear voice exchange. It would be unrealistic to consider travelling today without these modern aids. However, batteries are still vulnerable and equipment can easily be damaged. There are just as many crevasses as ever, and it is intriguing that

methods for their swift detection do not seem to have advanced. To construct a permanent, 'safe' highway, tractors are used to fill the crevasses. With crevasses, you must still be observant, and lucky.

Antarctica remains a dangerous place, and mistakes can generate swift repercussions. There are inspiring stories of survival by the early heroic explorers, but others had tragic outcomes. The spirit of human endeavour has been maintained, with extraordinary achievement, but human life remains as fragile as it ever was in the awesome Antarctic.

SCIENTIFIC ACHIEVEMENTS OF TAE

TAE set out to undertake a range of scientific work in conjunction with IGY. This included regular meteorological observations at Shackleton, South Ice and during the crossing journey. Glaciological work at South Ice involved Hal Lister's glaciology, especially his drift studies and work on snow accumulation. On the journey, Geoffrey Pratt made periodic seismic soundings using buried explosives to determine ice thickness, and also measured gravity with his gravimeter. Along the route, Hal Lister studied snow profiles with a rammsonde to estimate annual accumulation rates across the continent. Geologically, I investigated the rocks in each of the three mountain ranges we discovered. This work confirmed the nature of the rock formations, and plant fossils in the Theron Mountains and the Whichaway Nunataks showed their Gondwana affiliation and Permian age. Our two doctors studied aspects of human physiology and adaptation to cold. Our geographical discoveries were recorded accurately in maps by our surveyors.

The expedition published a series of scientific reports, listed in Appendix V, which Fuchs edited. A range of other scientific papers was published in professional journals.

TAE received a generally positive evaluation of its exploration and scientific work. However, there have been some less than complimentary assessments of the expedition. In 2003, S.J. Pyne published a review of Antarctica and the history of its exploration. He said, of TAE:

Self-styled as the 'last greatest land expedition on

earth' … a much-publicised trek that sought to realise Shackleton's ambition for an overland traverse of Antarctica … The expedition succeeded although it was difficult to weigh just what it succeeded in; its principal contributions to science were the gravity and seismic soundings it conducted on behalf of IGY. An enterprise separate from IGY — distinct not merely in its origins but in its emphasis on the personalities of its leaders — the Trans-Antarctic Expedition was an anachronism. Its meaning to exploration was defined less by its realisation of the transantarctic traverse than by the new matrix for discovery established through IGY.[2]

I find Stephen Pyne's book rather strange. It outlines exploration history, and attempts to summarise the progression of geology and glaciology as sciences. Its perspectives differ considerably from my own, and I do not agree that TAE was an anachronism. Granted, it did take place at the end of a traditional era of exploration and discovery in the Antarctic interior by travelling into it, to locate and investigate newly discovered mountain ranges, and found a passage through them and across the Polar Plateau. I consider that the study of the new features encountered occurred in the best traditions of exploration, and thorough ground investigation and survey provided long-lasting contributions to our knowledge of the continent.

After TAE, few significant major traverses were undertaken, except for seismic exploration to determine ice thickness by the USA, Russia and Australia. This early seismic research has been superseded by using airborne radar to profile virtually the whole continent.

IGY AND ITS AFTERMATH

The International Geophysical Year made a considerable contribution to the knowledge and understanding of Antarctica. The most important outcome was as a catalyst for international coordination and cooperation. The discoveries which resulted from IGY resulted in a scientific spotlight being turned on the continent. Subsequently, the development of methods of enquiry has been phenomenal, and I am amazed that this continues strongly today.

Other exploration undertaken during IGY was in the Weddell Sea region, and is outlined in Appendix IV. Subsequent exploration was undertaken in the

Shackleton Range as part of a long-term international enterprise. Later research involved the dolerite rocks in the Therons, Shackletons and Whichaway Nunataks.[3] I was fascinated to learn that a Twin Otter landed at the site of South Ice in December 1998, using Blaiklock's surveyed position. Forty years on, they could not find any trace of our home. More recently, another long-term project placed advanced GPS station markers in the Antarctic Peninsula and mountains to the east, including Sentinel and Pensacola Mountains, and Whichaway Nunataks. They used these to check their relative positions in relation to tectonic plate movements occurring between West and East Antarctica, and to confirm the relative positions of these features within centimetres. Recently, Ian Dalziel, an American geophysicist from Texas, surprised me with his photograph of one of his sites in the Whichaways.[4] It was a dolerite nunatak further east from the main group where we travelled in 1957–58. Naturally, I was eager to hear about this research in our old territory.

The conviction, which some of us had at the time of TAE, that the late 1950s and the period of IGY would mark the climax and decline of Antarctic exploration was quite wrong. Later work from many nations has blossomed, and continues today. In geology, we have seen a revolution through plate tectonics, for which the Antarctic Ocean provided important data. It placed the results of centuries of painstaking geological mapping on the other, more accessible continents in an illuminating context.

The Antarctic Treaty: 1959

IGY was highly successful, as much for international cooperation as for science, even during the Cold War. But the future of Antarctica was in question, especially with the disputes arising from overlapping territorial claims in the Peninsula region. Historically, claims had been made by seven nations, which collectively covered only about two-thirds of the continent. Two major participants in IGY, the USA and Russia, had still made no claim.

IGY helped stimulate discussions leading to the Antarctic Treaty, which was opened for signature on 1 December 1959, signed by 12 countries, and officially entered into force on 23 June 1961. Under the Treaty, national claims were held in abeyance, and participants did not have to respect them.

Since 1961, another 28 nations signed the Treaty and a number of new international agreements about Antarctica have been reached, culminating in the Madrid Protocol on Environmental Protection in 1991, signed by 38 governments. Before this, other conventions were agreed upon, including the Conservation of Antarctic Seals (1972) and of Antarctic Marine Resources (1980). A Convention on the Regulation of Antarctic Mineral Resource Activities (CRAMRA, 1988) was adopted after six years of negotiation. However, within a few years, Australia and France declared their opposition to CRAMRA, arguing for Antarctica to become a world park or wilderness preserve.

International cooperation and coordination of Antarctic management constitutes one of the rare successes in international diplomacy for planet earth. This reflects the special characteristics of the Antarctic environment, the absence of permanent population, and the international commitment to coordinated scientific work there.

The Antarctic Treaty is available at http://www.nsf.gov/od/opp/antarct/anttrty.jsp. Simmonds noted that the Treaty continues to play a central and dominant role in Antarctic protocols.[5] Scientific endeavours continue in Antarctica, and a special year of coordinated scientific work, the fourth Polar Year, is scheduled for 2007–09.[6]

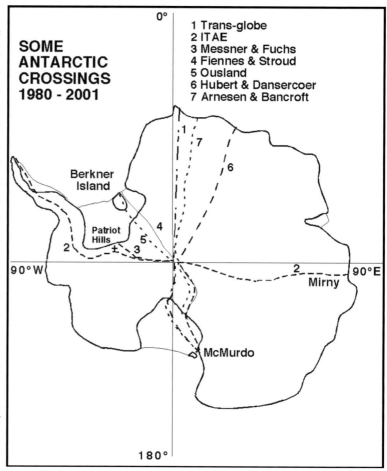

Figure 21 Some subsequent crossings made by different parties, described in the text.

CROSSING ANTARCTICA — ACHIEVEMENTS SINCE TAE

The major initiatives in Antarctica today are primarily national expeditions. Massive investment is required for long-term projects, such as the logistics needed to establish and maintain a new base. Many scientific projects have been national, and a few have been international endeavours. Some have involved extended land-based traverses, for example to access distant mountain regions for seismic and geological work. Understandably, air-supported projects have become more common.

In contrast to these national initiatives, all the crossings of Antarctica since 1958 were made by small, private expeditions. The last significant private expedition was probably the British Graham Land Expedition (BGLE, 1933–36). These small expeditions have evolved from early supported undertakings to subsequent unassisted crossings. A 'supported' enterprise might involve the use of vehicles, dogs or the use of air depots. Others crossings have been 'unassisted', which calls for remarkable self-contained performance.

The routes followed by different parties are shown on Figure 21. Other adventurers have made journeys from the coast to the South Pole by hauling small sledges, in the style of Scott and Shackleton. Incidentally, sledge dogs were banned in Antarctica, by international agreement, in 1991. The table below lists completed crossings, showing distances and duration.

TEN ANTARCTIC CROSSINGS
1980 to 2001

(Adapted from AdvertureStats 2003; ExplorersWeb Inc.)

NAME	YEAR	NATIONALITY	DAYS	DISTANCE
R. Fiennes	1980–81	UK	67	4800 km
C. Burton		UK		
O. Shepard		UK		
W. Steger	1989–90	USA	220	6000 km
J.-L. Etienne		France		
V. Boyarski		Russia		
G. Somers		UK		
Qin Dahe		China		
Keizo Funatsu		Japan		
R. Messner	1989–90	Italy	92	3000 km
A. Fuchs		Germany		
M. Hoibakk	1990–91	Norway	n.a	2930 km
S. Mordre		Norway		
S. Mordre		Norway		
R. Fiennes	1992–93	UK	95	2380 km
M. Stroud		UK		
B. Ousland	1996–97	Norway	64	2845 km
A. Hubert	1997–98	Belgium	99	3924 km
D. Dansercoer		Belgium		
M. Ohba	1998–1999	Japan	98	3824 km
R. Bae	2000–01	Norway	107	3800 km
E. Sonneland		Norway		
L. Arnesen	2000–01	Norway	93	2747 km
A. Bancroft		USA		

Seven of these expeditions will now be described, in outline, from their published accounts.

The Trans-Globe Expedition (TGE), 1980–82[7]

Virginia Fiennes, wife of the leader Ranulph Fiennes, conceived the idea for an unorthodox polar circling of the earth, following close to the 0°–180° longitudes, including an Antarctic crossing. This second Antarctic crossing used small, open vehicles. I was astonished to learn that three men made the overland journey riding skidoos, the equivalent of a motor bike for snow. Their radical planning revealed an imaginative understanding of Antarctic conditions.

The party prepared to winter near Ryvingen, 300 km inland from Sanae, the South African base in Dronning Maud Land. The experienced pilot, Giles Kershaw, and the aircraft maintenance engineer, Gerry Nicholson, arrived in a Twin Otter from England to join the expedition for the summer and fly supplies, fuel and the expedition huts up to Ryvingen. Two bases were established: a two-man station near Sanae (with Simon Grimes and Nicholson) and the inland station at Ryvingen. Ranulph Fiennes, Virginia Fiennes, Charles Barton and Oliver Shepard occupied the inland station. Ranulph Fiennes, Barton and Shepard rode their three Bombardier skidoos, pulling sledges, from Sanae across the narrow ice shelf and through the coastal mountains. The prefabricated huts at Ryvingen, 12 x 24 feet, were made of corrugated cardboard, an excellent insulator, and were erected in pits. The hut sections were easily transported and erected, and Kershaw and Nicholson then flew back to England to return the next summer.

When the Otter returned, Grimes was flown up from the station near Sanae to join Virginia Fiennes at Ryvingen and enable the crossing party to depart. The three skidoos set off on 29 October 1980 for the Pole in -50°C and a 20 knot wind. The immediate test was to climb the Kirwan Escarpment, a rise of 460 metres to the edge of the Polar Plateau. Fiennes describes this as a testing performance for his 640 cc skidoo engine, pulling two bouncing sledges, each carrying 544 kg. The skidoo's rubber tracks provided marginal grip on what proved to be ice inclines. The climb up the escarpment began from near 2130 metres, but after 60 km they reached the ridgeline, past the last nunatak.

Advancing steadily and moving under virtually any conditions, including whiteout, they travelled for about 10 hours each day and camped in a three-man tent. In the course of the crossing, in spite of consuming 6500 calories per day, their weight loss ranging from 3 to 26 pounds. Fiennes used compass bearings for navigation, sighting on clouds ahead or on horizon details, and he took theodolite sun shots to check their position. Later, he improvised a sun compass, scratching directions onto his plastic windscreen and engine cowling. The vehicles travelled about a mile apart, allowing him to check a back compass bearing every hour. Travel on the skidoos was very exposed, particularly for the right hand; the hand throttle had to be kept open or the vehicle would stop. They endured 'bitter, vicious cold'.

The TGE crossing party reached the Pole on 15 December 1980, seven weeks ahead of schedule. They were welcomed at the American Base at the Pole and camped in two pyramid tents, 100 yards from the station entrance. They were invited to dine at the base in exchange for dishwashing and general clean-up duties. Their air support had supplied fuel depots and from a depot he established at 86°S, Kershaw reached the Pole before them. No sooner had he arrived than he answered an emergency rescue call from the South Africans back near the coast and rescued four men. After five years negotiations, the expedition was assured of air fuel at the Pole. Kershaw flew the remainder of the team, including Virginia Fiennes, to the Pole.

After a week, the crossing party left the Pole on 23 December. Their descent to the Ross Ice Shelf followed the Scott Glacier, west of Amundsen's Axel Heiberg Glacier route in 1911–12. The Scott Glacier proved to be as heavily crevassed as was Amundsen's route. Shepard wrote in his diary, 'Quite the nastiest and most dangerous experience in my life'.

The skidoos arrived at Scott Base on 11 January 1981. It had been a bold, imaginative expedition and Kershaw's flying skills had been brilliant. The expedition went on to complete its trans-globe route by making a North Pole traverse.

The International Trans-Antarctica Expedition (ITAE) 1989–90[8]

The ITAE traverse party comprised six men, from the US, France, Britain, Russia, China and Japan. It achieved the longest possible traverse of Antarctica, 3700 miles (nearly 6000 km), from near the tip of the Antarctic Peninsula, via the South Pole to the Russian station at Mirny. This route was almost at 90 degrees to Fiennes' crossing.

The journey began at dawn on 27 July 1989 with three dog teams, in warm weather, in the region where Nordenskjold travelled in 1904. They used two navigation systems: a conventional compass and sextant, and an Argos satellite transmitter which sent a signal to Toulouse where their position was calculated and available next day via Punta Arenas. There was some dispute over the relative reliability of the two methods, and knowing their accurate location was at times critical for navigation.

They slowly progressed down the east side of the Peninsula in difficult, stormy weather. Depots had been put in by air the previous season, but some could not be found. They had serious crevasse incidents and were extremely fortunate not to lose any dogs, or men.

In November, they reached the Adventure Network International (ANI) base at Patriot Hills. ANI was providing Antarctic air transport for small expeditions. Reinhold Messner and Arvid Fuchs arrived at Patriot Hills with ANI around the same time, and were about to commence their ski crossing.

ITAE continued, and with improving weather they were able to travel faster and arrived at the Pole on 11 December 1981. They were 2071 miles into their journey. They stayed three days and continued, to face the higher part of the Polar Plateau and the 'area of inaccessibility', which some had predicted might prove impossible to negotiate because of expected deep, soft snow. Fortunately, they found hard, wind-packed surfaces.

The party reached Vostok, the inland Russian station, on 18 January 1990, to a boisterous welcome and a longed-for shower. The temperature inside the station was +60°F, which they found uncomfortably warm. The six men and their dogs continued along the route used by Russian tractors between Vostok and Mirny, their destination at the coast, and the vehicles left food depots for them. This is the region where the world's lowest temperature, -89.2°C, was recorded in 1983, and the travelling conditions were extreme because of the cold.

As they approached Mirny on the coast, it began to get warmer. Steger describes waking one morning, bewildered, unable to believe his ears. He could hear the chirp and warble of birds! His tent mate, Jean-Louis Etienne, was playing a tape of birdsongs, which he had saved until then.

This was a dangerous time, so close to the finish, and

just two days from reaching Mirny they experienced bad storms and poor visibility. Keizo Funatsu became lost after going outside to attend to his dog team. He dug a hole and sheltered in it until found, unhurt, after nearly 14 hours.

The group crossed a 'finishing line' at Mirny on 3 March 1990. This journey was another remarkable achievement, by men from six different nations. The whole venture, at a cost of around $11 million, was intended to focus world attention and cooperation on fragile Antarctica. The team returned via Australia, and I had the pleasure of meeting these fine men in Sydney.

Tragically, Giles Kershaw of ANI was killed in a plane crash in the Antarctic Peninsula two weeks after ITAE left Mirny.

The Wurth Antarctica Transversale (1989–90)

Reinhold Messner and Arvid Fuchs made the first Antarctic crossing on skis. The Italian, Messner, is well known as a mountaineer, having scaled Everest without oxygen and other major peaks on all continents. Fuchs, a German, had completed a number of dangerous, arduous journeys in Patagonia and across Greenland, and in 1989 walked with a party to the North Pole. Messner was 45 and Fuchs 10 years younger.

The expedition became known as the Wurth Antarctica Transversale, with financial backing from the German industrialist, Reinhold Wurth.[9] The cost of the expedition was more than a million DM (approximately US$600,000).

They set out from the south edge of the Ronne Ice Shelf at 82°S 71°W, having flown in with ANI from Punta Arenas, via the Patriot Hills base. They planned to leave Punta Arenas much earlier and start their journey by the third week of October, but two flights were turned back by bad weather. Their planned starting point for the crossing was the coast of Antarctica, at the northern edge of the Filchner Ice Shelf, but a fuel shortage at Patriot Hills forced the change to 82°S.

The two men had an air supply from an ANI Twin Otter in the Thiel Mountains (87°S, 88°W), 2800 metres above sea level on 6 December 1989. Like ITAE, the men used an Argos transmitter each

night to send a signal to the French Space Agency in Toulouse, where their location was calculated from Doppler shifting and relayed to the expedition base at Punta Arenas. They could send a distress code to Toulouse, but the Argos signal was not always received. While their Argos satellite device could fix their position, Fuchs soon found their GPS functioned so well they put away their alternative, a sextant. Later, the GPS caused initial confusion after they left the Pole and moved from east to west longitudes. Fuchs' ski boots proved to be poorly fitted, and for the rest of the expedition his feet suffered from severe blistering. Later, Messner also had problems with his feet.

The revolution achieved by this team was in their use of para-sails, stimulated by Fuchs' experience with these devices crossing Greenland. Fuchs said he placed his faith almost exclusively in sailing. As time progressed, their sail handling improved, in spite of some dangerous falls to begin with. They each took two different sized kites for light and heavier winds. As they reached the higher altitudes on the plateau, the force of the wind decreased and the sound of the sails diminished. Before reaching the Pole, they unexpectedly experienced a favourable wind and one day travelled 57 km (36 miles), in spite of the sastrugi. After earlier doubts, Messner now believed they could complete their crossing.

They arrived at the Pole on 31 December 1989, meeting their photographer and press representative there. Messner was deeply upset by the existence of the Pole Station in the middle of the pristine Antarctic wilderness. The date automatically advanced a day, from GMT to NZ time. Under Pole Station protocol, they were 'not there', and the station commanding officer neither welcomed them officially nor visited them. Antarctic bases are remote and have limited facilities for emergency work and for visitors. Today, official attitudes are that they cannot take on any search, rescue or recovery role. The countries that maintain scientific bases in Antarctica are involved in very high expenses, and there is no provision for additional commitments. Explorers involved in a demanding and exciting personal undertaking, have very different perspectives, and must find the reception they receive puzzling. However, Messner and Fuchs were given many meals, a shower and the luxury of a table to write on. They rested for three days before continuing, following the Shackleton–Scott route down the Beardmore Glacier.

ANI had put in a food and fuel depot for them at the Pole. They repaired their skis and changed equipment, including a new tent and skis for Fuchs. On their last morning, the station commanding officer invited them in for breakfast before they set off, though denied enough wind to sail off in style.

Fuchs was still hampered by sore feet and often arrived at camp an hour after Messner. On 18 January 1990, they were able to sail again and climbed to a notch in the ridge above the tributary Mill Glacier. The spectacular scenery awed even Messner, a legend in the world of mountaineering, who wrote 'nowhere on earth is there a landscape which is as grandiose as the route from the interior to the coast of the Ross Sea.' Their route down the Beardmore provided extreme crevasse difficulties, just as it had done for the early explorers over 75 years earlier, and one hellish icefall particularly impressed Messner.

Throughout the journey, they experienced constant doubts, including reaching the Pole, negotiating the Beardmore exit Gateway, and crossing the Ross Ice Shelf. Having left the Pole with only 45 days supplies, their food supply became 'painfully short' and they rationed their food, marching long hard days for two weeks, achieving 15 to 18 miles a day. Fortunately, suitable winds eventually came. Their kites were far more successful than Shackleton and Scott's efforts to use simple sails for wind assistance across the Ross Ice Shelf. With favourable winds from the south, Messner and Fuchs suddenly achieved some remarkable distances on the Ross Ice Shelf, including 440 km over two weeks, and more than 100 km in one day. Messner refers to their travelling at three speeds — 'donkey' (2 mph), 'penguin' (3–4 mph) and 'swallow' (5–8 mph)!

Messner and Fuchs reached McMurdo Sound on 12 February 1990 and were flown to the Italian Terra Nova station north of McMurdo. They sailed to Christchurch on the *Backen*.

Ranulph Fiennes and Mike Stroud (1992–93)

This British expedition set out from Berkner Island on the Weddell Sea coast to cross the continent to the Ross Sea.[10] Their aim was to make the first unassisted crossing — in other words, without any mechanical assistance, depots or air supply.

Fiennes, aged 49, had already crossed Antarctica by skidoo and crossed the North Pole on his Trans-Globe Expedition. Later, he made an unsuccessful attempt to reach the North Pole a second time. The 39-year-old Stroud was a doctor, who had carried out polar physiological research, and who wanted to test extreme performance. He was also an experienced mountaineer. While previous Antarctic crossings had been made, some without mechanical assistance, no one had crossed unassisted. Other ventures had reached the Pole, but for an unassisted crossing, twice the quantity of food and fuel are required.

Their original plan was to charter ANI, now managed by Annie Kershaw, Giles Kershaw's widow. This was for three people to be flown from Chile to the Atlantic coast of Antarctica, south of Cape Town, for £150,000. An alternative plan to cross, starting from McMurdo Sound, would have been much more costly. To mount any expedition to Antarctica remains an expensive exercise.

Fiennes and Stroud were flown from Punta Arenas to Patriot Hills and then to the east side of Berkner Island, at the edge of the Weddell Sea. With supplies for a complete crossing, their sledges weighed 485 pounds (220 kg). They had to overcome a series of initial misfortunes. Under sail, Stroud was carried at speed into a crevasse depression, but luckily the snow bridge did not collapse.

They experienced serious physical deterioration throughout their journey. They lost weight, which they checked on a miniature scale, and the effects of their ordeal increased. Their feet blistered and later developed abscesses and they experienced serious altitude effects on the plateau. Stroud was debilitated by hypoglycaemia, low blood sugar. Later he became vulnerable to hypothermia, exhibiting poor balance and slurred speech, and Fiennes had to watch him carefully.

By the time they reached the Pole, where they stayed only two hours, they had lost an incredible 25 percent of their body weight. Both their thermos flasks had broken, and they had problems caused by insufficient fluid. Sledging north to descend the Beardmore Glacier, they crossed the highest part of their journey at around 11,000 feet (3350 metes).

At such low temperatures, this altitude is said to be equivalent to 15,000 feet in temperate latitudes. They found the cold extreme, having abandoned some warm clothing to lighten their loads soon after starting their journey.

They made their difficult way down the crevassed course of the Beardmore and finally reached the Gateway crossing at its end. They were five days behind schedule, with an additional nine days lost before the start.

Their situation had become desperate. After descending the glacier, Fiennes and Stroud reduced their rations by 50 percent. Whether they would reach McMurdo in time to rendezvous with the *Seaquest* cruise ship was doubtful and the last US plane had left Antarctica. With their satellite transmitter broken, Fiennes was forced to make radio contact with ANI at Patriot Hills. The Twin Otter picked them up and flew them back to Patriot Hills and they were in Punta Arenas a week later. It must have been a disappointing decision to evacuate, because for every mile they covered, thousands of pounds were being pledged for the cause of multiple sclerosis research.

Fiennes and Stroud had technically crossed the Antarctic continent, getting beyond its edge and out onto the Ross Ice Shelf. *The Guinness Book of Records* notes their achievement as 2170-km (1350 miles) equivalent straight-line distance. Amundsen's dogs averaged 16.3 miles per day, while Fiennes and Stroud achieved an average of 15.7 miles. The physiological research fraternity must have been grateful for their voluntary ordeal and Stroud analysed their human performance in his subsequent book.

Few have suffered more in the Antarctic than Fiennes and Stroud.

Børge Ousland (1996–97)

This remarkable Norwegian explorer completed the first unassisted solo crossing of Antarctica.[11] He had previously made a solo crossing of the North Pole in 1995, and in 1995–96 made a solo trip to the South Pole. Shackleton inspired him, and to cross Antarctica alone had been a dream for some time. He wanted to be the first and states that if someone had already done it he would not have mounted his expedition. At the time of his crossing, Ousland was 34.

Ousland's account of his 1996–97 crossing contains interesting details, enhanced by his own photographs. He used specially designed equipment and his preparations recall Amundsen's thoroughness. He always obtained good advice, left nothing untested, and was fanatical about saving weight with his gear. He took two sets of skis as sailing skis and for cross-country skiing. His food was all freeze-dried and he even reduced the number of daily rations to only 87. He trained regularly, by towing three tyres through the forest. An expert skier, he practised with his para-wing sails, modifying their design in collaboration with a German sail expert.

He had reached the South Pole early in 1996 on his solo first journey of over 1000 kilometres. When frostbite and blisters made the continuation of the journey impossible, Ousland was evacuated by plane. His achievement stimulated two other men to attempt the first solo crossing, Marek Kaminsky (Poland) and Ranulph Fiennes (Britain). The announcement of their plans prompted Ousland to make another attempt. Both Kaminsky and Fiennes had previously been to each Pole, and Fiennes had already crossed Antarctica twice.

The various parties assembled in Punta Arenas. In addition to the three solo travellers, there were six Korean mountaineers led by Young Ho Heo, who had climbed on Everest. They flew off together for Patriot Hills in ANI's Hercules, a six-hour flight, and arrived on 13 November. Kjell Ove Storvik travelled with Ousland as his radio contact, to remain at Patriot Hills. Fiennes set off straight away and was flown independently to an undisclosed point, presumably near Berkner Island. Two days later the Pole and Norwegian were put down on opposite sides of Berkner Island, which divides the Ronne and Filchner Ice shelves. Kaminsky started his journey from the west side and Ousland from the east side, climbing over the axis of the island. From his previous visit, Ousland knew he had a better chance of more favourable wind directions.

The initial weight of Ousland's sledge was 180 kg and he knew it would become 1.2 kg lighter each day. He had his first sail next day in light wind and in three days was halfway across Berkner Island. He travelled along its relatively crevasse-free axis, heading for the transition from the island down onto the shelf ice beyond. Ousland had two sails, which he called

Baby Boy and Big Boy. These sails demanded expert handling and almost daily maintenance. Descending to the ice shelf beyond, he crossed it safely to reach the ridge on the east side of the Dufek Massif. The year before he had climbed Frost Spur, further west, but this time he climbed Wujek Ridge, which proved to be less steep. He walked across to the rock outcrops to the west and was surprised to discover a US Survey marker on the rock, 'Point Dorothy 1965'.

He carried three communication devices — a lightweight compact radio, an Argos satellite communicator and an emergency beacon. Having climbed the Dufek ridge on his 14th day, he was already about 300 miles from the start and at an altitude of 1100 metres. He continued south and entered a sastrugi area, where each day he sought to find and photograph at least one 'artwork' sculpted by the wind.

Ousland reached 84°S on 3 December 1996. Fiennes had climbed Frost Spur the day before, about 100 miles behind, and Kaminsky was still on the shelf ice. By 5 December, Ousland was at 85°40'S, with the sastrugi getting worse. It was like a long obstacle course; he could go around the large ones but found the small ones more of a problem. He found the weight of his sledge to be at the limit of manageability, and surmised that an extra 10 kg would have been a problem. From his radio he learned that Fiennes had been forced to stop in great pain with kidney stones, and was evacuated to Patriot Hills.

Ousland's route crossed a crevasse field he had seen the year before. There were no open crevasses, but he routinely looked for sastrugi crossings. The crevasses were up to 15 metres wide, and he was careful to drag the sledge behind him on long sledge shafts, designed to slide free in the event of a fall. The sledge was four metres behind, and he carried his climbing gear, rope and emergency beacon inside his anorak. He wore a balaclava around his neck and a facemask and, thankfully, his double-glass goggles did not mist up. He wore windproof mitts, large enough to wear over several pairs of woollen mitts, and toe-to-knee gaiters, fastened with Velcro. When he needed it, he wore his down vest on top of everything. He contrasts this with his North Pole journey, where there was constant polar bear danger and splitting ice floes drifting in the current.

Ousland reached an elevation of 2500 metres and noted a decrease in the sastrugi. December 16 brought a weather change. Initially the winds were from the east and too strong for sailing. Next morning, there was a fitful tail wind so he removed the skins from the sail skis and for the next seven hours sailed across the sastrugi with his big sail, under a gentle wind. In the thin air at the higher altitude, the sail behaved differently, with less noise, and it was easier to tack into the wind. Later that day, he changed to his smaller sail in a stronger wind and continued for 16 hours, taking only four short rests. Ousland had reached 88°S, and sailed 103 km. His sails were made of extremely light material with thin cords, like a rectangular parachute. The larger sail would respond in wind of only a few metres per second (four miles per hour). Even if the wind was insufficient to pull both Ousland and his sledge, it would still take some of the strain.

Ousland reached the Pole on 19 December 1996 and photographed himself reflected in the small metal globe marking the Pole. His sledge weight was now down to 133 kg and he had arrived on the 35th day, within the planned 38. He spent five hours there, had his passport stamped, but did not go inside the station. Although his GPS gave his position as 20 km from the Pole, with west longitude, further on he continued to use it each evening to check his position. In whiteout, he travelled using a compass, and in sunshine he used his watch to set his course and directed his skis relative to the shadow of a ski stick. He still had food for another 52 days and good fuel reserves.

Ousland decided to head for the Axel Heiberg Glacier, Amundsen's route, rather than the Beardmore. Continuing, he washed his socks on Christmas Eve, and on Christmas Day, with his sail just working, he travelled 18 km. He noticed a long split in his right boot and repaired it with parachute cord. Regretting that he had not brought a drill, he used a nail with pliers — 50 twists per hole!

The Axel Heiberg is extensively crevassed and, since Amundsen's journey in 1912, had been traversed only by Wally Herbert, also with dog teams. The route is a tricky Z-shaped course, in places through deep snow, and Ousland kept his climbing gear easily accessible.

Reaching the Ross Ice Shelf, he had favourable winds on some days and made a sequence of remarkable distances, including a staggering 226 km in 16 hours. Reaching the crevasse zone north of White Island, contact with McMurdo Base helped him find and follow a flagged route through it. He made radio contact with Kjell Ove Stirvik at Patriot Hills, with his last battery almost flat. He reached Scott Base on 17 January, having completed his 2845-km crossing in 64 days.

A few days later, Ed Hillary and others arrived to celebrate the 40th anniversary of the New Zealand IGY achievements. Ousland and Hillary flew to the Pole together, each for their third visit. The Koreans and Kaminsky had reached the Pole shortly beforehand.

Ousland's crossing had been remarkable. His preparations were meticulous and he was able to cope with any eventuality. His mastery with sails and skis was the keys to his success.

Alain Hubert and Dixie Dansercoer (1997–98)

These two Belgians, aged 44 and 35, set out in 1997 on a long Antarctic crossing from near the former IGY Belgian base, Roi Badouin, in Dronning Maud Land.[12] Their expedition honoured the centenary of Adrian de Gerlache's first Antarctic wintering expedition in *Belgica*. Both men were experienced polar travellers and their route was to cover about 4000 km and cross unexplored areas and two mountain ranges. The journey was to be unassisted.

They started from Blue One, the ANI tourist base, after being flown in on a C130 ANI aircraft. There were 30 people on the flight, including a team of South African technicians working at the SANAE base. Two days later, a Twin Otter landed them near the former Belgian base. They set off at 3 pm and were able to sail 26 km, at speeds reaching 30 km/h in a temperature of -15°C. Both were experienced in wind sailing, Dansercoer being a champion windsurfer. They carried three kites, 6, 12 and 21 square metres in size. These sophisticated sails, which were developed in Greenland and Canada, were lightweight and the men regularly had to sort the suspension lines and repair the sails. Each of their sledges initially weighed around 200 kg. Their food had been specially developed in a 'digestibility laboratory', to reduce weight. It included biscuits made from ground cereals

and anhydrous milk fats, which tasted like chocolate. The Americans at the Pole later called them 'Belgian pralines', referring to their high protein content. Their soup mixes were also apparently delicious.

They each had two pairs of skis, one pair being wide mountain skis giving good lateral stability with the sails, and the other, narrower backcountry skis with a central adhesive skin for friction, following Ousland. Their giant, 21 square metre sails had never really been tested and required special wind conditions. They weighed only 650 grams and had a single instead of the customary double membrane surface. Later, these sails were to transform their rate of travel and prove critical for success.

By the time the men had reached 3000 metre elevation they were experiencing bad headaches. The stove was also producing fumes, but when they checked it, all appeared to be in order. On 29 November 1997, they experienced winds up to 100 km/h and could only progress for two hours. Back in the tent, the stove was releasing bad fumes and Hubert lost consciousness. Dansercoer opened the tent at once and was able to revive him. They sent an Argos message, code A9B11, meaning stove malfunction. Their MSR stove was apparently producing carbon monoxide, though they had been using that type for years. It was housed in a Kevlar box and Hubert realised it must have a combustion problem, so he cut a hole in the box and solved it.

On 4 December they made an early start, but Dansercoer was suddenly lifted several metres off the surface by the strong wind and fell heavily. His sledge overturned, he was knocked unconscious and the sail ripped and collapsed. Fortunately, he sustained only a cracked rib, though was badly bruised and managed to continue the following day, in spite of a painful back and chest.

Their skill in mastering the use of the big sail improved and they began to make real progress, averaging 70 km per day, with successive distances of 90 and 101 km. They achieved speeds up to 33 km/h, and found the wind directions conformed to modelling predictions. One day they achieved 202 km in 10 hours and 303 km in two days, averaging 78 km a day. Although the plateau was flat, the sastrugi were up to 30 centimetres high. After 50 days they had consumed half their food and their sledges were

60 kg lighter. However, they were still 870 km from the Pole. On Christmas Day they sailed for ten and a half hours, covering 128 km. Despite only 100 metre visibility, next day they achieved 84 km in eight hours to cross the 84°S latitude. Their pattern of good distances continued, though travelling at an angle of 30 degrees across the sastrugi, and they reached the 88th parallel. As they approached the Pole, the surface became smoother and they exceeded 45 km/h on several occasions and camped 19 km from the Pole.

Using their sails, Hubert and Dansercoer headed for a black speck on the horizon, which began to resolve as buildings. Although on the lookout for the dome of the US South Pole Station, in the fog they missed it and were continuing until a Hercules C 130 cut across their path. It proved to be landing, and they realised they had overshot and had to turn back for four hours. Their GPS location was confused, just as Ousland found on his journey.

Hubert and Dansercoer then descended the Axel Heiberg glacier, through snow over a metre thick, and one night they experienced a further 20 centimetres snowfall. Their sledges made a furrow 50 centimetres deep and there were avalanches off Mount Nansen, six km away. They described the mountains as primeval and made the difficult route down the glacier, a 1000 metre descent in 32 km, along the same route followed by Ousland the year before. Having finally emerged from the glacier onto the Ross Ice Shelf, they became concerned about their slow progress, after more than 10 days of bad weather, which prevented the use of their sails. If they did not reach McMurdo before 30 January, their insurance would increase from $1500 to $49,500 per week!

Still with 670 kilometres to travel, they puzzled over Ousland's assurances that the shelf was 'a piece of cake'. However, conditions are not the same from year to year and there was only the prospect of adopting half-rations. Then, suddenly, the winds changed to follow them and three dramatic sailing days followed.

Their record progress continued, achieving 411 km in 72 hours. One can only think of the contrast with Shackleton, struggling home using an improvised sail, and of the Scott tragedy. Eventually, with Mount Erebus in close sight, the wind dropped and after their last camp they pulled their sledges, entering McMurdo Base on 10 February in a snowstorm.

The Hubert–Dansercoer journey of 3924 km had taken 99 days, the same period as TAE's original crossing. It was a great achievement and a wonderful tribute to the de Gerlache centenary.

Liv Arnesen and Ann Bancroft (2000–01)

Both these women were former schoolteachers. Arnesen (Norway) was 47 years of age and Bancroft (USA) 45. Each had previously skied to the South Pole from Patriot Hills, Arnesen solo and Bancroft in a team of four women. Bancroft had also been with Will Steger and others on a walk to the North Pole.[13]

They practised ski sailing for a year beforehand, testing four different sails. Arnesen observed that most sails are designed for men, who are usually heavier than women. Their sail areas were 4, 11, 15 and 32 square metres; the largest was their sail wing, developed by NASA, the US space agency.

Their crossing route started from the edge of Antarctica near Blue One, the ANI tourism base in Dronning Maud Land. They each set off with 113 kg (250 pounds) sledges across blue ice, wearing their crampons. During the first two weeks, they were unable to sail because of unsuitable wind. They also used two sets of skis — a narrow pair with moleskin inserts for hauling and wider skis for sailing. After the first fortnight on the ice, when they had hoped to be well on the way, they were still only about 140 km inland. Up to the 167 km point, their progress averaged only 11 km/day, but they had reached the edge of the Polar Plateau. Sailing was strenuous and the women sustained painful injuries, namely a torn shoulder muscle and a strained knee, which persisted through the trip. After travelling for a month, they entered the usual plateau sastrugi fields, but started to make better progress of between 140 and 200 km per day.

Their progress was spasmodic and they felt increasing concern they might not reach the Pole before 20 January, their deadline for completing the crossing. But sailing with their 15 square metre sails they made a run of 113 km in 10 hours, and several good days followed. Bancroft had an accident on 12 January, while using her big NASA sail. It launched her two metres above the ground, but fortunately she only suffered bruising. A 14-hour sail brought them to within a day of the Pole and they arrived on 16 January 2001. They were given a hot breakfast but, as usual, received no official assistance. They, too, found the heat inside the base oppressive and spent only one night there, camped outside beside the ceremonial Pole marker. They had both lost nine kilograms in weight.

They had arranged a food depot at the Pole beforehand and restocked from it. Their sledges returned to their original 113 kg (250 pounds) weight, having reduced to 40 kg when they arrived at the Pole. The second stage of their journey started on 18 January. In the first week of February they lost two days, confined to their tent by blizzards, and were entering heavily crevassed areas and finding travelling almost 'beyond endurance'. Their chosen route was down the Shackleton Glacier, and on the first day its surface appeared deceptively smooth. They expected this glacier to be faster and safer than the Beardmore or the Axel Heiberg. However, they found the crevassed areas were unsafe under sail, and descending one hill was a nightmare because of the crevasses. They progressed by keeping very close together, tying their sledges together over one section. Despite these measures, they still had a number of serious crevasse incidents. They had each broken a crampon, and it was a welcome relief to travel on their skis on their last day on the glacier.

On the 90th day Arnesen and Bancroft were 24 km from the Ross Ice Shelf. They crossed onto the Shelf and realised they had completed the crossing of the continent. The distance to McMurdo was nearly 800 km and they knew they would need a sequence of very good sailing days to arrive there in time. They had one day with wind, but then experienced windless conditions. The last icebreaker was due to leave McMurdo on 23 February and, with only nine days left and still 644 km to be traversed, they were

forced to contact ANI for a plane to evacuate them. Several days later, the plane arrived after a long flight from Patriot Hills. ANI had warned them the weather might force them to fly back to Patriot Hills, but after the plane had refuelled from the drums it carried, conditions allowed them to fly on to McMurdo.

This noteworthy and difficult crossing was the first by women. Their web site (www.yourexpedition.com) was particularly successful, scoring 23 million hits, and they got 20,000 email messages on the trip.

These short summaries describe seven of the 10 Antarctic crossings known to have been completed since TAE. All were noteworthy, and the different routes have followed virtually every conceivable direction. Interestingly, Fuchs' original TAE route has still be to be repeated. Though hazardous, it would provide no insurmountable difficulties for a modern party. The stimulus for making crossings seems largely to have involved creating an original achievement, a first.

It is difficult to see what challenges remain. With the progression from supported to unsupported expeditions, increasing skill has been shown in self-sufficiency and in utilising the wind. There is always the incentive of making a crossing in record time, but one of the most outstanding journeys, the solo crossing by Børge Ousland in only 64 days, is a benchmark that may be unassailable.

The spirit of human endeavour clearly lives on in the modern era; may it never be seen as an anachronism. As I read accounts of challenging journeys such as those undertaken by these modern day adventurers, it is pleasing to look forward with optimism, as well as to look back with satisfaction.

This spirit, I confidently assert, characterised TAE half a century ago.

Appendix I Previous Explorers in the Weddell Sea Region

Descriptions of Antarctic exploration history tend to give short accounts of explorers in the Weddell Sea region, because they did not provide the desired access for the South Pole.[1] The quest to reach the Pole became the focus of endeavours from the early twentieth century, until Amundsen and Scott finally attained it in 1911–12.

Fuchs' TAE expedition planning made careful use of what knowledge the previous explorers had established. The purpose of this appendix is to provide a more detailed summary of these explorations in the Weddell Sea region.

The expeditions are those listed in the table on page 17.

James Cook (1728–79)

Cook's ships were the first to penetrate the Antarctic Circle and to circumnavigate the continent in 1772–75. After he discovered South Georgia and South Sandwich Land he wrote, on 6 February 1775:

> We continued to steer to the South and SE till noon at which time we were on the Latitude of 58°15'S, Longitude 21°34' West and seeing neither land nor signs or any, I concluded that what we had seen, which I named *Sandwich Land* was either a group of Islands or else a point of the Continent, for I firmly believe that there is a tract of land near the Pole, which is the Source of most of the ice which is spread over this vast Southern Ocean.[2]

The second voyage made by Cook extended the exploration he began in *Endeavour* when he charted the New Zealand coastline and the east coast of Australia. This second voyage was to search for 'Terra Australis Incognita', the unknown southern land which some still believed was there, undetected. *Resolution* and *Adventure* left Plymouth in July 1772 and the voyage is wonderfully documented in Cook's journal.

On this second voyage he visited Tierra del Fuego and then set off, sighting new land on 16 January 1775, which he called the Isle of Georgia (now South Georgia). He was disappointed when he proved South Georgia was only an island. Continuing further southeast, he encountered the South Sandwich Islands. Cook reached what is now called the Scotia Sea, the gateway to the Weddell Sea. He was in the third year of his voyage and *Resolution* was alone. He and his men must have been exhausted and his ship no longer in a condition to continue further on a strenuous voyage in unknown waters. He chose to turn north to search for Bouvet's Cape Circumcision but could not find it because its reported position was inaccurate.

H.E.P. Herdman, one of the first authorities on Antarctic sea ice, considered that if Cook had continued further south he might have sighted or even reached the Antarctic continent.[3]

Cook's achievements on this second voyage were remarkable. Figure 22 shows his discoveries in the Scotia Sea. He showed how to manage exploration to extreme southern latitudes in long summer campaigns, even with fragile wooden ships under sail. He was a skilled navigator and always knew his geographic position. This was the case even before he used Harrison's 'miraculous' clock, for the first time on this voyage, to calculate longitude.[4] His earlier Australian voyage had also recorded accurate positions, by using

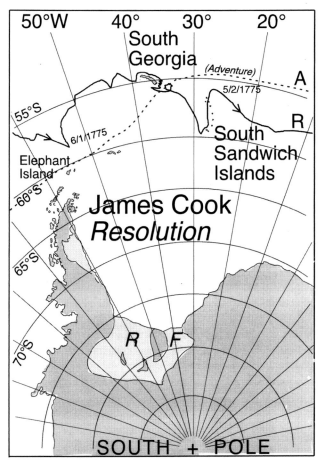

Figure 22 Cook's route in *Resolution* (R), across the Scotia Sea when he discovered South Georgia and the South Sandwich Islands. Route A was taken by his second ship, *Adventure*, under Furneaux. R: Ronne Ice Shelf; F: Filchner Ice Shelf.

lunar methods. Today, quartz clocks, checked against radio time signals, have superseded the chronometers invented by Harrison. Satellite global positioning devices (GPS) have now supplanted these navigation systems.

Long voyages in Cook's era were renowned for the death and debilitation caused by scurvy. Cook suppressed this disease successfully on *Resolution*, although it persisted on his sister ship, Furneaux' *Adventure*. He was elected a Fellow of the Royal Society in February 1776 and his scientific paper on the health of seamen was published in the *Transactions of the Royal Society*. He was awarded the Society's Copley Gold Medal. Scientists who were later awarded this medal included Rutherford and Einstein. Cook used a range of procedures to guard against scurvy, but he failed to rule out some which are not effective, such as the use of malt.[5] A fuller understanding of scurvy and overcoming this scourge with doses of ascorbic acid,

Vitamin C, was not achieved until 1928. Cook also knew how to keep his seamen content and many came with him again on his third, tragic voyage to Hawaii.

Cook's name is prominent in many maritime nations around the globe and his genius left a legacy for those who followed. His explorations revised and corrected the map of the world at large, including Antarctica, even though he never saw it.

James Weddell (1797–1834)

By age 30 Weddell was already experienced, having sailed in icy seas near Greenland, and he advocated the potential for sealing in the southern ocean. William Smith had just discovered new land south of Cape Horn and Weddell undertook several voyages for sealing.[6] On his third voyage he was captain of *Jane* (160 tons), sailing with the much smaller *Beaufoy* (65 tons) under Matthew Brisbane.

The voyage was to seek new sealing grounds, but if this proved unproductive Weddell was to explore for new lands. After spending a week in the South Orkney Island group, north-east of the Antarctic Peninsula, Weddell concluded that the few seals they found had migrated from further afield, probably not far away.

By late January 1823, after looking for islands between the Orkneys and 'Sandwich Land', they turned south, passing numerous icebergs. After lying to during a gale, they continued further south and in early February sailed in dark, foggy weather and one night narrowly missed colliding with an iceberg. By 16 February at 70°S, icebergs had almost disappeared and they continued further south in an open sea.

On 29 February 1823, they reached their furthest point, 74°15'S. The wind was freshening from the south and Weddell prudently turned back and returned to South Georgia. Weddell named the sea King George the Fourth's Sea, but it was later named in his own honour. Figure 23 shows his route, deep into the Weddell Sea. He felt convinced there was an open ocean at the South Pole.

Several later explorers tried to follow Weddell's route but consistently met impassable pack-ice. Ross concluded that Weddell was favoured by an unusually fine season in 1823 and Sir Vivian Fuchs records that the sea was open early in the years 1967–69.[7] In some years exceptional ice conditions do exist, with little

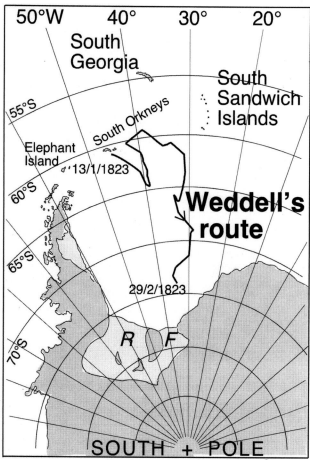

Figure 23 The route followed by James Weddell In 1823, deep into the sea now named after him. He had two small wooden ships. R: Ronne Ice Shelf; F: Filchner Ice Shelf.

pack-ice, as they did for Weddell in 1823. Satellite images confirm this (see Appendix II). Pack-ice conditions are usually intractable and later led to the destruction of *Antarctic* and *Endurance*.

Weddell's voyage and discoveries had a major influence on expeditions which followed, but they could not repeat his route. It was not until 1904 that William Bruce discovered the key to entering the Weddell Sea, down its east coast.

James Clerk Ross (1800–62)
Three national expeditions set off for Antarctica in 1840 and 1841 and each made remarkable discoveries — Dumont d'Urville (France), Charles Wilkes (USA) and James Clark Ross (Britain). Their major discoveries were all in East Antarctica.

Ross made three summer voyages between 1840 and 1843 with two ships, *Erebus* (built in 1826, 372 tons) and *Terror* (1813, 326 tons), which had been built

with thick hulls, massive enough to carry mortars, and known as bombs. They were three-masted, with double decks, and strengthened internally with massive timber beams.[8]

The expedition reached Hobart in August 1840 and sailed south in November. Ross made two successful visits into what is now called the Ross Sea, the second major indentation into the Antarctic continent. The highly successful first season established what became the easiest approach towards the South Pole and named McMurdo Sound, Mount Erebus and the Great Ice Barrier.

Ross's ships returned to Hobart and spent a relaxed winter there, continuing scientific work and enjoying the hospitality of Governor and Mrs Franklin and local society. The following spring, the expedition returned south to explore the 'Barrier' further east, forcing a way through the pack-ice of the Ross Sea and surviving several challenges. They then sailed east to winter in the Falkland Islands, less enjoyably than at Hobart.

Ross hoped to penetrate deeper into the Weddell Sea than did Weddell in 1823. The route sailed by the Ross expedition in shown in Figure 24. Because of tight Weddell Sea pack-ice, the ships could not get far south. Ross must have been wary of becoming beset in the ice and there were serious threats from icebergs. He followed the edge of the pack-ice to the east into the region of Weddell's entry 20 years before, near 45°W. Though the pack-ice conditions were very different that summer, *Erebus* and *Terror* finally reached beyond 71°S.

Ross must have felt disappointed by the Weddell voyage, but his contributions were significant. The expedition sailed home to England after a remarkable record of Antarctic discovery. They had been away nearly four years.

The two ships took part in Sir John Franklin's last, tragic expedition to the Arctic, again seeking the Northwest Passage. Franklin died on the expedition and his senior captain, the Antarctic veteran Francis Crozier, disappeared with all the expedition's men. Later, searches gradually pieced together their tragic fate; no one had survived and the two ships had also vanished.

Otto Nordenskjold and Carl Larsen
Larsen and Nordenskjold contributed to the

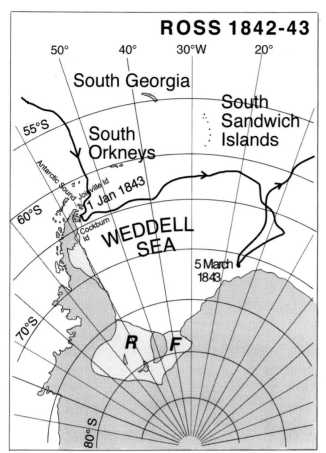

Figure 24 The route of discovery made by James Clark Ross, trying to re-enter the Weddell Sea, thwarted by pack-ice. His expedition had two very heavy wooden ships. R: Ronne Ice Shelf; F: Filchner Ice Shelf.

exploration of the north-west corner of the Weddell Sea and the generally inaccessible east coast of the Antarctic Peninsula. They worked together on Nordenskjold's Swedish expedition in 1902–04, but in trying to relieve the expedition after its first winter, Larsen lost *Antarctic*, crushed in the Weddell pack-ice. Their explorations are shown on Figure 25.

Carl Anton Larsen (1860–1924), a Norwegian, visited the Antarctic Peninsula in *Jason* in 1892–93, on whale and seal exploration and returned in *Jason* in 1894 to explore down the east side of the Peninsula.[9] He succeeded in penetrating 400 miles (640 km) south of Joinville Island, against the circulating currents of the Weddell Gyre, where the pack-ice is forced against the peninsula and where Shackleton's *Endurance* was later destroyed. Larsen was a keen field observer and reported the first Antarctic fossils, on Seymour Island.

After the Swedish expedition, in 1904 Larsen

established the whaling industry on South Georgia with Argentinean investment. Much later, he took part in a whaling venture to the Ross Sea, where he died on board one of his whalers.

Nils Otto Gustaf Nordenskjold (1869–1928) was born in southern Sweden. His uncle, Baron Adolf Erik Nordenskjold, had been the first to navigate the Northeast Passage (north of Arctic Russia) in *Vega* in 1878–80. Norenskjold studied geology for his doctorate and on an earlier expedition visited the Magellan region of Tierra del Fuego, where he studied the younger geological formations and the extent of former glaciations. He also took part in a Danish expedition to north-eastern Greenland in 1900.

Nordenskjold was stimulated by Larsen's recent discoveries in *Jason* along the east coast of the peninsula and by the fossils Larsen saw on Seymour Island. He selected a versatile team of eight scientists, including a fellow geologist, for his Swedish expedition.

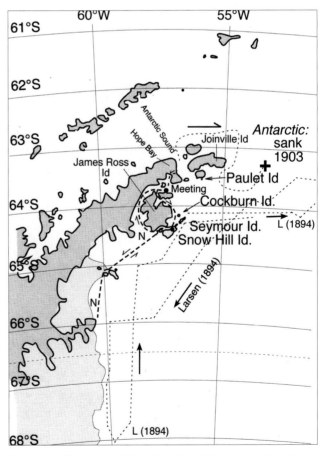

Figure 25 The routes followed by Otto Nordenskjold on the Swedish Expedition in 1902–04. His winter base was on Snow Hill Island. Larsen, who had previously penetrated south in Jason in 1894, lost Antarctic in 1903.

The Nordenskjold expedition ship was a whaler, originally *Cap Nor* (226 tonnes), which had been built at Drammen in 1871 and renamed *Antarctic*.

Antarctic left from Gøteborg on 16 October 1901.[10] The ship sailed through the Antarctic Sound to Paulet Island on the edge of the Weddell Sea. Nordenskjold landed on Paulet on 15 January 1902 and recorded a large penguin colony. This island was to play a critical role in survival after the loss of *Antarctic*.

Nordenskjold made the most of the remaining summer in the region near where Weddell had first penetrated 80 years before, by following the edge of the pack-ice eastwards. They reached 63°30′S, 45°7′W on 1 February 1902, and returned to construct a base on Snow Hill Island, south of Seymour Island. *Antarctic* left on 22 February and wintered in the Falklands, with plans to return in the spring.

Nordenskjold's party spent two winters working from the base hut on Snow Hill Island, undertaking exploration to the south, geological work on Snow Hill Island and the geologically very productive Seymour Island. The expedition had not planned on a two-year stay, but *Antarctic* had failed to return for them in the 1902–03 summer and the party spent a second winter at Snow Hill Island.

Unknown to Nordenskjold, *Antarctic* had been caught and crushed in the pack-ice north of Paulet Island. Larsen and all his party survived and wintered in a rock hut on Paulet Island, living on penguins. One man died during their awful winter. *Antarctic* had previously left three men at Hope Bay, at the northern tip of the Antarctic Peninsula, in the hope they could reach Nordenskjold to tell him that *Antarctic* had been unable to reach Snow Hill Island. These men could not reach the island and wintered under very primitive circumstances at Hope Bay, living on penguins and using a blubber stove.

The expedition enjoyed unexpected relief by the Argentinean vessel, *Uruguay*, which came out to search for *Antarctic* when she failed to return with the expedition. Three remarkable meetings, amongst the most renowned in Antarctic history, then occurred at or near the Snow Hill Base. Nordenskjold and his men were completely surprised — first by the three Hope Bay survivors, then by a party from *Uruguay*, and finally by Larsen and five of his *Antarctic* survivors. The remaining survivors on Paulet Island were picked

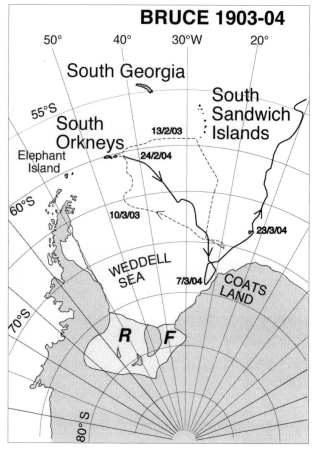

Figure 26 The critical discovery by William Bruce in *Scotia* after wintering on Lawrie Island. The first to sight the ice cliffs bordering Coats Land, he discovered the key to penetrating the pack-ice of the Weddell Sea, followed by later explorers. R: Ronne Ice Shelf; F: Filchner Ice Shelf.

up by *Uruguay*. The expedition made a triumphant return to South America and Sweden.

Nordenskjold had led a surprisingly successful and productive expedition, in spite of losing *Antarctic*, and with a relatively small party.[11] The scientific results were published over time in a comprehensive expedition series in seven volumes.

Nordenskjold's discoveries were influential in geological science and his good judgment in locating his base at Snow Hill, in the midst of the fossiliferous Mesozoic–Tertiary basin, was masterly. Sadly, Nordenskjold died in 1928 after a traffic accident near his home in Gøteborg. He was 59.

The geology of the Antarctic continent was unknown in 1902. Nordensjkold collected and recorded the first comprehensive evidence showing Antarctica was not essentially different to the other, temperate continents. The fossil plants and therefore their evidence of a previous warm climate were a revelation. He also found giant fossil penguins and the bones of an extinct whale.

William Bruce (1867–1921)

William Speirs Bruce led the Scottish National Expedition in a notable Weddell Sea exploration. He found a way down its eastern coast, the key to deeper penetration into Antarctica from this side. Peter Speak has written a fine biography of Bruce. The expedition routes are shown on Figure 26.

Bruce already had considerable expedition and scientific experience in the Scotia Sea and had been on several Arctic expeditions. Around this time, preparations for the first British Antarctic Expedition, in *Discovery*, were finally taking shape. Bruce wanted to join as a scientist, but dissension arose with Clements Markham of the Royal Geographic Society, who was organising the expedition. Bruce made alternative plans for a Scottish National Expedition in 1900. By the time Markham finally invited Bruce to join *Discovery*, Bruce was already occupied in recruiting his own expedition team. Significant grants from the Coats family of Paisley of over £30,000 and smaller donations from over 170 Scottish firms and individuals supported the expedition. He obtained no financial support from the British government.

Bruce sought advice from Colin Archer in Norway about finding a suitable expedition ship. Archer had built the *Fram* for Fridjof Nansen for his long Arctic Ocean drift and Roald Amundsen later used her on his South Pole expedition. They chose a Norwegian whaler, *Hekla*, which cost a mere £2620 but needed extensive rebuilding. She was renamed *Scotia*.

The expedition stayed at Laurie Island in the South Orkney Islands. After a successful scientific winter, *Scotia* left in November 1903, leaving a party to continue summer observations, and went to Buenos Aires. There Bruce discussed the future of his base with the British Minister and the British Consul, as well as with senior officers of the Argentinean Meteorological Office. At that time, Britain had no interest in continuing observations at Bruce's base but had no objection to Argentina's interest in taking it over. After World War II, Argentina and Chile declared their territorial claims over the Antarctic Peninsula and numerous confrontations occurred when Britain intensified its own sovereignty claims over the Falkland Islands Dependency area. After the International Geophysical Year, 1957–58, the first Antarctic Treaty held all territorial claims in Antarctica in abeyance.

Scotia returned briefly to Laurie Island and left a party under Robert Mossman to man the base during the following year. She then made another attempt to get into the eastern part of the Weddell Sea, forcing her way south near the 32°W meridian until beset, close to 72°S. The water depth was much shallower than expected and when the captain climbed to the crow's nest he reported visible land and they sailed on to reach the ice cliffs, which form the edge of the continent.

There was a risk they might be caught for the winter and, when a storm threatened to crush the ship, *Scotia* did become beset in the pack-ice. Bruce, who seems to have been a leader who could reassure his men in perilous situations, organised football on the ice. He also had a bagpipe player, Gilbert Kerr, play music for an emperor penguin, which proved oblivious to a range of different music. Bizarre photos were taken with Kerr wearing a kilt and full highland dress. The photographs show the unfortunate bird as captive, tethered to the ice at Kerr's feet.

Bruce correctly surmised they had indeed seen the edge of the continent, declaring it an extension of Enderby Land, over 2000 km further west. He called his new discovery Coats Land, after the expedition's financial supporters.

Scotia escaped from the newly discovered Coats Land coast, sailed to Cape Town and returned to Scotland to a welcome as polar heroes. The Scottish National Antarctic Expedition was ignored in London. While it could not rank with Scott's *Discovery* expedition, Bruce had achieved remarkable scientific results and discovered new land. Bruce found the key for penetrating the Weddell Sea, down its eastern coast. In normal conditions, an open lead commonly develops next to the ice-cliffed coast, enticing bold vessels to sail further south.

Wilhelm Filchner (1877–1957)

As a young man Filchner achieved recognition for some daring and resourceful travel in Russia and central Asia. He obtained support for his Antarctic

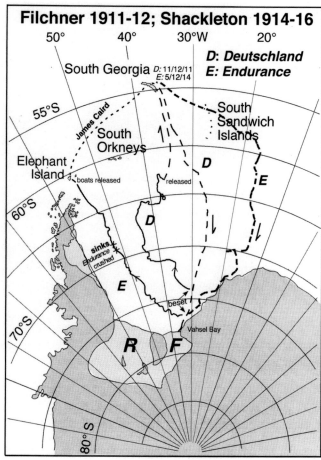

Filchner 1911-12; Shackleton 1914-16

D: Deutschland
E: Endurance

Figure 27 Filchner penetrated to Vahsel Bay in 1912 in *Deutschland* (D). Shackleton almost reached Vahsel Bay in 1915 in *Endurance* (E). Both ships were beset and drifted but *Endurance* was crushed and sank. Shackleton then achieved his famous survival. While his party waited precariously on Elephant Island, Shackleton made an open boat journey to South Georgia and returned to Elephant island to rescue all the party in *Yelcho*. R: Ronne Ice Shelf; F: Filchner Ice Shelf.

plans in 1909 and funds were raised, relatively quickly, through a lottery. He purchased a suitable Norwegian ice-vessel, renamed *Deutschland*, and had her considerably strengthened.

In Filchner's 1922 account of his expedition, Nordenskjold's introduction emphasised that the major reason for Filchner going to the Weddell Sea was to investigate the hypothesis of a possible strait across the Antarctic continent to the Ross Sea.[12] It had been surmised the Weddell was a continuation of the Atlantic Ocean, forming a deep indentation like that of the Ross Sea on the other side, probably with a similar ice barrier. Filchner wanted to attempt a crossing to examine the 'strait'. The question of this hypothetical strait was not fully settled for another 50 years and had to address the

disposition of the mountains and the sub-glacial topography with seismic sounding. The seismic and topographic results from several American traverse expeditions, during and following the IGY, from Ellsworth and Byrd Bases, showed there is no strait.[13]

Deutschland's Captain was Richard Vahsel, reported to be 'a bold ice captain', who was to die on board in the Weddell Sea. The expedition sailed from Hamburg in early May 1911, spent 48 days on South Georgia and made a cruise down to the South Sandwich Islands. The Norwegian Antarctic veteran, Carl Larsen, had established whaling on South Georgia in 1904 and was very helpful to the expedition.

Twelve ponies from Manchuria for the expedition reached South Georgia on the schooner *Harpon*, from Buenos Aires. They had spent 10 weeks in the Zoological Gardens there, and were in superb condition. The expedition left South Georgia on 10 November 1911, with 33 men, eight ponies, numerous dogs and a cat. It planned to proceed south, generally east of the 20°W meridian, to reach Coats Land and follow it south as far as possible. However, they encountered pack-ice just after leaving South Georgia and went further west, closer to 33°W, between the routes followed by Weddell and Bruce. They slowly pushed south through the pack, burning seal blubber and penguins to save coal. They sighted the coast, the southern continuation of Bruce's Coats Land, and finally an ice-covered ridge rising in a gentle slope to 600 metres with a coastal ice cliff 400 metres high. Finding no place to land, they continued south. Filchner named this new coast Prinzregent Luitpold Land, and a projecting cape, Cape Vahsel, close to which the water depth was only 114 metres. The route of the *Deutschland* is shown on Figure 27.

At the end of January 1912, *Deutschland* reached a bay in the south-east corner of the Weddell Sea, where the visible ice cap rose to over 1000 metres, and continued further to the south-east. A complex ice barrier extended to the west, equivalent to the barrier which Ross discovered at the south edge of the Ross Sea. Filchner had discovered the southern edge of the Weddell Sea, against what is now the Filchner Ice Shelf. Small nunataks (rock outcrops) were visible in the ice cliffs, south of the feature, which Filchner called Vahsel Bay.

Filchner started searching for a suitable place to build

his main base hut and finally decided to erect it on a 'stable' iceberg, the so-called Station Iceberg, cemented into the south edge of the bay. The hut materials, dogs and ponies were landed successfully and the hut was virtually finished by 17 February in only eight days.

Filchner planned three exploratory sledging trips in the spring of 1912, to address other questions which he seems to have regarded as more important than investigating the unexplored land towards the South Pole. However, the Station Iceberg was affected by spring tides and began to drift away to the north. The base building was quickly recovered, with the hope of building it elsewhere, and Filchner had ideas of wintering at the foot of the ice cap to the east, and commenced successful steps to do so. Ultimately, he accepted there was no question of establishing a landing that season and was resigned to returning to Grytviken to winter there and attempt a return late in the year for a significantly reduced program.

Pack-ice blocked *Deutschland*'s progress north and on 6 March the ship had to follow a course away from the coast. By the next afternoon she was beset, and even under full power could progress only three miles in over nine hours and they were beset on 15 March at 73°34'S. Filchner wondered if they would be crushed like *Antarctic* in 1903.

Over the next eight months, the ship drifted north in a somewhat irregular course. They were lucky to avoid major ice pressure, which occasionally came near them, but never as disastrously as *Endurance* was to experience three years later, further west. Filchner believed their efforts to get through some thicker pack-ice might have helped to protect them by surrounding them. Captain Vahsel became ill early in June and died in August, when they were close to the Antarctic Circle.

Filchner appreciated that the drift of the ship had brought them relatively close to the position where Benjamin Morrell had reported evidence of land in 1823. This American sealer had described his voyage into the Weddell Sea and a number of other remarkable travels in tropical latitudes. His Weddell Sea accounts seemed to parallel those of James Weddell, but were received with scepticism because of lack of detail and inconsistencies. Filchner and two companions made a long traverse with dogs to visit Morrell's reported locality, 65 km west of the ship's position. As the ship continued to drift, the party travelled an actual distance of 157 km across the pack-ice in 10 days and returned to find the ship. They had taken considerable risks and seen no hint of land, and they confirmed that the sea depth was more than 1000 metres.

Deutschland finally emerged from the pack-ice on 18 December. She was intact and reached Grytviken in South Georgia in mid-December. Filchner decided to return to Germany and left for Buenos Aires on another boat. The expedition had been racked by controversies, especially involving dissension between Filchner, an army man, and Vahsel who was in the German Navy. After she returned, there were plans to use *Deutschland* on an Austro-Hungarian Antarctic expedition being organised by Felix König. König invited Filchner to take part but he declined. Filchner had seen enough of Antarctica, and chose to return to central Asia, where he pursued a long, interesting exploration career. The war blocked König's plans.

The achievements of the *Deutschland* expedition have largely been ignored, but this exploration was much more significant than Shackleton's, three years later. Filchner was the first to confirm the position of the southern edge of the Weddell Sea and he accurately predicted that its ice barrier, the edge of a large ice shelf, ran west to impinge on the eastern side of the Antarctic Peninsula.

It is remarkable that *Deutschland* survived her winter drift in the pack-ice, whereas *Endurance* did not. The different circumstances might have been largely fortuitous. A comparison of the designs of *Fram*, *Deutschland* and *Endurance* is given in Appendix III.

One must wonder how Filchner reacted when he heard of Shackleton's remarkable survival after losing his ship, *Endurance*.

Ernest Shackleton (1876–1922)

Shackleton astonished Amundsen by travelling to within 180 km of the South Pole in 1909 on his *Nimrod* expedition. However, Shackleton's most famous grapple with Antarctica was still to come, in the Weddell Sea in 1914–16. The expedition's route is shown in Figure 27.

Endurance was caught in the pack-ice trying to reach the south-east corner of the Weddell Sea to commence an Antarctic crossing. Like Filchner's *Deutschland*, *Endurance* was beset and drifted through the winter. Whereas *Deutschland* emerged undamaged and returned to South Georgia, *Endurance* drifted north for 10 months before she was crushed and sank. No one knew of their predicament; she had no functioning radio.

Shackleton and all his *Endurance* men survived and their story is well known and described in many accounts.[14] This summary recounts some aspects of the Imperial Trans-Antarctic Expedition, based on the writing of Shackleton and his captain, Frank Worsley.

William Bruce had made the first crossing proposal for a New Scottish Expedition in 1910.[15] He was unsuccessful in getting finance but was happy for Shackleton to adopt the proposal for his Imperial Trans-Antarctic Expedition in 1914.

It was not a good time for Shackleton to mount a new expedition, but he was famous after nearly reaching the South Pole on his *Nimrod* Expedition, especially for his decision to turn back safely. Robert Falcon Scott's last expedition reached the South Pole in 1912 only to find that Roald Amundsen had arrived five weeks earlier, and Scott's party died heroically during their return.

Shackleton's expedition plan comprised two sections. The main one was to establish a base on the Filchner Ice Shelf in the Weddell Sea, following Filchner's 1911 discoveries. It would establish a route south to reach the Pole and continue beyond to McMurdo Sound on the Ross Sea, following the known Shackleton–Scott route. The second section of the expedition was to lay depots inland from McMurdo Sound, across the Ross Ice Shelf, to the foot of the Beardmore Glacier for the crossing party to use after passing the Pole.

Shackleton found two ships, *Endurance* and *Aurora*. *Endurance* was a new wooden barquentine built at Sandefjord in Norway and completed in the 1913 summer. Lars Christensen constructed her and intended her for a new enterprise with Adrien de Gerlache, for Arctic tourism cruises ('polar safaris'). When de Gerlache withdrew financially, Shackleton had the opportunity to purchase the 300 tonne ship for around £14,000. She was regarded as 'one of the strongest ice ships ever built' and had triple expansion engines, capable of giving her a speed of 9 to 10 knots. She was built as *Polaris* but Shackleton renamed her *Endurance* following his family motto — 'By endurance we conquer'.

Aurora was purchased for £3200 from Douglas Mawson, who had used her on his Australasian Antarctic Expedition, 1911–13, when her captain was J.K. Davis. Davis had been with Shackleton's *Nimrod* Expedition.

Financial backing for the Imperial Trans-Antarctic Expedition was fragile, but Shackleton obtained £10,000 from the government, £1000 from the Royal Geographical Society and significant assistance from Dudley Docker, Elizabeth Dawson-Lambton, Dame Janet Stancomb Wills, and many smaller donors. A critical grant of £24,000 from Sir James Caird ensured the expedition could go ahead, but by the time *Endurance* reached Buenos Aires the expedition had run short of funds for stores.

The ship sailed from London on 1 August 1914 as war started in Europe and with Britain mobilising. At Margate, Shackleton sent a telegram to the Admiralty offering the expedition as a unit to the nation. If this offer was not accepted, it would continue. Two messages were received from the First Lord of the Admiralty, Winston Churchill. The first, by telegram, 'Proceed'; the second an explanatory letter stating it was best to continue in view of the public money involved.

Endurance left Southampton on 8 August and Shackleton followed independently to meet it in Buenos Aires in mid-October. In a remarkable letter to his wife from Buenos Aires, Shackleton mentioned that he felt the ship was 'not as strong as the *Nimrod* constructionally this I have seen from her way of behaving when in a gale pressing against the dock wall though there is nothing to be scared of as I think she will go through the ice all right only I would exchange her for the old *Nimrod* any day except for comfort'.[16]

Endurance left for South Georgia on 26 October and reached Grytviken on 5 November after a good passage. There were 28 men on board, including a stowaway, Percy Blackborrow. Frank Hurley, photographer, was also on the expedition, having just taken part in Mawson's expedition. His photographic record of the *Endurance* and his accounts are well known.[17] South Georgia was busy with its whaling, out of reach of a world at war, and had no wireless communication. Shackleton was able to take on stores, clothing and more coal, unrestricted by questions about credit.

On learning from the whaling men that the southern ice conditions were extremely severe, Shackleton decided to wait, to exercise and train the dogs, complete all preparations, and set off after a month. They sailed on 5 December 1914 and within three days met pack-ice. *Endurance* negotiated her way through it and reached Bruce's furthest south position by 12 January. Further on, they were passing new land, named the Caird Coast, before they expected to see Filchner's Luitpold Land at 77°S. Unexpectedly, they reached a polynya (a wide, open lead) late on 15 January and progressed swiftly covering over 300 km under sail and motor over the next three days. But four days later they became beset at 76°34′S, for the last time. *Endurance* began her long drift. They were still 160 km from Filchner's Vahsel Bay. Although the ship had a radio receiver, it heard nothing.

The 'impossible' escape of all Shackleton's team after *Endurance* was lost is the most famous in Antarctic history. *Endurance* drifted unharmed for seven months until, in August, an ice floe which had surrounded them began to break up suddenly during a moderate gale, and the ship was unprotected. In mid-October, harder ice pressure developed and the ship quickly heeled 30 degrees, the lifeboats on the lee side almost resting on the ice. Some of the dog kennels broke away and Shackleton wondered if the ship would be 'thrown on her beam ends'. The end for *Endurance* began on 24 October and Shackleton sketched his ship in a local pool of young ice, with pressure ridges providing a vice-like grip from three directions.[18] Over the next few days in bright, early summer sunshine, pressures steadily opened the ship's timbers and her leaks increased, beyond control. On 27 October 1915, in latitude 69°5′S, *Endurance* was crushed with frightening destruction. She finally sank on 21 November.

Shackleton tried hauling their three lifeboats across the ice, until the carpenter Harry McNish (or McNeish) 'mutinied' because of the risk of damaging them. They quietly drifted north and Shackleton's hopes now lay on reaching either Elephant Island or Clarence Island, still 100 miles north of them. They now launched their three lifeboats to perilously try to reach one of them. These were their last possible landfall, as the whole party could not realistically consider attempting a further voyage across the open ocean to South Georgia. They first landed at Cape Valentine on Elephant Island but, noting that it was unprotected from storm waves, they sailed

anticlockwise around the coast to Cape Wild on the north coast, landing on 17 April 1916. Cape Wild is a gravel spit between a craggy island and the precipitous slopes of the main island, with an adjacent glacier to the west. They set up their camp on an unoccupied penguin rookery on the spit.

To be able to land at Cape Wild is still a very rare occurrence because of adverse weather and turbulent sea. The penguin rookery is still there but the adjacent glacier has receded. The spit is narrow, but from a Hurley photo one can see where two adjacent boats were inverted, with sails draped over them to provide their 'home'.

Shackleton decided to use the best boat, *James Caird*, to sail with five men to South Georgia for help, leaving the others to await a rescue ship that he would organise. The alternative would have been to winter and then set out to reach Deception Island 200 miles to the south-west. At Elephant Island he left the others under the leadership of Frank Wild. They loaded two casks of fresh water and provisions for four weeks. The carpenter, McNish, had made *James Caird* as seaworthy as he could.

Harding has described *James Caird* in detail. She was 23 feet 6 inches long, double-ended and carvel-built. McNeish built up the sides by 15 inches, added two more strakes (lengthwise, along the sides), raised the thwarts (transverse seats) and finally put in half decks, fore and aft. McNeish used sledge runners for the decks, with box lids and frozen canvas, which Greenstreet and Bakewell painfully sewed, having thawed the canvas over a blubber stove. They had to work carefully so as not to break their few needles. She was caulked using cotton and threadwick, wool from a muffler, kneaded with the artist Marston's oil paints. Frank Hurley made a pump from the casing of the ship's compass. The lug sail from the second cutter, the *Stanscomb Wills*, was cut down into a mizzen for *James Caird*, to fit a small mast cut down from the cutter. She was already fitted with a standing lug and jib. The boat's cockpit was 5′ x 2 feet 6 inches (1.5 x 0.76 metres). Stones and bags of shingle were placed inside to serve as ballast.[19]

They set off on 24 April, threading out through scattered ice on the vital survival voyage. The five men with Shackleton were Frank Worsley, navigator; Tom Crean, an indestructible, strong individual well distinguished on both Scott's expeditions; Tim

McCarty, utterly reliable; Harry McNish, carpenter; and the bosun John Vincent, said to be the strongest man on *Endurance*.

The voyage took 16 days. Worsley had very few weather opportunities to get sun sights with his sextant, made difficult because of the boat's constant movement. His navigation was accurate, but a severe storm nearly wrecked them close to the wide entrance to King Haakon Bay and drove them south almost to Annenkov Island. The gale eased and almost simultaneously the pin locking the mast fell out. Had it come out during the storm, they would have been lost. In late afternoon they entered the bay, searching for some sheltered landing and, with dusk approaching, unexpectedly found Cave Cove, a narrow entrance in the cliffs. Today, this cove is relatively easy to visit from a nearby ship and is one of the more remarkable Shackleton 'shrines'.

After resting and sustaining themselves by eating albatross chicks, they sailed well up into King Haakon Bay, to prepare for a journey to reach a whaling settlement across the island. They transferred to a place Shackleton refers to as their 'cabin *à la Peggotty*', on the north coast near a distinctive bluff. Today, no sign remains, but they hauled the boat well up on shore and inverted it for shelter. Three of the men were utterly 'spent', and the strong man, Vincent, seemed broken.

To get help to rescue the men on Elephant Island, Shackleton had to contact the whaling community on the east coast of South Georgia, 39 km across the formidable alpine terrain. Shackleton, Worsley and Crean set off at 3 am on 19 May 1916, carrying minimal material — three days' rations carried in socks, an adze as an ice axe, a small compass and a basic blueprint chart of the island. Ironically, this was a copy of the map Filchner's expedition had prepared in 1911. They first climbed the adjacent glacier to reach what is now called Shackleton Pass. Some fog dissipated and they could see the east coast and Cook's Possession Bay. They knew of the small whaling station at Prince Olav Harbour to the north, but were sure it would be unoccupied for winter. In fact, there were still people there, and they could have reached it that day. The weather was miraculously fine and 36 hours later they stumbled into Stromness, after a nearly continuous traverse. They were not climbers and some have felt the journey was a not fully

challenging, mountaineering achievement. In the last decade the crossing has been repeated many times, though in the summer, and some attempts have had to be terminated. Shackleton's crossing was in early winter. Providence gave Shackleton a short window of gentle weather; otherwise he would have had to turn back or might have perished.

When they walked into Stromness they were completely unkempt and they were shunned by the first men they met. This initial encounter is movingly described by Huntford.[20] Huntford also refers to the feeling Shackleton described about a fourth presence on their crossing, which inspired T.S. Eliot to write some haunting lines in *The Waste Land*.

Shackleton now set out to rescue the men from Elephant Island. It took four difficult attempts because of fragile ships and the winter ice conditions. Finally Shackleton asked the Chileans for assistance and they provided the tug *Yelcho* for another rescue attempt. Fortunately the ice conditions were favourable and the boat slipped through and picked up the 22 men, all still alive, from Elephant Island, on 30 August. Shackleton and his party were fittingly welcomed and acclaimed in Punta Arenas. He had asked his men not to change their clothes or shave. They went on to Valparaiso and Santiago; it was an historic time for the Chilean nation and they were similarly honoured in Buenos Aires and Montevideo. The South Americans will never forget Shackleton.

The other half of Shackleton's expedition, the Ross Sea party, struggled through its own problems. The story of their continual crises and final disaster is less well known, but has been carefully documented.[21] Their supply ship, *Aurora*, was torn from her moorings at Cape Royds and in a disabled state reached Lyttleton. These accounts describe a disaster-prone party, which nevertheless did establish the depots inland for the anticipated arrival of Shackleton's crossing party. Ultimately J.K. Davis (Shackleton's last *Nimrod* captain) commanded the restored *Aurora* in a relief voyage south, with Shackleton signed on as a supernumerary officer. Shackleton was shocked to discover the condition of the survivors, and to learn that three men had died.

Ernest Shackleton was a striking personality in Antarctic history. Sent home in 1903 during Scott's

Discovery expedition with advanced scurvy, his life and Antarctic destiny were by then crystallised. Slighted and being invalided from the Scott expedition, he organised his *Nimrod* expedition into 'Scott's territory' and made important new discoveries. He discovered and climbed the Beardmore Glacier to reach the Polar Plateau and the threshold of the South Pole itself. His judgment in not pressing on the last hundred miles was wise. If the party had not lost their last pony, Socks, down a crevasse, perhaps they might have reached the Pole.

Logistically, the *Endurance* expedition was less impressive. It had a complicated plan, which was not adequately designed. It was hatched and developed at the worst possible time and proceeded through World War I. In terms of discovery it contributed very little.

Could Shackleton have achieved an Antarctic crossing, if he had been able to land on the Filchner Ice Shelf? Sir Vivian Fuchs has discussed this question, convincingly. His conclusion is an unequivocal 'no'.[22]

The survival after the loss of *Endurance* is one of the most amazing survival stories in Antarctic history. It could be said that Shackleton had an 'unsuccessful' life and career, but the survival of all his *Endurance* men is an inspiration for mankind.

He had strained his health, presumably on the *Nimrod* expedition and then on *Endurance* and its aftermath. He went on to fulfil his final Antarctic destiny on his last expedition with the loyal Worsley, Wild, and others who were with him previously. He died on board *Quest*, at Grytviken, early in 1922 and he was buried in the cemetery there on 5 March. *Quest* returned from a voyage to the Weddell Sea and his men erected a simple memorial on a headland looking out on the fiord. On the back of the massive granite headstone that now marks his grave are words from his admired Robert Browning: 'I hold that a man should strive to the uttermost for his life's set prize'.

Cruises by the Royal Research Ship *Discovery II* (1929–33)

The UK Discovery Committee was set up in 1923 to help the International Whaling Conferences frame regulations to protect the stock of whales being harvested in the southern oceans. The committee fulfilled two main tasks: to provide accurate charts of the Falkland Island Dependencies area and to acquire information on the life histories of the different species of whales.[23] The whale information would enable their hunting to be regulated, in the best interests of the industry.

Discovery, Scott's first expedition ship, was used for the committee's work from 1925 to 1926 and a new ship, RRS *Discovery II*, was built in 1929. She was 1036 tonnes and was strengthened for light pack-ice work. She had special laboratories and equipment for oceanographic work. In her first season, 1929–30, she completed a survey of the South Sandwich Islands, originally mapped by Cook and Bellingshausen. *Discovery II* took 21 days to chart the 11 islands, confirming the general accuracy of the earlier charting.

During her second commission, 1931 to 1933, *Discovery II* circumnavigated the continent in a series of voyages reaching the edge of the pack-ice. This was only the fifth Antarctic circumnavigation and the first during the winter. The voyage reached 70°S in the Weddell Sea. A major scientific achievement of this voyage was recording the approximate positions of the Antarctic Convergence.

Exploring the Southern Antarctic Peninsula

The main exploration, which extended knowledge of the Weddell Sea involved its southern edge and its coast against the Antarctic Peninsula. This work was achieved in 1947 in a joint American–British operation. Their work is shown in Figure 28.

Finn Ronne, who led the Ronne Antarctic Expedition (RARE) in 1946–48, migrated to the US from Norway in 1923. Ronne (1901–80) had a very good Antarctic pedigree as his father, Martin Ronne, was Amundsen's sail-maker on the Norwegian South Pole expedition (1911–12). Ronne took part in the US Antarctic Service Expedition (1941–42) to the western side of the southern Antarctic Peninsula, which built a new base at Stonington Island, also known as East Base. Ronne served in the US Navy in the Pacific War and quickly organised his private expedition, RARE, after the war.

FIDS, the Falkland Islands Dependency Survey, continued the exploratory survey in the Antarctic Peninsula, having established its first bases there during the war to monitor possible German naval supply efforts. At the time of Ronne's expedition, FIDS had built another base on Stonington Island, close to the unoccupied American East Base.

The joint work FIDS-RARE achieved has been described by Ronne and by Walton.[24] These books have such differences they might, initially, seem to describe different expeditions. Ronne was a controversial character and his expedition experienced unusual mishaps.

RARE had strong air facilities, good photographic survey equipment and personnel, but was weak in its ground travel. Its dog teams had been decimated by distemper on the voyage down. FIDS, on the other hand, had lost its one small aircraft, but had well-trained dog teams and experienced field survey men. This marriage of air operations and survey ground control worked happily. The FIDS ground team provided some measure of safety for the aircraft and established survey control points. Safety is one thing, but too often aircraft have achieved major exploration discoveries without establishing just where the new-discovered mountains actually were. We were to experience this on Trans-Antarctic. When we were provided with American photos of some of the new mountains we would encounter on our journey into the unknown, the new features were so far out of position that we never saw them.

Two RARE aircraft, a Beechcraft and a Norseman, coordinated with the FIDS ground support. Operations involved establishing an aircraft fuel depot by air at Cape Keeler on the Weddell coast and the crossing of the Plateau by the sledge party. The Norseman, piloted by Chuck Adams, provisioned the depot and the Beechcraft, piloted by Bill Lassiter, undertook the survey exploration with the photographer, Latardy. The supporting ground party used the best two FIDS dog teams. They supplied ground safety control for the air photography. Ken Butler was the leader, with Duggie Mason (FIDS surveyor) and two Americans, Walter Smith (survey) and Art Owen.

Ronne's flights with pilot James Lassiter established the southern configuration of the coast and followed the Antarctic Peninsula 200 miles (320 km) further south. They traced the edge of the great ice shelf to the east, almost reaching Vahsel Bay, and confirmed Filchner's prediction in 1912 that the great ice barrier he had discovered continued west to the Peninsula. Ronne named the barrier the Lassiter Ice Shelf and

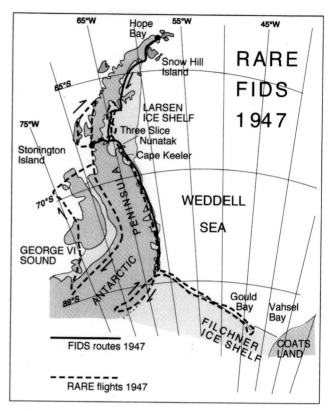

Figure 28 The explorations achieved by FIDS and the Ronne Antarctic Research Expedition in 1947.

the mountains to the south Edith Ronne Land, for his wife. Today, the Ice Shelf is called the Ronne Ice Shelf (in honour of Finn and Edith) and is separated by ice-covered Berkner Island from the smaller Filchner Ice Shelf further east.

The exploration routes by RARE and FIDS in 1947–48 are shown in Figure 28.

Air exploration without ground control can involve naming numerous new topographic details. Ronne (1949) listed over 80 unvisited but 'approved' features. To help confirm their discoveries, Ronne and Lassiter made ritualistic landings in two places, effectively in the middle of nowhere, to say they had actually set foot on the newly discovered ground. On other occasions, an American flag was dropped from the plane. Ronne believed that his expedition had shown that Antarctica was one continent and that there was no strait between East and West Antarctica. However, the final confirmation that this was true had to wait until seismic soundings established the bedrock levels beneath the ice.

A noteworthy feature of Ronne's expedition was the fact that it included two women, Edith Ronne and Jennie Darlington. Jennie had married one of the pilots, Jim Darlington, shortly before the expedition's ship, *Port of Beaumont*, sailed from the US. The presence of the two women produced some interesting reactions by the FIDS' men, some of whom were surprised by the presence of these women in Antarctica, and some amusing incidents are well described by Darlington.[25]

At the end of the expedition, *Beaumont* was still firmly iced in near East Base, with no prospect of a late season release. An emergency arose when Jenny Darlington announced she was pregnant. This special event was a first in Antarctica. The assistance of two American icebreakers, *Burton Island* and *Edisto*, which happened to be in the region was requested and they broke the ice out around *Beaumont* and towed her out on 20 February 1948. Jennie Darlington and her husband travelled back to the US and their daughter, Cynthia, was born.

Benefiting from the icebreakers' presence, Vivian Fuchs arrived on *John Biscoe* with a relief FIDS party for the Stonington Island Base. Fuchs' subsequent sledge journey with Ray Adie down King George VI Sound stimulated his ideas for TAE.

The Norwegian-British-Swedish Expedition (NBS) (1949–52)

This expedition worked from a base in Dronning Maud Land to the east of the Weddell Sea. The area had been first explored by Norwegian whaling expeditions in the 1930s. NBS, in *Norsel*, was a highly successful international expedition that undertook pioneering research in glaciology, geology, meteorology and the measurement of ice thickness by seismic sounding.[26] NBS inspired the scientific plans and influenced the logistics used by Fuchs' TAE. The exploration achieved by NBS is shown on Figure 29.

The leader of the expedition was John Giaever, a Norwegian. The senior Swedish member was glaciologist Valter Schytt and the senior British member, geophysicist Gordon Robin, was an Australian. The 15 men in the first wintering party included five Norwegians, three Swedes, two Englishmen and a Canadian. Light aircraft were used in all three summer seasons for taking aerial photographs. Together with a triangulation network made by a Norwegian surveyor, the photographs later

served as the basis for a published series of topographic maps. The air units were, in successive summers, British, Swedish and Norwegian. Brian Walford led a Royal Air Force group the first season, using two Auster aircraft equipped with floats, and later with skis. Peter Weston was one of the RAF engineers and eight years later he served on Fuchs' TAE expedition.

The NBS expedition's work included meteorological observations on the coastal ice shelf. Glaciologists Valter Schytt and Charles Swithinbank studied the structure of the ice shelf to a depth of 100 metres. Microscope study of cross-sections of the ice enabled them to interpret snow strata to determine the rate of snow accumulation, supplementing their measurements at the base and inland. These glaciologists completed a 1000 km inland traverse and measured the glacier movement. The geologists Fred Roots and Alan Reece studied the geology of the

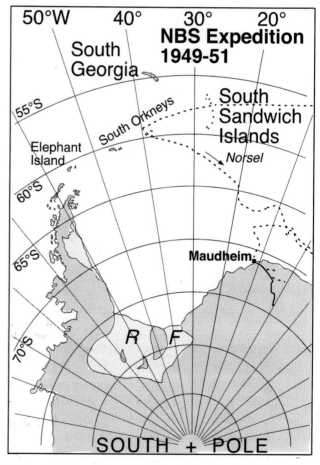

Figure 29 Norwegian-British-Swedish Expedition's explorations in 1949–51. The glaciological and geological traverses are dotted, and the seismic journey is shown by a solid line. R: Ronne Ice Shelf; F: Filchner Ice Shelf.

inland mountain ranges during two summer seasons. Allan Reece's right eye was injured when a small chip of rock flew into it. Several months later the Swedish doctor at Maudheim had to remove the eye to save Reece's sight.

NBS completed an important traverse south of Maudheim, lasting over two months, to reach a point 600 km inland (74°18′S 0°48′E). This, led by Gordon Robin, used two weasels (discontinued American war-time ice vehicles) with a dog team in support for essential safety. Earlier, Robin had toyed with a scheme to drive from Maudheim right across the continent to the Ross Sea with weasels and dog teams, making ice soundings along the way.[27] Robin's seismic soundings showed that the ice thickness in some places was nearly 3000 metres and his results helped to revise earlier estimates of the volume of ice in Antarctica.

The NBS expedition proved the value of international collaboration and had an important influence on later Antarctic science. It was to become a model for the International Geophysical Year (IGY) in 1957–58, and later for the central tenets of the Antarctic Treaty. The Treaty succeeded in marginalising some claims to sovereignty, including the Norwegian claim to the Dronning Maud Land sector.

Appendix II The Weddell Sea and its Special Character

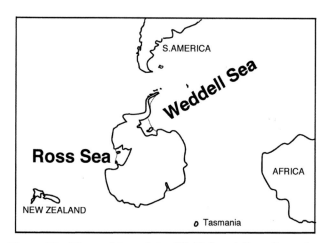

Figure 30 The position of the Weddell and Ross Seas, the major sea-ice-filled embayments in Antarctica. The Weddell Sea was discovered 28 years before the Ross Sea, but proved to be much more difficult for ships to penetrate.

Two major intra-continental seas, the Ross and Weddell, indent the outline of the Antarctic continent (Figure 30). They have provided important access routes for early endeavours to explore into the heart of the continent, and each was named for their discoverers: James Weddell in 1823, and James Ross in 1840. Both are choked by the pack-ice, together with large icebergs, which surround the whole Antarctic continent. Access from the Ross Sea has proved consistently more straightforward than from the Weddell. Why is this the case?

Pack-Ice in the Weddell Sea

The Weddell Sea is usually impenetrable for most ships, except along its east side. James Weddell discovered the sea, with two small wooden ships, when he experienced a freak year in 1823 and penetrated deep into what was a sea free of pack-ice. He surmised it extended to the South Pole, but wisely turned back north.

Later explorers were stimulated by Weddell to continue his pioneering penetration, hoping to reach the coast of the continent, if not the South Pole. But none could follow his route because they met impenetrable pack-ice and some may have suspected Weddell's veracity, though his documentation was careful and complete. He simply experienced a freak year.

The Weddell Sea is about 2000 km across and penetrates over 1000 km southwards towards the South Pole. In the south it is limited by the edge of the Filchner–Ronne Ice Shelves, about 1300 km from the Pole. This Weddell Sea Barrier is equivalent to that which confines the Ross Sea, which Ross discovered in 1841 and named the Great Barrier. The distances from each barrier to the Pole are similar. They are the edges of great ice shelves, fed by glaciers, which descend from the higher interior. The relatively thick ice flows north to the coast where it floats on the sea, periodically breaking off as very large tabular icebergs.

The pack-ice forms as the sea freezes in winter. This forms ice up to two metres thick in some places, every year, and in successive years can produce thicker ice and complex ice floes. In the north, ice floes break away and melt in summer, establishing an irregular and changing edge to the pack-ice. Sea currents and winds drive the floating pack-ice, forming pressure ridges. Careful studies have established that a strong current flows west around the Antarctic continent. This current continues, deep into the Weddell Sea, along the Barrier and then continues north against the Antarctic Peninsula. The movements generate a very tight icepack, usually difficult or impossible to penetrate by ship. The pack can easily entrap any ship and endanger it by pressure. In two famous instances, the *Antarctic* (1904) and *Endurance* (1915) were crushed and sank. Fuchs' Trans-Antarctic Expedition vessels in 1955 (*Theron*) and 1956 (*Magga Dan*) had to find a route though the pack-ice and experienced its potential treachery and hazards. Relatively fewer ships have come to grief in the Ross Sea.

The patterns of the drifting pack-ice were first established from the drifts of *Deutschland* (1912) and *Endurance* (1915). In recent years, several drift markers have been placed on the pack-ice, and followed by radio and satellite, to provide the collective results shown Figures 31 and 32. Many research workers, to understand Antarctic sea-ice behaviour, have closely studied the results of these drift-ice projects. Harder and Fischer have calculated that the mean northward sea ice volume exported out of the Southern Weddell Sea annually is around 2000 cubic kilometres.[1] This compares with the largest freshwater runoff, for example from the Amazon. A major hypothesis in relation to global warming is that the inland Antarctic ice could start to disperse if its ice shelves, including the Ross and Ronne–Filchner, were to break up. Ice

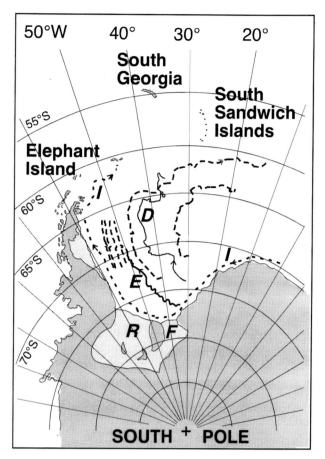

Figure 31 Weddell Sea pack-ice drift paths from various sources: ship drifts (D *Deutschland*, and E *Endurance*) and drift buoy markers. I shows the paths followed by icebergs, followed on satellite imagery. R: Ronne Ice Shelf; F: Filchner Ice Shelf.

shelves at the margins of the Antarctic Peninsula, such as the Larsen, have shown rapid decreases in recent decades, in conjunction with temperature warming measured in the Peninsula. By contrast, much of East Antarctica has been getting slightly colder.

The tracking of tabular icebergs by satellite imagery has provided remarkable demonstrations of sea-ice drift. These have included the Amery and Trolltunga icebergs, each over 100 km long, which were carried west from their ice shelf sources further to the east, and swept down through the Weddell Sea to reach the northern Peninsula (Figure 31).

An important insight into the annual variations in sea ice in the Weddell Sea has been provided by satellite imagery. In a monograph containing a collection of scientific papers about Antarctic Sea Ice, Cominso and Gordon illustrate the patterns of minimum sea ice in successive years, using satellite images between 1979 and 1994 (Figure 33).[2] There are remarkable

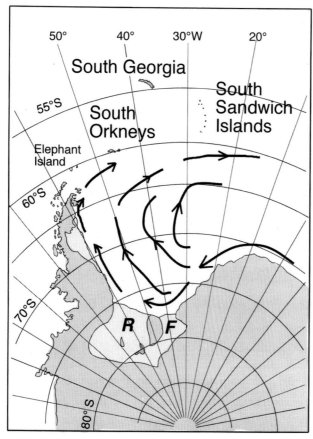

Figure 32 The gyre followed by pack-ice drift paths in the Weddell Sea. Redrawn from *Antarctic Research Series* No 74, 1998, p. 274. R: Ronne Ice Shelf; F: Filchner Ice Shelf.

differences from year to year, and one can understand how Weddell happened to experience a very fortunate season in 1823. A more pronounced summer minimum tends to follow a high winter maximum year, possibly affected by the Antarctic Circumpolar Wave recognised by White and Peterson.[3]

These variations in summer sea ice in the Weddell Sea help to account for the considerable contrasts in different years which vessels have experienced. Weather effects, particularly wind, can aggravate the conditions. Expedition supply cruise ships now make very effective use of satellite imagery.

The Geological Formation of the Weddell and Scotia Seas Between Antarctica and South America

Antarctic rocks resemble those found in all the other continents. Any geologist will immediately recognise familiar rock types, including common granite and other continental rocks, and exciting fossils occur in some places. In 1957, I was privileged to be first to examine the rocks of the Theron Mountains the Shackleton Range and the Whichaway Nunataks further inland, and found fossil plants, which confirmed the Gondwana association for this corner of the Weddell Sea. These parts of Antarctica, south and east of the Weddell Sea (including Dronning Maud Land) are within East Antarctica, which contrasts with the geology of the Antarctic Peninsula, known as West Antarctica. Otto Nordenskjold found good evidence during his geological studies in Patagonia and his subsequent 1901–03 Antarctic Peninsula expedition, that the East Antarctic region has geological affinities with the Andean chain of South

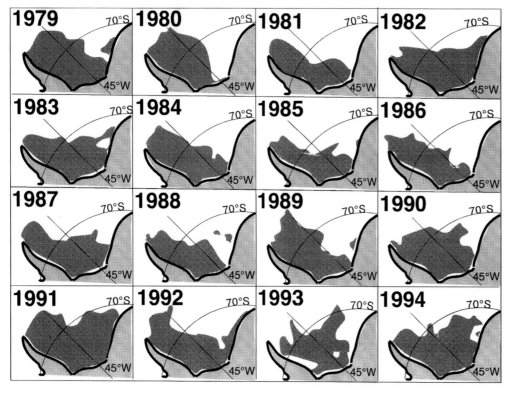

Figure 33 Sea ice distri-butions from satellite imagery, to show the tremendous differences from year to year (1979–94). Redrawn from Cominso and Gordon, Antarctic Research Series No 74, 1998, p 296.

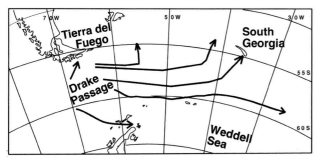

Figure 34 The movement vectors in the Scotia Arc, interpreted from plate tectonics (redrawn from P.F. Barker, *Earth Science Reviews*, 2001, 55, 1–39).

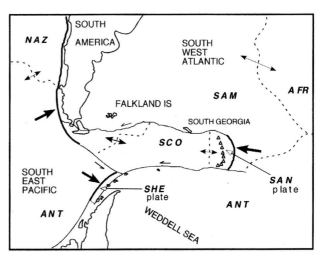

Figure 35 Sketch of tectonic plates in the Scotia region. Compare with Plate 71. Redrawn from P.F. Barker, *Earth Science Reviews*, 2001, 55, 1–39. The movement vectors are indicated. An older spreading ridge existed inside the Scotia Arc.

America. So, too, has South Georgia. But further north, the Falkland Islands are a different fragment of Gondwanaland.

The floor of the Weddell Sea provides evidence about its formation as an oceanic basin formed by 'spreading' within a plate-tectonic model, 160 to 100 million years ago. The adjacent Scotia Sea contains the Scotia Arc, which has an unusual geometry.

This arc includes the north-east pointing Antarctic Peninsula. It then sweeps east through the South Orkney Islands, the South Sandwich Islands at the turn of the arc, north-west through South Georgia and finally a westward trend to link with the Andes through Tierra del Fuego.

The Scotia Arc exhibits an extraordinary geological arrangement (Plate 71). Evidence confirms a long history of its astonishing geological development.[4] As well as using the rock types and their ages, P.F. Barker used the magnetic stripe evidence on the sea floor to unravel the previous movement directions. Figure 34 shows the disruption of a former connection between South America and Antarctica, with some parts moving towards the north but, especially, the central

part towards the east. Barker believes this disruption commenced about 40 million years ago. Through sea floor spreading and plate dislocation, South Georgia has been moved about 2000 km to the east! The interpreted tectonic plates are shown in Figure 35.

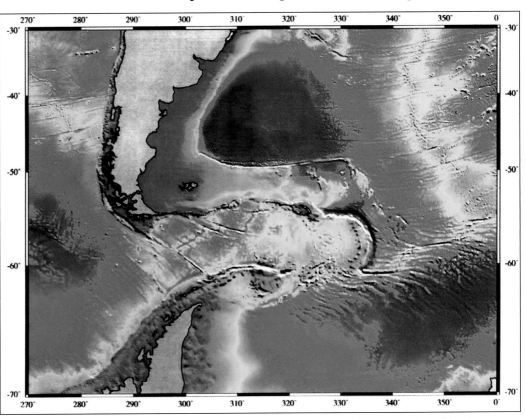

71 Scotia Arc: a sea-surface height, enhanced satellite image. It shows South America, the Falkland Islands, South Georgia, the South Sandwich trench and volcanic arc linking with the Antarctic Peninsula. See text and Figure 35. Seasat, Geosat, ERS 1. (NASA image)

The South Sandwich volcanic arc is adjacent to a deep-sea trench, where the South American Plate is being pushed under the adjacent Scotia Sea further east in a 'subduction zone'. Earthquakes occur along this zone, under the volcanic arc.

Further north, the Falkland Islands group is part of the former Gondwanaland continent. Most of its rocks are near-horizontal sandstones, in complete contrast with the metamorphic rocks found in the Antarctic Peninsula and the Scotia Sea. But its closest affiliations are with southern Africa and this fragment of Gondwanaland has migrated a vast distance.

Appendix III Dimensions and Construction of Three Polar Ships

	Length	Max. width	Max. tonnage	Hull thickness
Fram	132 ft	36 ft	402	24–28 in
Deutschland	121 ft	25 ft	344	21–26 in
Endurance	128 ft	25 ft	350	18–24 in

Fram

The Norwegian Colin Archer designed her for purposes outlined to him by Fridtjof Nansen. Some details and quotes are given in Nansen's *Furthest North*. *Fram* was the ship Fridjof Nansen used for his ice drift expedition across the Arctic Ocean in 1893–96. She was built to withstand the pressure of the ice, with sloping sides to rise it out of the water instead of being nipped by the ice. 'A ship of the form and size here indicated will not be a good or comfortable seaboat, but that is of minor importance in waters filled with ice such as we are here speaking of.'

Archer made plan after plan for the ship and successive models were built and abandoned. Improvements were constantly being considered. Archer noted two points were especially studied: '1) that the shape of the hull be such as to offer as small a vulnerable target as possible to the attacks of the ice: and 2) that it be built so solidly as to be able to withstand the greatest possible pressure from without in any direction whatsoever'. The intention was to make the ship as small as possible, lighter than a larger ship and also stronger in proportion to her weight. Nansen was of the opinion that a vessel of 170 tons register would suffice, but *Fram* was considerably larger, 402 tons gross (307 tons net). The plan was to build a short, broad vessel with smooth sides and without projecting edges. The hull was pointed fore and aft, a special characteristic already introduced by Archer in his revolutionary lifeboat designs. The ends were exceptionally strong, and Fram had a specially designed bow and stern, with wells for the screw and rudder, so that both could be hoisted up on deck.

Nansen describes how the outside planking consisted of three layers of oak and greenheart. The diagrams of *Fram* show the details of her very careful timber construction. She had diagonal stay supports, placed as nearly as possible at right angles to the sides of the ship, and a triple expansion engine.

Fram survived her three-year Arctic drift voyage intact. She was severely tested on several occasions by ice pressure ridges up to 22 feet high. In March 1894

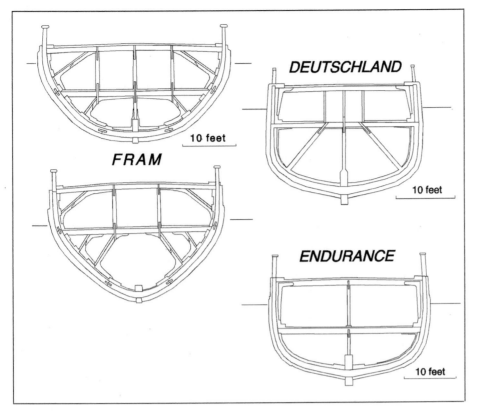

Figure 36 Transverse cross-sections of three polar ships: Nansen's *Fram*, Filchner's *Deutschland*, and Shackleton's *Endurance*.

a week was spent removing one of these. On several occasions, blasting was used to try to relieve the ice pressure. In August, *Fram* was subjected to sudden ice pressure and 'in stately fashion' was 'lifted in the course of a few minutes, 22 inches at the stern and 14 inches by the bow … without heeling over in the least … swiftly and lightly raised as if she had been a feather.'

Nansen had hopes of undertaking an Antarctic expedition in *Fram* but was never able to do so. However, he made her available to Roald Amundsen for his South Pole expedition in 1911. *Fram* performed well in the Ross Sea, for Amundsen to establish his base, Framheim. *Fram* returned for him the next year after his journey to the Pole.

Deutschland

Built in 1905 at the Risor shipyard in Lindstol, *Deutschland*'s original name was *Bjorn* (Bear). After purchasing her, Wilhelm Filchner had modifications made in the Framnaes yard in Norway before the second German South Pole expedition of 1911–13.

On Ernest Shackleton's advice, the hull was strengthened with braces and a propeller well was built so the screw could be hoisted on deck. Later, strong iron plates and bands were fastened across the stern and alterations were made to the main boiler and engine in Hamburg. Her engine was a two-cylinder expansion engine.[1]

Deutschland travelled to the Antarctic via Buenos Aires and South Georgia. After a survey visit to the northern South Sandwich Islands, she set off for the Weddell Sea, following the route shown on Figure 27. The problems which affected the expedition in trying to establish a base, are described in Appendix I.

Deutschland became beset and drifted in the Weddell Sea pack-ice for over eight months before getting free and returning to South Georgia. She emerged undamaged. Filchner's log of her drift indicates that she escaped the threats of ice pressure ridges and icebergs.

Endurance

Like *Fram* before her, *Endurance* was built in the Framnaes yard in Sandefjord, in 1911–12. Her original name was *Polaris* and she was built for 'polar safaris' in the Arctic. However, the enterprise never proceeded for financial reasons. Shackleton purchased her in early 1914 for his Imperial Trans-Antarctic Expedition. She was delivered to London in June and the shipbuilders James Pollock & Sons did some unconfirmed work on her.[2]

Endurance sailed from Southampton on 8 August 1914, under Captain Frank Worsley. Her route to South Georgia was via Buenos Aires. In a letter to his wife, written from Buenos Aires, Shackleton wrote:

this ship is not as strong as the Nimrod constructionally this I have seen from her way of behaving when in a gale pressing against the dock wall here though there is nothing to be scared of as I think she will go through the ice all right only I would exchange her for the old Nimrod any day now except for comfort … it seems to be a very bad season after all and I think the wisest thing is to winter her.[3]

Because of the bad ice season reported by the whalers in the Weddell Sea, *Endurance* spent a month at South Georgia and did not leave until 5 December. She met the pack-ice within three days, but sailed through the South Sandwich Islands and followed a course similar to that used by Bruce in 1904. They passed Bruce's southernmost point and continued south to see previously unseen land named as the Caird Coast. They were finally beset in 76°34', still 160 km from Filchner's Vahsel Bay, on 22 January 1915.

Endurance began a long drift in the pack-ice, starting from a point south of where *Deutschland* had been beset. The paths of the two ships is shown in Figure 27. The regions of the Weddell Sea they traversed were different, but essential contrasts in the conditions they experienced may relate to the individual ice seasons, three years apart. The weather circumstances would also have been different. In June 1915 Shackleton referred to pressure near the ship, and in July the ship was heaved over to port. She settled with no hull damage, but the rudder had been violently forced out of position. Pressure continued to move closer to the ship and in October severe pressure gave her a 30-degree list to port. One of Hurley's photographs taken on 19 October shows *Endurance* listing, and lifted by the ice pressure.[4] Five days later she began to leak, the pumps were manned and the ship was continually bending and straining. A higher pressure wave approached *Endurance* on 27 October and began to crush the ship. The water gained on the pumps and as Hurley described:

> I am quickly down on the moving ice with the cinema, expecting every minute to see the sides, which are springing and buckling, stave in. The line of pressure now assaults the ship, and she is heaved to the crest of the ridge like a toy. Immense fragments are forced under the counter and wrench away the stern post.[5]

That evening, the men returned for their last meal, to a background of groaning timbers and crunching ice. Tongues of ice could be seen protruding from the ship's side. That night, the men all camped on the ice. *Endurance* was progressively destroyed and sank on 21 November 1915.

Reading the descriptions of the last weeks of *Endurance*, it is hard not to feel *Deutschland* might also have succumbed under these ice circumstances. Could *Fram* have survived? Would her hull shape and internal construction strengths have allowed her to ride above the ice?

Appendix IV Other IGY Expeditions in the Weddell Sea Region

At the time of the Trans-Antarctic Expedition, there were three other expeditions which occupied bases for the International Geophysical Year, shown on Figure 37: Halley Bay (Royal Society), General Belgrano (Argentine Government) and Ellsworth (US Navy). The exploration carried out from these bases is summarised.

FROM HALLEY BAY

This base had no vehicles to enable travel, but during 1956, from dark images to the east occasionally visible by refraction, the men at the base surmised that mountains probably existed inland. Fuchs undertook

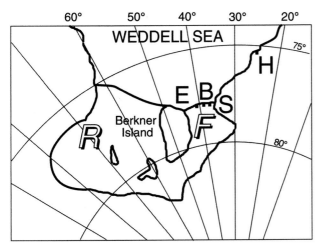

Figure 37 The other Weddell Sea IGY bases in 1957–58: Ellsworth (US), Belgrano (Argentina), Shackleton (TAE) and Halley Bay (UK). R: Ronne Ice Shelf; F: Filchner Ice Shelf.

an exploratory flight in 1957 from Halley Bay in the TAE Otter aircraft, which discovered mountains well inland, in Norwegian territory. They were estimated as rising to over 7000 feet (2400 metres) and were named Tottanfjella after the Royal Society's supply vessel, *Tottan*.

The following summary of the later field exploration inland is taken from several sources.[1] The map, Figure 38, shows the routes followed.

Survey and geological mapping and research largely stimulated the exploration. The Shackleton Range lies between the stable, older 'shield' (or craton) of East Antarctica, the Transantartic Mountains and the tectonic mountain belts of West Antarctica, which include the Peninsula.

Ground exploration from Halley Bay did not take place until after 1959 when the base was handed over by the Royal Society to FIDS. Explorations with dog teams and vehicles took place from 1961 to 1966, especially involving geological work, survey and later radio-echo sounding of ice sheet thickness. Three men were killed in a major crevasse accident in Mannefallknausane in 1965, when their Muskeg tractor fell into a deep, narrowing crevasse.

After work in the eastern mountains, Heimefrontfjella, had been completed, vehicles and dog teams concentrated on the Theron Mountains in 1966 and 1967. Subsequent work continued further south into the eastern Shackleton Range in 1968–69.

The next stage of survey and geological exploration in the Shackleton Range involved three seasons with

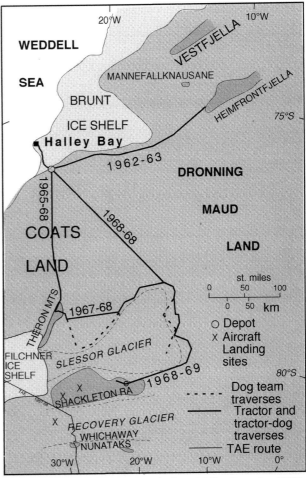

Figure 38 The explorations made from Halley Bay after IGY. Some of the Shackleton Range parties were established by air.

American aircraft to fly in dog teams for several months' work. BAS surveyors erected the ground control for the US air photography completed in 1967. The ground exploration of the Shackleton Range from 1968–69 was a return to the small-scale, air-supported explorations which were so successful on TAE 10 years before. Ken Blaiklock and in later years, Peter Clarkson, led the dog-team survey and geological work. Clarkson led the major part of the long-term geological work in this extensive mountain range, which extends over 200 km (124 miles), east to west, and is up to 70 km (43 miles) wide. In 1968–69, the American aircraft also supported a Norwegian geological expedition, which worked in Heimefrontfjella.

The Soviet exploration in 1975–76 and 1976–77 was based on air support, including the use of long-range MI-8 helicopters from their Druznaja-1 base on the Filchner Ice Shelf. Further Soviet geological fieldwork was undertaken in the Shackletons in three later seasons. German scientists took part on some of the Soviet expeditions. In 1977–78, a British geological party used motor toboggans for the first time, having been flown in from Halley Bay by a Twin Otter. A German geological expedition (GEISHA) took place in 1987–88, when 27 scientists and support staff established a base camp on the Brunt Ice Shelf near Halley Bay. A second base camp was established with two Dornier 228–100 aircraft and two twin-engined Bolkow 105 helicopters. Helicopters and motor toboggans were used from satellite field camps.

The final geological map of Shackleton Range marked a significant international achievement.

ARGENTINE EXPLORATION FROM BELGRANO

General Belgrano Station was established near the coast, on the Filchner Ice Shelf, in January 1955. The site was 25 miles (40 km) west of the site for the TAE Shackleton Base, established in 1956.

Belgrano Station had vehicles and made traverses east to the region of Vahsel Bay. Later, they made a number of flights in 1955 and were the first to observe the inland mountains later known as the Theron Mountains and the Shackleton Range. TAE saw these a few months later and visited them the following year. The following information is from Hernán Pujato.[2] The air reconnaissance routes are shown on Figure 39.

From 1942, the Argentine army had a broad plan to install bases in the region claimed by Argentina, especially after World War II. Their first bases were established on the islands and mainland down the West Coast of the Antarctic Peninsula. An important step later in the plan was to travel to the south-east corner of the Weddell Sea. A new icebreaker, *General San Martin*, reached the Filchner Ice Shelf on 3 January 1955, the first vessel to do so since Filchner in *Deutschland* in 1911. Argentina operated Belgrano Station through the International Geophysical Year (1957–58) and the US turned over its Ellsworth Base to Argentina in February 1959. Ellsworth was 35 miles (56 km) west of Belgrano and was occupied until 1961. *San Martin* had experienced difficulty

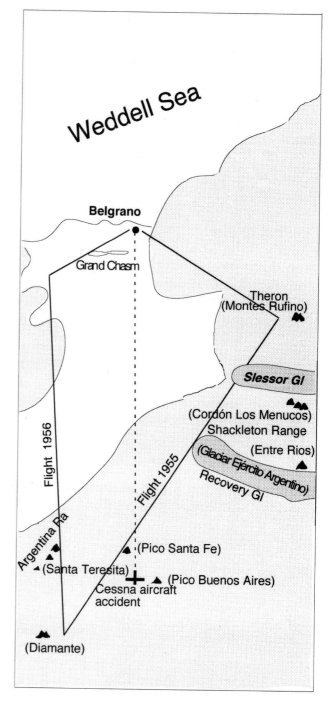

Figure 38 The air exploration achieved by the Argentines from General Belgrano Base. These names were never registered, although they preceded TAE discoveries.

reaching these stations because of pack-ice, and Belgrano was moved to a bedrock site east of Vahsel Bay, as first seen by Filchner in 1911.

Pujato wanted to use Belgrano as a starting point for a surface traverse to the South Pole. He was forced to abandon this plan, but believed that aircraft could be used to reach parts of the region south of Belgrano. The base was officially opened on 18 January 1955, when a Cessna 180 aircraft was brought down on *San Martin*. A second plane, a De Havilland Beaver, arrived the next season. Local flights were made the first year, but with two aircraft, extensive flights were undertaken in 1955–56. Belgrano had no hangars for the aircraft and they were secured in excavations through the winter, as were our two planes at Shackleton. Four men were responsible for the flying from Belgrano including two pilots: Hernán Pujato and Domingo Molinari.

During 1956 the aircraft made 24 flights over the region, including the area from Moltke Nunatak (near Vahsel Bay), west to Gould Bay and inland to 83°S. On an early flight described by Molinari, the aircraft were apparently away for five hours and recognised the new mountains for the first time. They landed at 83°10′S, 39°30′W and established a depot (Caferio Namuncura). Pujato does not give the date of this first long inland flight, but it was probably late in 1955. On TAE, Haslop and Blaiklock flew past the Therons and saw the Shackletons in an Auster from Shackleton Base on 7 February 1956.

The Argentines gave many names to the new topographic features: San Lorenzo Plain, Rufino Mountains (the Therons), Entre Rios Chain, Argentine Army Glacier, Menucos Mountains (the Shackletons), Peak Buenos Aires, Diamente Chain and Santa Terista.

Later, the Cessna crashed on the way to 83°S. Miraculously, the two men on board were not injured but the aircraft was wrecked. The Beaver rescued them, but no further long-distance flight exploration could be undertaken. The discovery of the mountains was never documented and the original Argentine discovery and suggested names were unrecorded. Pujato met Finn Ronne, leader of the US Navy IGY Expedition, when he visited Belgrano on 31 December 1956 and told him of the mountain discoveries. He says Ronne suggested the Argentines should officially record their discoveries, but apparently this was not done.

Later, in 1965, an Argentine vehicle party led by Colonel Jorge Leal made a return traverse to the South Pole. The following summary is from *Polar Record* in 1967: 'A party of ten men travelling in six Sno-Cats left Belgrano on 26th October 1965 and reached the Pole on 10th December. They returned on 31 December in a total journey of 2600 km. Four men with two dog sledges accompanied the party as far as the Pensacola Mountains.'

A C-47 and two Beaver aircraft flew from Belgrano to the Pole on 4 November 1965. The C-47 continued to McMurdo Base on the 12th. It returned via the Pole, joined there by the two Beavers, to Belgrano. In September 1965, a Cessna aircraft, returning from a new army station (Alfarez de Navio Sobral at 81°04′S, 40°36′W) to Belgrano could not land at either station owing to fog and crash-landed 20 km south of Belgrano. The crew were not injured but were not rescued until 7 October. In attempting to walk to Belgrano they had become lost.

All these achievements seem to be largely unknown outside Argentina.

ELLSWORTH BASE (US), 1957–58

The Traverse to Dufek Massif

The expedition and this long traverse, past the Dufek Massif 370 miles (600 km) inland from Ellsworth, have been well described by Behrendt.[3] It was an outstanding journey and achieved important scientific results. This summary is based on Behrendt's account.

The expedition arrived in two US Navy vessels, *Wyandot* (the supply vessel) and *Staten Island* (an icebreaker built in 1940). *Staten Island* had some ice-breaking capacity, but *Wyandot* did not, and in the course of the voyage through pack-ice in the Weddell Sea, though following *Staten Island*, *Wyandot* suffered some serious damage and developed significant leaks. Her captain, F.M. Gambacorta, was increasingly anxious for the survival of his ship.

The two vessels, with the icebreaker leading, entered the pack-ice near 62°S on 17 December. After being beset for five days, they eventually reached open water next to Coats Land on 28 December at 72°S and proceeded south past Halley Bay to the edge of the Filchner Ice Shelf. They passed the TAE Shackleton Base and General Belgrano, the Argentine base where Ronne made a courtesy call. Ellsworth was to be the seventh US IGY base and their most isolated station. There was a bold intention to position the base as strategically as possible for weather and other scientific observations and to enable access for a geophysical traverse inland with vehicles. With considerable determination, the vessels travelled 425 miles (680 km) further west. On 15 January they reached to within 42 miles (68 km) of the south-west corner of the Weddell Sea, against the Antarctic Peninsula. The last traverse west was along the edge of the Ronne Ice Shelf, which is characterised by ice cliffs and a lack of places to offload materials for a base. The ships' routes are shown in Figure 40.

The expedition was a part of Operation Deep Freeze, under the overall command of Admiral George Dufek, based at McMurdo Base on the Ross Sea. From this distance, Dufek became increasingly concerned about getting Ellsworth established early enough for the station to be fully built, and for the two vessels to leave the Weddell Sea safely, well before the approach of winter. Dufek referred to 15 February as the last

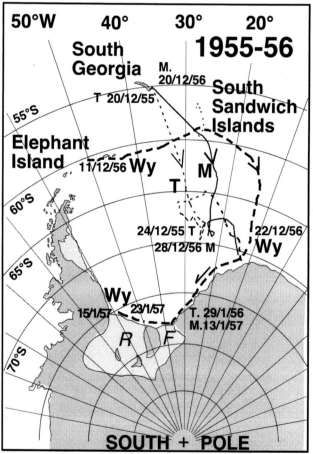

Figure 40 The routes taken by the US IGY vessels in 1956–57: *Wyandot* and *Staten Island* (Wy). *Theron* (T) and *Magga Dan* (M) routes are shown for comparison. R: Ronne Ice Shelf; F: Filchner Ice Shelf.

possible day for withdrawal. Progress in getting so far west of Shackleton and Belgrano and finding a site for Ellsworth was taking much longer than desirable, and there must have been questions about remoteness, in relation to re-supply the next year.

The Ellsworth leader was Commander Finn Ronne, who had been a member of three previous Antarctic expeditions, most recently 10 years before. His RARE expedition was described in Appendix I. Ronne must have been keen to continue his 1947 exploration, and have access to the southern Antarctic Peninsula and the unknown country south of the Weddell Sea. However, the height of the ice-shelf cliffs (120 feet, 42 metres) along the south-western coast of the Weddell towards the Peninsula made unloading impossible. Behrendt quotes the very interesting communication exchanges between Dufek and the expedition, and the alternatives Dufek raised for putting in a smaller expedition base. Placing the base much further north, near Cape Norwegia, was suggested. This would have been close to the site of Maudheim, the International Norwegian-British-Swedish Expedition's base of 1949–52. That expedition had made traverses inland, with pioneering geophysical work, including seismic, ice-depth sounding. Dufek's proposals were strenuously resisted. The *Staten Island* and *Wyandot* had difficulty returning back towards Belgrano and *Staten Island* had to negotiate some of the most severe pack-ice encountered on the cruise. Both ships sustained damage, including propeller damage, and *Wyandot* had significant hull damage, causing leakage.

A site for the base was finally selected on 26 January, 35 miles (56 km) west of General Belgrano, at a place on the Filchner Ice Shelf where there was a natural loading ramp leading up 45 metres onto the shelf. Similar ramps existed at Shackleton and Belgrano, and Behrendt later published his conclusions that they all resulted from high melt rates beneath the ice shelf in this region. There was no such ramp at the edge of the Ronne Ice Shelf further west. *Wyandot* was unloaded within 11 days and the base was quickly erected two miles (3 km) inland. The final handover took place on 11 February, when the ships departed.

Captain Finn Ronne was 57. In command at Ellsworth, he had a dual role: as civilian station scientific leader and as naval officer in charge. He was the only member of the party of 39 who had been to Antarctica previously. Ellsworth had an unhappy winter under its complicated leader, whose approach seemed to have become even more difficult than on RARE. Some of his rulings were bizarre, and the greatest difficulties probably resulted from his inflated opinion of his own experience and knowledge. As the only person with previous Antarctic experience and much older than other members of the expedition, he believed that as leader he should make all planning decisions. These included where and how the inland scientific traverse should be organised. Doubtless, he wanted to explore 'Edith Ronne Land', which he had originally seen in the distance with Jim Lassiter and Bill Latady in 1947. He had his own immutable ideas for the vehicle geophysical traverse, and obstinately disagreed with his capable geophysical–glaciological team. Ronne had no experience with vehicles and his perspectives continued to obstruct the planning. Sadly, the achievements of the traverse party had little to do with his leadership. Vivian Fuchs and others on TAE had first observed the nature of the Filchner Ice Shelf inland from Shackleton. On 31 January 1956 they saw the east end of the Grand Chasm, a narrow, severely broken zone 25 miles (40 km) inland. When the Americans saw it from the air on 16 March 1957 they instantly recognised it as a severe obstacle and Behrendt wonders if Ellsworth would have been located where it was, had the existence of the chasm been known. The chasm was a major fracture on the Shelf, which would eventually fracture completely in 1986 to release three large icebergs.

A number of scientific projects were successfully completed at Ellsworth. They included the excavation of a deep pit to 100 feet (31 metres), from which drilling continued to reach 182 feet (55 metres) below the surface, well below sea level. Thorough preparations were made for the seismic and gravity traverse, and a range of other geophysical projects.

A major problem arose for one of the two Sno-Cat vehicles intended for the spring traverse. Its clutch overheated, damaging the tempering of the clutch springs. They did not have a replacement clutch and after removal of the clutch assembly, the senior base mechanic declared it beyond repair. One solution offered to the traverse party was to replace the disabled Sno-Cat with two Weasel vehicles for their

journey. Hugo Neuberg, the senior glaciologist, set out to re-temper the springs. Fuchs offered David Pratt's help but David was extremely busy preparing for the TAE journey. However, he lent Neuberg an intact spring. A suitable furnace had to be improvised at Ellsworth and the early attempts to use this were unsuccessful (fire brick oven, pipes, blowtorches …). But with his fellow glaciologist, Paul Walker, Neuberg was finally successful. The spring was held in the flames of the oil galley range firebox until it reached a cherry-red colour and it was then quenched in kerosene. It was then annealed in a regular oven around 500°F. Unfortunately, this was later found to have damaged the stove! The colour was compared with the TAE spring.

Neuberg went on to re-temper all the 16 springs, and the clutch assembly tested successfully! 'This was Hugo's proudest accomplishment during the entire year and possibly in his life. He is legendary among Antarcticians who know him.' Unbelievably, Ronne seems to have blocked efforts to arrange for a replacement clutch to be brought down on Jim Lassiter's flight, expected in the spring.

On 21 October, an Otter reconnaissance flight about 350 miles (560 km) west of south from Ellsworth reached a significant range of mountains, the Dufek Massif, part of the extensive Pensacola Mountains. These ranges had been seen and photographed on a long return Neptune flight from McMurdo early in 1956. Ronne was complimented on his discoveries but was severely criticised by Dufek. The single-engine Otter flight had gone beyond its defined range limit and Ellsworth had inadequate search and rescue facilities. However, Ed Thiel had seen the spectacular Dufek Mountains and determined the forthcoming traverse should reach them.

The Geophysical Traverse From Ellsworth

The traverse set off at the end of October with five men in two Sno-Cats and sledges. One Sno-Cat had a crevasse detector, but this was found not to be of much assistance when negotiating some severe crevasse country.

The traverse route is shown in Figure 41. The party made a route around the eastern end of the Chasm, south-west over the wide ice rise of Berkner Island, which divides the Filchner from the Ronne Ice Shelf, and then on to reach the Dufek Massif. Sections of

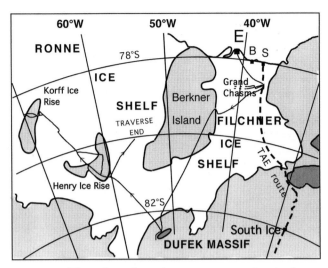

Figure 41 The US geophysical traverse route, 1957–58, from Ellsworth Base to the Dufek Massif.

the journey were hazardous, with frequent crevasse incidents, mostly involving sledges but occasionally, men. With only two Sno-Cats, the capability for vehicle recovery was severely limited and they were forced to proceed with great caution. Air surveillance was critical in helping find a safe route over some sections, including the route past the end of the Grand Chasm. They set off to follow Fuchs' TAE route, but never saw any of the black TAE flags. Their Otter air support was restricted to a 250-mile range, without refuelling depots, and the vehicles moved on beyond this distance. The party had only a low-power, 7.5-watt 'angry-nine' radio transmitter, and soon reached a point on the floating ice shelf where they had no communication with Ellsworth.

The traverse vehicles needed fuel resupply. Jim Lassiter's 10-man group had reached Ellsworth in November with two C-47 (Douglas DC-3) aircraft, after flying down from the US via Punta Arenas and the southern Antarctic Peninsula. Their mission involved a planned 200,000 square mile mapping project in 40-mile wide strips, to an accuracy of a mile. Lassiter's aircraft re-supplied the traverse team several times.

On the first re-supply, Lassiter flew out with Ronne and, as well as the vehicle fuel, they brought a more powerful, 125-watt radio transmitter which would have solved their communication problems, especially enabling the aircraft to find them. Instead, they had to agree on a confirmed location for a given day, well in advance. Perversely, Ronne took the new radio back

with him, allegedly because he did not have approval from the overall commander, Admiral Dufek.

The vehicle party remained out of radio contact for three weeks. The traverse carried out regular seismic soundings to determine the ice depth to bedrock. Gravity and magnetometer measurements were also undertaken. The glaciologists made regular pit excavations to log the snow stratigraphy and estimate annual accumulation rates, and drilled a nine-metre hole to measure the deep temperature overnight, which is a good indication of the annual average.

Ed Thiel was co-leader of the party and worked as chief seismologist with John Behrendt. Nolan Aughenbaugh was assistant seismologist and also geologist when they finally reached outcrops in the Dufek Massif. Hugo Neuberg was the senior glaciologist and co-leader. Paul Walker was his assistant glaciologist. A versatile team member, Neuberg made the sun sightings to fix their travel positions, was the party's best Morse radio operator, and was the party's vehicle mechanic.

On 6 December they could see the mountains, still 70 miles ahead, with spectacular jagged peaks and spires. Behrendt surmised that the peaks looked like igneous rock, but geologist Aughenbaugh was affronted by his gall, a mere geophysicist, in trying to identify the rocks from that distance. Augie bet him the rocks were sedimentary. Two days later, they were close enough to see that the mountains appeared to be made of flat-lying, dark sedimentary rock.

The first Lassiter flight arrived with mail and 12 drums of fuel. It also brought a spare Sno-Cat clutch from the US, which was stored at Ellsworth because Neuberg's repaired clutch was working well. Ronne was also on the plane and had a 125-watt transmitter, as mentioned earlier.

Members of the party climbed several of the peaks; the layered rocks proved to be igneous gabbros and related rocks. Behrendt won the igneous vs sedimentary bet. They were layered gabbros, about 175 million years old. The rocks contained perplexing fine details in their layering and for a time Aughenbaugh entertained a theory that a granitisation process from original sandstones had formed them. Granitisation was a somewhat heretical controversy in geology at the time. The gabbros showed some mineralisation and stimulated later investigations (US, Soviet and

Argentine) in relation to the potential for platinum and related elements, but fortunately no economic deposits were found. Behrendt observes that, even with the latest technology, the cost of mineral development would be prohibitive: 'Consider building and maintaining a railroad across the rapidly moving, crevassed Filchner Ice Shelf!'

Exploration in these spectacular ranges must have been a delight, and one of the places was named Enchanted Valley. Behrendt describes their drive up the valley between two parts of the range as being one of the most beautiful and scenic mountain drives he had ever taken. The few later visitors to the region have all been entranced. The Davis Valley, named for the cook at Ellsworth, and Forlidas Pond, named for a radio operator there, are 'dry valleys', five to seven kilometres across. It is a large ice-free area with small lakes. The lakes contain unusual pink algal plants, one identified as the alga *Phormidium incrustatum* (Naeg.). This area has become recognised as Special Protected Area No. 119, under the Antarctic Treaty, because of its special scientific significance and biological sensitivity. Research access to it is by special permit, and only on foot.

The party reached the south-west end of the Dufek Massif in mid-December 1957 and could see another range, now called the Cordiner Peaks, 15–30 miles (24–48 km) away. They wanted to visit this range but were deterred from doing so by crevassing. This was the southernmost point reached on their traverse.

Afterwards, Behrendt says he often regretted that they had not enjoyed better cooperation with Finn Ronne. Behrendt writes that they could have gone on to the Pole, only about 450 miles (720 km) away:

the sort of adventure that would have excited Ronne. I am sure George Dufek would have been supportive, and we probably would have beaten Fuchs and the Transantarctic Expedition to the Pole. This probably would not have been viewed favorably by Hugh Odishaw and Bert Crary but still would have been scientifically very worthwhile … Adventure tourist parties routinely use this route today to ski to the South Pole or across Antarctica.[4]

After leaving the Dufeks, the traverse proceeded another 300 miles to the east, across several ice-buried islands in the ice shelf, the Henry and Korff Ice Rises. The party was given a final visit on 29 December by one of Lassiter's C-47 aircraft from Ellsworth, with seven drums of fuel and Christmas food. They had also brought the 125-watt radio transmitter, now with Dufek's permission. The traverse party had been 24 days without any radio contact since the last air supply and had travelled 400 miles (640 km) along a complex traverse route. From then on, with the stronger transmitter, radio contact with Ellsworth was always successful.

The vehicles completed the traverse, proceeding north towards Berkner Island. They had been issued a directive to return north to Gould Bay, west of Ellsworth. The relief vessels, *Westwind* and *Wyandot*, were approaching Ellsworth to exchange a new party at the base. The vehicles finally ran out of fuel and two Otters flew in from Ellsworth with a new geophysical team. The original traverse team flew back to Ellsworth and within a few days sailed on the return north.

The exchange geophysical team continued their work for another month with the vehicles, but then was evacuated for the winter. The next season (1958–59) the exchange traverse team used four new Sno-Cats and followed the route inland past the end of the Grand Chasm. This traverse, led by Father Bradley, a Jesuit seismologist, and John Pirrit, glaciologist, also accomplished a notable, long journey to reach Byrd Station, another US IGY base. The original Sno-Cats used in 1957–58 were abandoned.

The 1957–58 traverse travelled about 1200 miles (1931 km) in 80 days. Scientifically, it achieved important results, especially contributing to the international effort towards mapping ice thickness across Antarctica. The men all went on with expedition work. Behrendt has made over 12 trips to Antarctica in 40 years. Paul Walker died of a brain tumour in 1959, in the Arctic, and Ed Thiel was killed in a plane crash at Wilkes Station in 1961.

Despite the erratic leadership of Finn Ronne, the American party made significant discoveries.

Appendix V TAE Publications

Trans-Antarctic Expedition Scientific Reports

No. 1: *Synopsis of Results*, V.E. Fuchs.

No. 2: *A Gravity Traverse of Antarctica*, J.G.D. Pratt.

No. 3: *Seismic Soundings Across Antarctica*, J.G.D. Pratt.

No. 4: *Tides at Shackleton, Weddell Sea*, J.D.G. Pratt.

No. 5: *Glaciology: 1) Solid Precipitation and Drift Snow*, H. Lister.

No. 7: *Distribution of Surface Phytoplankton Between New Zealand and Antarctica*, Vivienne Cassie.

No. 8: *Geology: 1) Theron Mountains, Shackleton Range and Whichaway Nunataks*, P.J. Stephenson, *With a Section on Palaeomagnetism of the Dolerite Intrusions* by D.J. Blundell.

No. 9: *Geology: 2) Fossil Floras*, E. Plumstead, *With an Appendix on Antarctic Fossil Wood* by Richard Krausel.

No. 10: *Geology: 3) Archaeocyatha From Antarctica and a Review of the Phylum*, Dorothy Hill.

No. 11: *Geology: 4) Geology of Victoria Land Between the Mawson and Mulock Glaciers, Antarctica*, B.M. Gunn and Guyon Warren.

No. 12: *Metamorphosed Coal From the Theron Mountain*, H.R. Brown and G.H. Tay.

No. 13: *Meteorology: 1) Shackleton, Southice and the Journey Across Antarctica*, J.J. la Grange.

No. 14: *Meteorology: 2) Scott Base, McMurdo Sound*, R.W. Balham.

No. 15: *Survey*, K.V. Blaiklock, D.G. Stratton and J.H. Miller. Includes 12 map sheets on a scale of 1:200,000 covering the greater part of the area from 77°S to 82°S between 38°W and 22°W. A single sheet on a scale of 1:2,000,000 shows the trans-Antarctic traverse and the various scientific stations occupied. There are also two sheets on scales of 1:1,000,000 and 1:508,384 covering the areas worked by the Ross Sea party.

No. 16: *Geology: 5) Devonian Fishes of the Mawson-Mulock Area, Victoria Land, Antarctica*, Errol I. White.

Some Other TAE Publications

Blundell, D.J., and P.J. Stephenson, 'Palaeomagnetism of Some Dolerite Intrusions From the Theron Mountains and Whichaway Nunataks, Antarctica', *Nature*, Vol. 184, 1960, p. 1860.

Goldsmith, R., 'The Commonwealth Trans-Antarctic Expedition: Medical and Physiological Aspects of the Advance Party', *Lancet*, 11 Aril 1959, pp. 741–44.

Goldsmith, R., 'Use of Clothing Records to Demonstrate Acclimatisation to Cold in Man', *Journal of Applied Physiology*, Vol. 15, 1960, pp. 776–80.

Homard, D.E.L., 'The British Trans-Antarctic Expedition, 1956–58', *British Army Review*, No. 7, 1958, pp. 34–47.

Homard, D.E.L., 'The R.E.M.E. Contribution to Polar Exploration', *Journal of the Royal Electrical and Mechanical Engineers*, Vol. 5, No. 1, 1959, pp. 2–11.

Lister H., and G. Pratt, 'Geophysical Investigations of the Commonwealth Trans-Antarctic Expedition', *Geographical Journal*, Vol. CXXV (3–4), 1959, pp. 343–56.

Pratt, D.L., 'Sub-Zero Welding in the Antarctic', Parts I and II, *Torch*, No. 18 Summer 1958, pp. 2–6, and No. 20 Winter 1958, pp.2–8.

Pratt, D.L., 'Performance of Vehicles Under Trans-Antarctic Conditions', The Institution of Mechanical Engineers, *Proceedings of the Automobile Division*, 1958–59, No. 6.

Pratt, D.L., G.M. Christie, E.F. Coxon and J.R. Lodwick, 'Fuels and Lubricants for the Trans-Antarctic Expedition', *Journal of the Institute of Petroleum*, Vol. 45, No. 422, 1959, pp. 19–41.

Rogers, A.F., 'Antarctic Climate, Clothing and Acclimatisation', in O.G. Edholm and E.K.E. Gunderson (eds), *Polar Human Biology*, Heinemann, London, 1973.

Rogers, A.F., and R.J. Sutherland, *Antarctic Climate, Clothing and Acclimatisation*, E.O.A.R. 69-0068, AD734.071, N.T.I.S. Springfield, Virginia, 1971.

Stephenson, J., 'Patterned Ground in Antarctica', *Journal of Glaciology*, Vol. 3, 1961, pp. 1163–64.

Stephenson, P.J., 'Some Considerations of Snow Metamorphism in the Light of Ice Crystal Studies', in H. Ōura (ed.), *Physics of Snow and Ice*, Vol. 1, Pt 2 [Sapporo], Institute of Low Temperature Science, Hokkaido University, 1967, pp. 725–40.

Stephenson, P.J., 'Some Aspects of Shallow Snow Metamorphism at Southice, Antarctica'. in A.J. Gow, C. Keeler, C.C. Langway and W.F. Weeks (eds), *International Symposium on Antarctic Glaciological Exploration (ISAGE)*, IASH Publication No. 86, Proceedings of SCAR/IASH Symposium. Hanover, New Hampshire, 3–7 September 1968, pp. 231–42.

Stephenson, P.J., and H. Lister, 'Preliminary Results of the Glaciological Work of the Trans-Antarctic Expedition, 1955–58', *Journal of Glaciology*, Vol. 3, 1959, pp. 426–31.

Stewart, R.H.A., 'Summary of Observations at Shackleton, Antarctica', *Quarterly Journal of the Royal Meteorological Society*, Vol. 84, No. 360, 1958, pp. 176–79.

Glossary

Anorak: a garment worn over everything to keep the wind out from the top of your body. Our anoraks were made of ventile. A hood is essential. Complements wind-proof pants.

Aurora (australis): glows or curtains of light in various usually somewhat muted colours, white, greenish or red. Caused by interactions of charged particles of the solar wind with upper atmosphere.

Balaclava: a head protector. Mine was a lined leather one with tie-down earflaps. A woollen beanie serves in warmer weather. Usually, one has to keep the ears covered. A scarf is a useful accessory.

Beset: a term describing a ship which gets itself caught in pack-ice.

Blizzard: a storm with wind or drift snow. A bad blizzard can completely overwhelm attempts to get on with things.

Chasm: a wide crevasse in the ice.

Cornice: a snow feature which can form at the edge of cliffs from wind-borne snow drift. Delicately beautiful and dangerous, they can easily collapse with you, or avalanche onto you.

Crevasse: a fracture in a glacier, formed where the movement of the ice causes it to crack. Crevasses vary in width, depth and length. Many are concealed by a snow bridge formed over them by drift snow. The deepest are perhaps between 30 and 60 metres, and the widest we saw were 25 metres. The depths of a crevasse are exquisitely blue, but very dangerous, for men, dogs or vehicles.

Dead man: A baulk of timber buried in the snow for use as an anchor for a rope or wire with a winch.

Depth hoar: A layer beneath the surface of the snow which has larger grains and lower density. These layers contain faceted hoar crystals. As one skis or runs a dog sledge over them, they are prone to collapse, with a distinctive sound which frightened our dogs.

Dolerite: an igneous rock injected as molten material, parallel to the older rock structure (a sill) or across it (a dyke). Of any thickness up to hundreds of metres, or more. Horizontal sills are characteristic of the Trans Antarctic Mountains and parts of Gondwanaland (especially Tasmania and South Africa).

Drift: wind-borne snow. Drift can block visibility on the ground even when the sky is clear above. Given the opportunity, it can get into clothing, equipment and buildings. It can penetrate through a nail hole. Drift can look quite sinister at lower winds, slithering across the ground.

Duffles: booties or gloves made of blanket material to help keep the feet and hands warm, inside footwear and gloves. Thick normal socks and gloves are worn as well.

Escarpment: a linear, very steep topographic feature in the landscape, in rock or ice.

Fast ice: sea ice which has formed against the coast. It may be several years old and can look deceptively permanent.

Floe: a free piece of sea ice of various thickness. Their sizes range up to kilometres.

Frostbite: a menace for all Antarctic visitors. Whether nipping, inflammation, blistering or actual white frozen flesh it is very serious. It should be mutually searched for in one another's faces, when outside under cold conditions. Fingers and toes need personal monitoring. In emergency one tries to thaw it by rubbing or placing in an armpit or crotch.

GPS: an instrument capable of giving accurate latitude and longitude quickly from satellite signals. It was not developed until about 1985.

Ice: technically, contains disconnected bubbles of air which get more compressed at deeper levels. The old trapped air is invaluable for careful studies of former atmospheric compositions, such as of methane and carbon dioxide.

Ice edge: The boundary between sea ice and the open sea.

Ice front: The cliff forming the seaward edge of an ice shelf.

Ice sheet: Extensive ice which smothers the land, in some places inland from an ice shelf. Some are up to thousands of metres thick.

Ice shelf: An extensive flat ice feature which occurs in many coastal regions of Antarctica. The feature can be many hundred metres thick. Ice shelves are fed by inland glaciers and flow towards the edge of the continent, where they can start floating on the adjacent sea. They have ice cliffs against the sea and periodically break away, forming characteristic, tabular icebergs. The edge of the Ross Ice Shelf was originally referred to as the 'Barrier'.

Ice wall: an ice escarpment.

Iceberg: a large-size floating ice feature in the ocean. James Cook called them ice islands. They are formed from glacial ice breaking off at the coast, from either glaciers or ice-shelves. Only about a seventh of their mass is exposed. Penguins and sea birds love to free-ride them. The most common Antarctic icebergs are tabular icebergs, formed from ice shelves.

Insulation jacket, and pants: essentials for colder conditions. Insulation can be down, or other fibres. Deliciously comforting.

Katabatic wind: wind which can blow habitually, or come and go in its intensity. The winds result from cold air descending downhill, from higher elevations. Mawson knew a lot about them at his base at Commonwealth Bay, where the wind decreases dramatically a few kilometres offshore. Wind-assisted skiers have make very clever use of such winds in crossing Antarctica.

Kurta: a very compact manual arithmetic calculator. Ken Blaiklock frequently used one.

Lead: an open channel through pack-ice. Some leads form close to the edge of the continent under the influence of wind and tide.

Longjohns: long woollen underwear. Complemented by long-sleeved woollen underwear tops.

Magnetic compass: a traditional device used for indicating direction. They work over much of Antarctica, except in the region near the Magnetic Pole, where the horizontal response is weak.

Moccasin: footwear made of soft leather, laced up over many socks, duffles, etc. Warm and comfortable on snow, but less useful walking on rock or ice.

Nunatak: an isolated mountain which protrudes through the ice. From an Eskimo word.

Pack-ice: a complex of areas of floating sea ice which can vary from tight to more open, and range from accessible to impenetrable.

Polar Plateau: an extensive high region which forms most of inland Antarctica.

Polynya: a Russian word for open water in the pack-ice, which may range in size from a pool to an extensive lake. Good size is essential for floatplane take-off.

Pyramid tent: a traditional tent design, made to survive strong winds. Usually four sides. Hard to erect in strong wind. If it gets really windy you sit up all night inside, hanging onto the poles. Quite heavy and intended to be rip-proof. Ours was double-walled.

Rammsonde: an instrument used for measuring the density of snow layers, by driving it into the snow with a dropped weight, and noting the penetration each time. The layers can be rhythmic, allowing the annual accumulation to be estimated.

Sastrugi: Eskimo term for wind-carved snow ridges. They may be up to more than a metre high. They are hard on vehicle tracks and on some skiers. Can be iron hard, with fluted undercut edges. Many are works of art, with a sharkfin-like end which can droop.

Scurvy: the awful disease long-distance early sailors often succumbed to and did not understand. Due to deficiency of vitamin C, which humans cannot generate; they must rely on eating the right foods. James Cook was successful in controlling it, using some unhelpful routines as well as vital ones. Fresh seal meat was recognised as a cure by Shackleton and others and people on the edge of death made dramatic recoveries once they were given fresh meat.

Sea ice: ice floes formed by freezing of the sea, and carried along with it, distributed by winds and currents. Over several winters can get formidably thick and form pack-ice.

Shadow compass: a simple device for navigating a course, as long as the sun is shining. The direction is based on the time and your position.

Skin: This can be a nuisance in cold Antarctica. The face can be a problem. Fingers can give trouble, and fingertips have a bad tendency to dry out and crack painfully next to fingernails. It is subject to frostbite, even inside many glove layers in extreme cold. After time in the cold, the thickening of one's skin is remarkable. Suncream or other creams can be helpful, especially for finger cracking.

Snow blindness: a very uncomfortable experience when

one goes without eye protection. It can be all too easy to go without goggles when the light is dull, to 'see better'. Medication can alleviate the discomfort but time is needed for recovery.

Snow goggles: carefully made UV goggles to protect eyes from snow blindness and wind. I even had a colourless pair supplied for geological work.

Ventile: miraculous cloth made of very finely woven material. It is strong and windproof. Heavy material for tents, amazingly light material for anoraks and trousers.

Whiteout: a situation caused by diffused light, which can develop quite quickly through continuous cloud cover and other weather circumstances, when there are no shadows. It is extremely hazardous for people and especially aircraft because there is no horizon and vertical orientation can be lost. Walking about, one sees details which the mind fabricates into the most ridiculous objects at absurd distances. It can be very dangerous when travelling, with no sense of slope.

George Lowe likened it to the view inside a pingpong ball, and the opposite of being in a coal cellar with the light turned off.

Wind crust: a thin ice layer which is formed by wind metamorphism on the snow surface. At South Ice the wind crusts were very thin, one snow grain thick. They could form a glossy continuous surface which would crack audibly in colder weather, frightening our dogs on the run.

Wind-proof pants: complement an anorak. Two universal garments for Antarctica. Drawstring adjustments at the waist, pyjama-like, leading to indiscretions on return to civilisation in relation to zips.

Wind scoop: a hollow carved by the wind eddy, often next to a rock outcrop, designed to frustrate geologists and others. They can be very smooth, in hard ice.

WWV: the miraculous radio time from Washington which allowed setting of timepieces for survey observations on the sun or stars to fix positions.

Bibliography

Alexander, C., *The Endurance*, Bloomsbury, London, 1998.

Arnesen, Liv, and Ann Bancroft with Cheryl Dahle, *No Horizon is so Far*, Da Capo Press, New York, 2003.

Arnold, Anthea, *Eight Men in a Crate*, Bluntisham, Huntingdon, 2007.

Barber, N., *The White Desert*, Hodder & Stoughton, London, 1958.

Barker, P.F., 'Scotia Sea Regional Tectonic Evolution: Implications for Mantle Flow and Palaeocirculation', *Earth Science Reviews*, Vol. 55, 2001.

Beaglehole, J.C. (ed.), *The Voyages of the Resolution and Adventure, 1772-1775*, Hakluyt Society Extra Series, London, 1969.

Behrendt, J., *Innocents on the Ice*, University Press of Colorado, Niwot, 1998.

Broadway, J., J. Arendt and S. Folkerd, 'Bright Light Phase Shifts of the Phase Positioning of the Human Melatonin Rhythm During the Antarctic Winter', *Neuroscience Letters*, Vol. 79, 1987.

Brook, D., and J.R. Beck, 'Antarctic Petrels, Snow Petrels and South Polar Skuas Breeding in the Theron Mountains', *British Antarctic Survey Bulletin*, No. 27, 1972.

Bruce, W.S., 'The New Scottish National Antarctic Expedition 1911', *Royal Scottish Geographical Society Journal*, 1910.

Burke, D., *Moments of Terror*, NSW University Press, Sydney, 1993.

Carpenter, K.J., *The History of Scurvy and Vitamin C*, Cambridge University Press, Cambridge, 1968.

Cherry-Gerrard, A., *The Worst Journey in the World: An Account of Scott's Last Antarctic Expedition, 1910-13* (1922), Penguin Books, Harmondsworth, 1970.

Clarkson, P.D., et al., 'Explanatory Text', in J.W. Thomson (comp.), *Geological Map of Shackleton Range, Antarctica*, 1995, BAS GEOMAP Series, Sheet 4. Cambridge, British Antarctic Survey Natural Research Council.

Claydon, J.R., *Report by Officer Commanding R.N.Z.A.F. Flight, Trans-Antarctic Expedition*, Royal New Zealand Air Force, 1958.

Cominso, J.C., and A.L. Gordon, 'Interannual Variability in Summer, Sea Ice Minimum, Coastal Polynyas and Bottom Water Formation in the Weddell Sea', in M.O. Jeffries (ed.), *Antarctic Sea Ice: Physical Processes Interactions and Variability*, Antarctic Research Series, Vol. 74, American Geophysical Union, Washington, DC, 1998.

Crossley, Louise, *Explore Antarctica*, Cambridge University Press, Sydney, 1995.

Darlington, J., *My Antarctic Honeymoon*, Doubleday, Garden City, 1956.

Dutton, G., 'The Hero as Egoist', *The Bulletin*, 15 July 1961.

Edwards, P. (ed.), *The Journals of Captain Cook*, Penguin Books, Harmondsworth, 1999.

Elzinger, A., T. Nordin, D. Turner and U. Wrakberg, *Antarctic Challenges*, Royal Society of Arts and Sciences, Göteborg, 2004.

Ferrigno, J.G., and W.G. Gould, 'Substantial Changes in the Coastline of Antarctica Revealed by Satellite Imagery', *Polar Record*, Vol. 23, 1987.

Fiennes, Ranulph, *To the Ends of the Earth*, Hodder & Stoughton, London, 1984.

Fiennes, Ranulph, *Mind Over Matter*, Sinclair-Stevenson, London, 1993.

Filchner, W., *To the Sixth Continent* (1922), translated by William Barr, Bluntisham, Huntington, 1994.

Fisher, M., and J. Fisher, *Shackleton*, Barrie, London, 1957.

Fuchs, Vivian, *Antarctic Adventure*, Cassell, London, 1959.

Fuchs, Vivian, 'Shackleton', *Geographical Journal*, Vol. 141, 1975.

Fuchs, Vivian, *Of Ice and Men*, Anthony Nelson, Oswestry, 1982.

Fuchs, Vivian, *A Time to Speak*, Anthony Nelson, Oswestry, 1990.

Fuchs, Vivian, TAE Expedition Journal, Scott Polar Research Institute Archives.

Fuchs, Vivian, and Edmund Hillary, *The Crossing of Antarctica*, Cassell, London, 1958.

Giaver, J., *The White Desert*, Chatto & Windus, London, 1954.

Griffiths, Tom, *Slicing the Silence*, University of New South Wales Press, Sydney, 2007.

Harder, M., and H. Fischer, 'Sea Ice Dynamics in the Weddell Sea Simulated With an Optimised Model', *Journal of Geophysical Research*, Vol. 104, No. C5, 1999.

Harding, McG.D., *Shackleton's Boat: The Story of the James Caird*, Neville & Harding, Cranbrook, 1996.

Helm, A.S., and J.H. Miller, *Antarctica: The Story of the New Zealand Party of the Trans-Antarctic Expedition*, New Zealand Government Printer, Wellington, 1964.

Herdman, H.F.P., 'Early Discoverers XII: Some Notes on Sea Ice Observations by Captain James Cook, R.N., During his Circumnavigation of Antarctica, 1772-75', *Journal of Glaciology*, Vol. 3, 1959.

Hillary, Edmund, *No Latitude for Error*, Hodder & Stoughton, London, 1961.

Hillary, Edmund, *View From the Summit*, Random House, Auckland, 1999.

Hubert, Alain, Dixie Dansercoer and Michel Brent, *In the Teeth of the Wind*, Bluntisham Books, Huntingdon, 2001.

Hunter Christie, E.W., *The Antarctic Problem: An Historic and Political Study*, Allen & Unwin, London, 1951.

Huntford, R., *Shackleton*, Hodder & Stoughton, London, 1985.

Hurley, F., *Argonauts of the South*, G.P. Putnam's Sons, New York, 1925.

Hurley, F., *Shackleton's Argonauts: A Saga of the Antarctic Ice-Packs*, Angus & Robertson, Sydney, 1948.

la Grange, J.J., *Meteorology: 1) Shackleton, South Ice and the Journey Across Antarctica*, Trans-Antarctic Expedition Scientific Report No. 13, 1963.

Larsen, C.A., 'The Voyage of the Jason to the Antarctic Region', *Geographical Journal*, Vol. 4, 1894.

Lister, H., *Glaciology: 1) Solid Precipitation and Drift Snow*, Trans-Antarctic Expedition Scientific Report No. 5, 1960.

Lister, H., *Ice — High and Low*, privately published, 2005.

Lister, H., *Malham —Our Shangri-La*, privately published, 2005.

Lowe, George, *Because it is There*, Cassell, London, 1959.

McElrea, R., and D. Harrowfield, *Polar Castaways*, Canterbury University Press, Christchurch, 2004.

McKenzie, D., *Opposite Poles*, Robert Hale, London, 1963.

Martin, Stephen, *A History of Antarctica*, State Library of NSW Press, Sydney, 1996.

Messner, Reinhold, *Crossing Antarctica; Both Heaven and Hell*, translated by Jill Neate, The Mountaineers, Seattle, 1991.

Mill, H.R., *The Life of Sir Ernest Shackleton*, Heinemann, London, 1923.

Nansen, F., *Farthest North*, Constable, London, 1897.

Nordenskjold, O., *Antarctica, or Two Years Amongst the Ice of the South Pole* (1905), C. Hurst, London, 1977.

Ousland, Børge, *Alone Across Antarctica* (translation by James Anderson), ISBN 82-994379-1-1, 1997.

Pratt, J.D.G., *Tides at Shackleton, Weddell Sea*, Trans-Antarctic Expedition Scientific Report No. 4, 1958.

Pujato, H., 'Los vuelos precursors del General Pujato', *Antartida* (Buenos Aires), No. 8, 1977.

Pyne, Stephen J., *The Ice*, Weidenfeld & Nicolson, London, 2003.

Reader's Digest Services, *Antarctica*, Capricorn Press, Dee Why, 1985.

Ronne, F., *Antarctic Conquest: The Story of the Ronne Expedition*, G.P. Putnam's Sons, New York, 1949.

Ross, James Clark, *A Voyage of Discovery and Research in the Southern and Antarctic Regions During the Years 1839-43* (1847), David & Charles Reprints, Newton Abbot, 1969.

Shackleton, E.H., *South: The Endurance Expedition*, William Heinemann, London, 1919.

Simmonds, Kenneth R., *The Antarctic Conventions*, Simmonds & Hill, London, 1993.

Simpson, C.J.W., 'The British North Greenland Expedition', *Geographical Journal*, Vol. 121, 1955.

Sobel, D., *Longitude*, Fourth Estate, London, 1996.

Speak, P., *William Speirs Bruce: Polar Explorer and Scottish Nationalist*, National Museums of Scotland, Edinburgh, 2003.

Steger, Will, 'Six Men Across Antarctica', *National Geographic*, Vol. 178, No. 5, 1990.

Steger, Will, and Jon Bowermaster, *Crossing Antarctica*, New York, Knopf, 1991.

Stephenson, J., 'Fossil Polygons', *Journal of Glaciology*, Vol. 3, 1961.

Stephenson, P.J., *Geology: 1) Theron Mountains, Shackleton Range and Whichaway Nunataks*, Trans-Antarctic Expedition Scientific Report No. 8, 1966.

Stroud, M., *Shadows on the Wasteland*, Jonathan Cape, London, 1993.

Stroud, M., *Survival of the Fittest*. Jonathan Cape, London, 1998.

Theil, E., 'Antarctica, One Continent or Two?', *Polar Record*, Vol. 10, No. 67, 1961.

Trans-Antarctic Expedition Scientific Reports, see Appendix V.

Tyler-Lewis, K., *The Lost Men*, Bloomsbury, London, 2006.

Van der Kay, J., 'Fantasy, Hope and a Late Teenage Spirit of Adventure', *Victorious*, Summer 1999–2000.

Walton, K., *Two Years in the Antarctic*, Lutterworth, London, 1955.

Weddell, J., *A Voyage Towards the South Pole* (1827), David & Charles Reprints, Newton Abbot, 1970.

White, W.B., and R.G. Peterson, 'An Antarctic Circumpolar Wave in Surface Pressure, Wind, Temperature and Sea Ice Extent', *Nature*, Vol. 380 (6125), 1996.

Worsley, F.A., *Endurance*, Philip Allen, London, 1931.

Endnotes

Chapter 1 Unknown Antarctica

1 Martin, Stephen, *A History of Antarctica*, 1996, p. 33.

2 J.C. Beaglehole (ed.), *The Voyages of the Resolution and Adventure, 1772–1775*, Hakluyt Society Extra Series, 1969.

3 From James Cook's journal, in P. Edwards (ed.), *The Journals of Captain Cook*, 1999, p. 412.

Chapter 2 The Trans-Antarctic Expedition 1955–58

1 C.J.W Simpson, 'The British North Greenland Expedition', *Geographical Journal*, Vol. 121, 1955, pp. 274–80.

2 IGY: the International Geophysical Year, 1 July 1957–31 December 1958. An international, coordinated, third polar year which emphasised Antarctica.

3 V.E. Fuchs, *A Time to Speak*, 1990, p. 206.

4 Ibid., pp. 218–19.

5 Bass, notes of meetings (30 June and 15 September 1954) relating to proposals for a Trans Antarctic Expedition, Commonwealth Relations Office, Scott Polar Research Institute Archives, Cambridge.

6 A copy of Duncan Carse's plans for his Trans-Antarctic Expedition proposal was provided to me from his estate papers, through the courtesy of Dr A.F. Trendall.

7 K.V. Blaiklock, comments on Duncan Carse's proposal for a Trans-Antarctic Expedition, personal communication, 2006.

8 Estimated equivalents in 2006 from www.eh.net are as follows:1955 £187,000 = £3,385760 (retail price index) in 2006; £750,000 = £47,052,348; £500,000 = £ 9,052,854; £20,000 = £362,113 (~Australian $900,000). With acknowledgements to L.R. Officer and S.H. Williamson 2007.

9 *San Martin* was the Argentine icebreaker which was used to penetrate the Weddell Sea and establish the General Belgrano Base the previous season to prepare for IGY.

10 V.E. Fuchs, TAE Expedition Journal, Scott Polar Research Institute Archives.

11 This refers to the damage apparent in one of the Norwegian-British-Swedish Expedition huts (1949–52).

12 Vivian Fuchs and Edmund Hillary, *The Crossing of Antarctica*, 1958, pp. 300–13.

13 Derek Williams was on the *Theron* voyage as photographer for British Petroleum (BP), a major expedition supporter. BP produced his film, *Foothold on Antarctica*.

14 Fuchs, *A Time to Speak*, p. 238.

15 V.E. Fuchs, TAE Expedition Journal, Scott Polar Research Institute Archives.

16 The Grand Chasm moved open with the formation of several new icebergs in 1986. J.G. Ferrigno and W.G. Gould, *Polar Record*, Vol 23, 1987, pp. 577–83, described the final break-up. Satellite imagery recorded how the Chasm widened until the large block of the shelf to the north of it was seen to have started splitting (by September 1986). It quickly broke into three giant icebergs that rotated counterclockwise at the southern edge of the Weddell Sea. This large breakout from the Filchner Ice Shelf marked the end for the three Weddell coast IGY stations (Ellsworth, Belgrano and Shackleton). The site of our TAE Shackleton base had survived for 30 years.

17 This account is based on the following: Fuchs and Hillary's *The Crossing of Antarctica*, 1958; Edmund Hillary, *No Latitude for Error*, 1961; A.S. Helm and J.H. Miller, *Antarctica: The Story of the New Zealand Party of the Trans-Antarctic Expedition*, 1964; J.R. Claydon, *Report by Officer Commanding R.N.Z.A.F. Flight, Trans-Antarctic Expedition*, 1958.

18 Claydon, *Report*, p. 45.

19 Ibid., p. 48.

20 Edmund Hillary, *View From the Summit*, 1999, p. 128.

21 A. Cherry-Gerrard, *The Worst Journey in the World: An Account of Scott's Last Antarctic Expedition, 1910–13*, 1922 (reissued 1970).

22 J. Van der Kay, 'Fantasy, Hope and a Late Teenage Spirit of Adventure', *Victorious*, Summer 1999–2000.

Chapter 3 The Second Winter, 1967

1 Vivian Fuchs and Edmund Hillary, *The Crossing of Antarctica*, 1958; Edmund Hillary, *No Latitude for Error*, 1961.

2 J.D.G. Pratt, *Tides at Shackleton, Weddell Sea*. Trans-Antarctic

Expedition Scientific Report No. 4, 1958.

3 R.F. Scott's last expedition lectures, 1911, at the Cape Royds hut.

4 Considerable research has been directed to the problems of disrupted circadian rhythms. Light is an important cue for regulating our biological clock. The hormone, melatonin, is secreted in the pineal gland, also known to be involved in long-term biological rhythm. Melatonin was only isolated as recently as 1958. The pineal gland is a small, cone-shaped projection from the top of the mid-brain in most vertebrate animals. It is slightly larger than a pea. Professor Arendt established a Centre for Chronobiology at the University of Surrey and has conducted research with the British Antarctic Survey for many years. She states: 'In coping with the 24 hour day during the winter darkness there is a tendency for the internal clock to drift away from the 24 hour clock with consequent problems of sleeping and working'. Working with the base doctors at Halley Bay, 75°S, she has used measurements of the melatonin rhythm and sleep to show this winter delay, and in some circumstances complete resynchronisation from the 24th day in winter. An hour of bright, 2500 lux, white light in the morning around breakfast time and in the late afternoon, using light equipment designed to treat winter depression, was sufficient to prevent this delay ... Recently, she has explored the effect of increasing the light intensity of the whole base and changing the spectral composition of the light to include more short wavelengths. She considers these to be more powerful for resetting the internal clock than broad-spectrum white light. However, so far doubling the average overall exposure to light in winter, to around 60 lux, even with more short wavelengths, has not proved as potent as the two short bursts of very bright light used previously. Designs for the new base at Halley will take light considerations seriously. See J. Broadway, J. Arendt and S. Folkerd, 'Bright Light Phase Shifts of the Phase Positioning of the Human Melatonin Rhythm During the Antarctic Winter' Neuroscience Letters, Vol. 79, 1987, pp. 185–89.

5 H. Lister, Glaciology: 1) Solid Precipitation and Drift Snow, Trans-Antarctic Expedition Scientific Report No. 5, 1960.

6 J.J. la Grange, Meteorology: 1) Shackleton, Southice and the Journey Across Antarctica, Trans-Antarctic Expedition Scientific Report No. 13, 1963.

7 Tom Griffiths, Slicing the Silence, 2007, 'Wintering', pp. 162–85.

8 K. Walton, Two Years in the Antarctic, 1955.

9 J. Behrendt, Innocents on the Ice, 1998, p. 254. The Dufek Massif was about 470 miles south of Ellsworth Base, ~82°30 S.

10 P.D. Clarkson et al., 'Explanatory Text', in J.W. Thomson (comp.), Geological Map of Shackleton Range, Antarctica, 1995, BAS GEOMAP Series, Sheet 4. Cambridge, British Antarctic Survey Natural Research Council.

11 J. Stephenson, 'Fossil Polygons', Journal of Glaciology, Vol. 3, 1961, pp. 1163–64.

12 D. Brook and J.R. Beck, 'Antarctic Petrels, Snow Petrels and South Polar Skuas Breeding in the Theron Mountains', British Antarctic Survey Bulletin, No. 27, 1972, pp. 131–37.

13 P.J. Stephenson, Geology: 1) Theron Mountains, Shackleton Range and Whichaway Nunataks, Trans-Antarctic Expedition Scientific Report No. 8, 1966.

Chapter 4   Crossing the Continent

1 Vivian Fuchs and Edmund Hillary, The Crossing of Antarctica, 1958, pp. 167–88.

2 Ibid., p. 175.

3 Ibid., pp. 189–207; Edmund Hillary, No Latitude for Error, 1961.

Chapter 5   Hillary's Dash for the Pole

1 Edmund Hillary, No Latitude for Error, 1961.

2 Edmund Hillary, View From the Summit, 1999, p. 128.

3 Hillary, No Latitude, p. 100.

4 Ibid., p. 101.

5 A.S. Helm and J.H. Miller, Antarctica: The Story of the New Zealand Party of the Trans-Antarctic Expedition, 1964, pp. 325–40.

6 Hillary, No Latitude, p. 195.

7 Ibid., p. 205.

8 Ibid., p. 206.

9 Helm and Miller, Antarctica, p. 340.

10 Vivian Fuchs and Edmund Hillary, The Crossing of Antarctica, 1958, pp. 248–49.

11 N. Barber's entertaining The White Desert, 1958, describes his persevering enterprise in getting to the South Pole.

12 Ibid., p. 91.

13 Ibid., p. 129.

14 Ibid., p. 137.

15 Ibid., p. 141; D. McKenzie, Opposite Poles, 1963, p. 122.

16 J. Behrendt, Innocents on the Ice: A Memoir of Antarctic Exploration, 1998, p. 390.

17 Helm and Miller, Antarctica. The New Zealand survey journeys are described in the chapters 'The Darwin Journey', 'The Southern Survey Journey' and 'The Northern Journey'.

18 McKenzie, Opposite Poles, Chapter 19.

19 D. Burke, Moments of Terror, 1993.

20 Fuchs and Hillary, Crossing of Antarctica, pp. 289–91; Helm and Miller, Antarctica, pp. 325–40.

21 Fuchs and Hillary, p. 291.

22 Ibid., pp. 292–93.

Chapter 6   After TAE

1 Vivian Fuchs, A Time to Speak, 1990, Chapter 14.

2 Geoffrey Dutton, 'The Hero as Egoist', The Bulletin, 15 July 1961.

3 Edmund Hillary, View From the Summit, 1999, p. 127.

4 Ibid., p. 128.

5 Idem.,

6 Ibid., p. 129.

7 Ibid., p. 129. This suggestion, that Fuchs believed the Weddell Sea contained two areas of floating ice was also stated by Hillary, No Latitude for Error, 1961, p. 24.

8 Hillary, View From the Summit, p. 131.

9 Ibid., p. 133.

10 Ibid., p. 181.

11 Ibid., p. 183.
12 Ibid., p. 183.
13 Ibid., p. 184.
14 Idem.
15 Ibid., p. 187.
16 Ibid., p. 188.
17 J.G. Ferrigno and W.G. Gould, 'Substantial Changes in the Coastline of Antarctica Revealed by Satellite Images', *Polar Record*, Vol. 25, 1987, pp. 577–83.
18 *Polar Record*, Vol. 37, October 2001, p. 369.

Chapter 7   Then and Now

1 SAR: synthetic aperture radar. A satellite's motion and advanced signal processing techniques can simulate a larger radar antenna. The synthetic aperture is the distance travelled by the spacecraft while the radar antenna collects information about the object. SAR transmits radar pulses rapidly, often several hundred pulses while it passes over a particular object, and it receives many reflected pulses. After intensive signal processing, all of the responses can be analysed such that the resulting image appears to have been obtained from a large, stationary antenna. The ability of SAR to pass through clouds relatively unaffected, to illuminate the Earth's surface with its own signals, and to measure distances precisely makes it an especially useful sensor for many applications, including sea ice monitoring, cartography, surface deformation detection, glacier monitoring, crop production forecasting, forest cover mapping, ocean wave spectra, urban planning, coastal surveillance (erosion), and monitoring disasters such as forest fires, floods, volcanic eruptions and oil spills. (Summarised from information supplied by the Alaska Satellite Facility, http://www.asf.alaska.edu/, with the NASA-ASF information CD which contains SAR images from Antarctica and Alaska, *The Ends of the Earth*. The image, Figure 15, reproduced in this book, is acknowledged from this source.)
2 Stephen J. Pyne, *The Ice*, 2003, pp. 114–15.
3 Bryan Storey, personal communication, 2006. He was taking part in the joint BAS-USAP Ferrar Large Igneous Province (FLIPS) project.
4 Ian W.D. Dalziel, lecture given at James Cook University, Townsville, April 2007. Dalziel and his colleagues had been conducting a five-season GPS station project (WAGN), to measure the relative movements of prepared stations installed in the Antarctic Peninsula and to the east in East Antarctic mountain sites.
5 Kenneth R. Simmonds, *The Antarctic Conventions*, 1993, p. 29.
6 The fourth Polar Year, 2007–09. This international coordination of observation and research is concentrating on a range of environmental aspects of the changing polar regions. The other polar years took place in 1882–82, 1932–33 and 1957–58 (IGY). The fourth polar year commenced on 1 March 2007.
7 Ranulph Fiennes, *To the Ends of the Earth*, 1984.
8 Will Steger, 'Six Men Across Antarctica', *National Geographic*, Vol. 178, No. 5, 1990, pp. 66–93; Will Steger and Jon Bowermaster, *Crossing Antarctica*, 1991.
9 Reinhold Messner and Arved Fuchs, 'First to Ski Cross Continent', *National Geographic*, Vol. 178, No 5, 1990, pp. 94–95; Reinhold Messner, *Crossing Antarctica; Both Heaven and Hell*, 1991.
10 Ranulph Fiennes, *Mind Over Matter*, 1993; M. Stroud, *Shadows on the Wasteland*, 1993; M. Stroud, *Survival of the Fittest*, 1998.
11 Børge Ousland, *Alone Across Antarctica*, 1997.
12 Alain Hubert, Dixie Dansercoer and Michel Brent, *In the Teeth of the Wind*, 2001.
13 Liv Arnesen and Ann Bancroft with Cheryl Dahle, *No Horizon is so Far*, 2003.

Appendix I   Previous Explorers

1 Characteristics of Antarctica and the history of exploration are well described in many sources, including Louise Crossley, *Explore Antarctica*, 1995; Stephen Martin, *A History of Antarctica*, 1996; Reader's Digest Services, *Antarctica*, 1985.
2 From James Cook's journal, in P. Edwards (ed.), *The Journals of Captain Cook*. 1999, p. 411.
3 H.F.P. Herdman, 'Early Discoverers XII: Some Notes on Sea Ice Observations by Captain James Cook, R.N., During his Circumnavigation of Antarctica, 1772–75', *Journal of Glaciology*, Vol. 3, 1959, pp. 534–41.
4 D. Sobel, *Longitude*, 1996.
5 K.J. Carpenter, *The History of Scurvy and Vitamin C*, 1968.
6 J. Weddell, *A Voyage Towards the South Pole*, 1827, reprinted 1970.
7 V.E. Fuchs, *A Time to Speak*, 1990, p. 281.
8 James Clark Ross, *A Voyage of Discovery and Research in the Southern and Antarctic Regions During the Years 1839–43*, 1847, reprinted 1969.
9 C.A. Larsen, 'The Voyage of the Jason to the Antarctic Region', *Geographical Journal*, Vol. 4, 1894, pp. 333–44.
10 O. Nordenskjold, *Antarctica, or Two Years Amongst the Ice of the South Pole*, 1905, reprinted 1977. The loss of *Antarctic* is described in Chapters XVII and XVIII by C.J. Skottsberg.
11 A. Elzinger, T. Nordin, D. Turner and U. Wrakberg, *Antarctic Challenges*, 2004.
12 W. Filchner, *To the Sixth Continent*, 1922, translated 1994 by William Barr.
13 E. Theil, 'Antarctica, One Continent or Two?', *Polar Record*, Vol. 10, No. 67, 1961, pp. 335–48.
14 E.H. Shackleton, *South*, 1919; C. Alexander *The Endurance*, 1998; F.A. Worsley, *Endurance*, 1931. See also three Shackleton biographies: H.R. Mill, *The Life of Sir Ernest Shackleton*, 1923; M. Fisher and J. Fisher, *Shackleton*, 1957; R. Huntford: *Shackleton*, 1985.
15 W.S. Bruce, 'The New Scottish National Antarctic Expedition 1911', *Royal Scottish Geographical Society Journal*, 1910.
16 Fisher and Fisher, *Shackleton*, pp. 331–32.
17 F. Hurley, *Argonauts of the South*, 1925; F. Hurley, *Shackleton's*

Argonauts: A Saga of the Antarctic Ice-Packs, 1948.

18 Shackleton, *South*, Chapter IV.

19 McG.D. Harding, *Shackleton's Boat: The Story of the James Caird*, 1996.

20 Huntford, *Shackleton*, pp. 643–44.

21 R. McElrea and D. Harrowfield, *Polar Castaways*, 2004; K. Tyler-Lewis, *The Lost Men*, 2006.

22 Vivian Fuchs, 'Shackleton', *Geographical Journal*, Vol. 141, 1975, pp. 14–18.

23 E.W. Hunter Christie, *The Antarctic Problem: An Historic and Political Study*, 1951.

24 F. Ronne, *Antarctic Conquest: The Story of the Ronne Expedition*, 1949; K. Walton, *Two Years in the Antarctic*, 1955.

25 J. Darlington, *My Antarctic Honeymoon*, 1956.

26 J. Giaver, *The White Desert*, 1954.

27 Ibid., p. 205.

Appendix II The Weddell Sea

1 M. Harder and H. Fischer, 'Sea Ice Dynamics in the Weddell Sea Simulated With an Optimised Model', *Journal of Geophysical Research*, Vol. 104, No. C5, 1999, pp. 11151–61.

2 J.C. Cominso and A.L. Gordon, 'Interannual Variability in Summer, Sea Ice Minimum, Coastal Polynyas and Bottom Water Formation in the Weddell Sea', in M.O. Jeffries (ed.), *Antarctic Sea Ice: Physical Processes Interactions and Variability*, Antarctic Research Series, Vol 74, 1998, pp. 293–315.

3 W.B. White and R..G. Peterson, 'An Antarctic Circumpolar Wave in Surface Pressure, Wind, Temperature and Sea Ice Extent', *Nature*, Vol. 380 (6125), 1996, pp. 51–54.

4 P.F. Barker, 'Scotia Sea Regional Tectonic Evolution: Implications for Mantle Flow and Palaeocirculation', *Earth Science Reviews*, Vol. 55, 2001, pp. 1–39.

Appendix III Dimensions and Construction of Three Polar Ships

1 W. Filchner: *To the Sixth Continent*, 1922, translated 1994 by William Barr.

2 National Maritime Museum, Historic Photographs & Ship Plans Section (Brass Foundry, Woolwich Arsenal): '*Endurance*': Mid-tranverse section. Plan dated 21-4-1911, No 1805. Copied 17/3/1914, No. 7749, To James Pollock Sons & Co. Ltd., London. (originally built as *Polaris*).

3 M. Fisher and J. Fisher, *Shackleton*, 1957, p. 332.

4 C. Alexander, *The Endurance*, 1998, p. 48.

5 F. Hurley, *Shackleton's Argonauts*, 1948, p. 94.

Appendix IV Other IGY Expeditions

1 Sources: Vivian Fuchs, *Of Ice and Men*, 1982; P.D. Clarkson (manuscript); P.D. Clarkson, et al., 'Explanatory Text', in J.W. Thomson (comp.), *Geological Map of Shackleton Range, Antarctica*, 1995, BAS GEOMAP Series, Sheet 4. Cambridge, British Antarctic Survey Natural Research Council.

2 H. Pujato, 'Los vuelos precursors del General Pujato', *Antartida* (Buenos Aires), No. 8, 1977, pp. 32–39.

3 J. Behrendt, *Innocents on the Ice*, 1998.

4 Ibid., p. 366.

Index

(Plate and figure page numbers are in *italics*)